Rivers, Roads, & Rails

When the Midwest was still young...

J.L. Fredrick

Dedicated to

Robert Lee Erickson

CONTENTS

INTRODUCTION ... 1

A GREAT SEA TO THE WEST ... 3
Early exploration and settlement

STAGECOACHES, TAVERNS, &
ROADHOUSES ... 55
Development of overland roads and mail routes

THE RIVERS ... 103
Waterways were the first highways to the frontier

ENTER: THE RAILROAD ... 195
The iron horse altered the way to do business

CHANGING TIMES ... 268

REFERENCES & SOURCES ... 280

RIVERS,
ROADS,
&
RAILS

RIVERS, ROADS, & RAILS

Introduction

If we could go back a century, and ask one simple question of the old pioneers, we would learn that transportation of man and material remained the single most valuable ingredient in progress toward the future. It was true two hundred years ago, as it is still true today. The predecessors of modern-day mass and private transportation systems answered vital needs of a growing nation, and propelled our society into constant motion. That motion has never stopped.

In this day and age we traverse well-maintained highways that comprise a network of arteries spanning the states. Natural beauty is ours to behold from the comfort of our air-conditioned cars. Maps and signs provide effortless guidance anywhere we want to go. Restaurants and motels abound, and gas stations and convenience stores make a trip across town or the state nearly worry free. But it wasn't always as easy as jumping into the family sedan and turning a key. Imagine preparing for a trip that might take days or weeks to complete in an ox-drawn wagon, when the only accommodations along the way might be the protection of a big oak tree, or if you were lucky, a tiny log cabin with a little spare room on the floor.

Surrounded by constant danger, the pioneer endured unimaginable hardships as he cut his way into dense forests to make a home for himself and his family. We can look back with interest to that time when transportation was in its primal stages, and marvel at gradual, innovative advances.

This volume focuses on 19th Century transportation and its impact on the development of communities in Wisconsin, and the all-important links with the settlement and growth of a newer frontier in Minnesota and Iowa. Topics include travel upon the waterways and the development of various overland conveyances, although it is difficult to separate the stories of various modes of travel during the pioneer era. Chronologically, it is nearly impossible to clearly define a point in time

1

when the importance of one ended and another began, as conveyance progressed from canoes on natural waterways to overland wagon paths and stagecoaches, and to steamships and locomotives. Their significance overlapped and intermingled, and none were totally independent from the others.

The Grand Excursion of 1854 etched a pivotal milestone of great magnitude – a turning point in the development of the "Old Northwest." Although there had been settlements established in the frontier regions of Wisconsin, Minnesota, and Iowa prior to that time, nothing can compare to the influence that this event bestowed upon the pioneer territory.

More than two hundred years earlier, preparations had begun when the first European explorer set foot in what is now Wisconsin. A fascinating chain of events was set into motion that would shape the Upper Midwest.

Come with me now, on another grand journey, and ride the rivers, roads, and rails through our enchanting past.

A "Great Sea to the West..."

We can only imagine the sight that lay before Jean Nicolet, perhaps the first white visitor to Wisconsin in 1634. Nicolet, a French fur trader, came to Green Bay from Quebec as his government's representative to explore this vast territory with intentions of gaining control of the new land, and ultimately to discover a route to the China Sea. The Fox River presented the most logical path, as dense forest prevented easy overland travel. He followed the river through Lake Winnebago, continuing on to the site that is now Berlin, where a large Indian community of Mascoutin, Miami, and Kickapoo told him of a "great sea" to the west, however, a language misinterpretation prevented him from understanding that they really meant a "great river." They also told him of ferocious tribes inhabiting that area, and because Nicolet was acting under orders not to risk the loss of any information gathered so far, he returned to Quebec, fearing the hostility of the western tribes.

Nearly forty years later, Father Jacques Marquette was sent to the new territory as a missionary. He spent three years in various locations working with the Indians. During that time he met an old schoolmate from Quebec, Louis Joliet, operating a fur trading post at Sault Ste. Marie. They, too, had heard the stories of the great sea to the west, and began preparing for a voyage of discovery. Five companions were chosen, one of which was an Illinois Indian slave boy who had taught Marquette his language. It can be speculated that this choice was for the purpose of decreasing the chances of hostile confrontation in the new frontier.

In May 1673, the seven-man party departed from St. Ignace with two supply-laden canoes, destined for the unfamiliar territory beyond the Indian village where no white man had yet ventured. At the village, two Miami Indians were persuaded to guide the troupe to and across the portage between Fox River and Wisconsin River. The next day, Marquette and his band set out on the Wisconsin, in search of its mouth at the Mississippi. Several weeks later, and some distance down the

Mississippi, they determined that this was not the route to the Orient they had been searching for, and returned home. Nine years later another French explorer, LaSalle, reached the mouth. He sent a member of his party, Father Hennepin, to explore the upper Mississippi.

During the next century, the only thoroughfares across Wisconsin were the waterways. Access to military installations at Green Bay, Portage and Prairie du Chien was via the rivers, and the establishment of other settlements was limited mostly to the riverbanks by virtue of the lack of any other travel means.

First Flourmill on the New Frontier

Long before settlements of any size began to appear in Wisconsin, the Mississippi River played an important role in exploration to the north. Until the early 1800s, Prairie du Chien remained the only white settlement on the western edge of Wisconsin. Like the sawmills, taverns and blacksmith shops, flourmills, too, were among the first establishments to do early business in the fringe areas of civilization. Because Prairie du Chien was the first permanent settlement on the Upper Mississippi it's not surprising that a flour mill should appear there soon after its early inhabitants were hanging their coats on a peg behind the cabin door.

The year was 1818; the only settlements in the Wisconsin Territory were the fur trading posts at Green Bay and Prairie du Chien. The northern quarter of the United States remained known only to a few trappers and the Native Americans at the time John Shaw's Mill in Fisher's Coulee began grinding flour.

There had been a settlement of fur traders and their voyageurs since 1781, but it was not until the turn of the 19th century that farming in that region began to develop. Farming techniques quite primitive, a narrow strip of land beneath the high bluffs near Prairie du Chien was cultivated and wheat grown and harvested. Threshing was accomplished by treading oxen over the wheat spread out on the ground. At first, coffee mills were used for grinding, and it goes without saying that yields remained on a rather small scale.

John Shaw, a trader between St. Louis and the Upper Mississippi River region visited Prairie du Chien in 1815. He learned that the people there relied heavily on traders bringing in flour and other supplies from Mackinaw, but the remoteness from any other settlements would make it necessary to engage in farming on a larger scale in order to produce an adequate volume of wheat. Arrangements were already under way for that, and Shaw immediately saw the opportunity for a good location of a gristmill.

Three years later Mr. Shaw returned to make good his promise of 1815 to erect the mill in Fisher's Coulee where there was a sufficient waterpower supply. It eventually proved to be an expensive endeavor for Shaw, but a matter of great convenience to the people. In the fall of 1818 Shaw's Mill opened for business. Mill Creek rushed over the waterwheel and the stones began turning. Prairie du Chien had flour!

A strong garrison had been placed at the just-completed Fort Crawford under the command of Lieutenant Colonel Talbot Chambers. The commander showed little respect for the fur traders and their associates as they had sympathized and aided the British in the War of 1812. He vented his dislike for them and their un-American deeds with harsh treatment. Miller Shaw refused to be subject to such treatment; he wrote: "It was in consequence of petty tyrannies and the civil law not being much in force or very effectual, that I abandoned all idea of settlement at Prairie du Chien and all designs of improvements I had formed, and sold my mill at a sacrifice."

During the period of Shaw's Mill operation, flour became an important commodity of trade. Farmers traded their surplus to Indians for venison and dressed deerskins, or sold it to the traders in exchange for needed goods. The two most powerful traders and largest buyers of the flour were Michael Brisbois, an agent of the Hudson Bay Fur Company, and Joseph Rolette, a representative of the Astor Fur Company. As a sideline to trading, Brisbois ran a public bake shop. He issued tickets for 50 loaves of bread in return for 100 pounds of flour; these tickets soon became legal tender in the community for purchases of articles from the Indians and traders. The bake house – as well as the tickets – grew popular among the inhabitants of Prairie du Chien; no longer did anyone bake their own bread but depended entirely upon the bakery.

So much flour was made at Shaw's Mill in 1820 that Rolette contracted with the government to supply Fort Crawford. The soldiers preferred the coarse flour from the mill to the finely ground alternative brought on keelboats. The product from Pittsburgh was almost certain to be sour upon arrival after the long journey.

A bitter rivalry in trading and flour marketing ensued between Brisbois and Rolette. Younger and more aggressive, Rolette surpassed Brisbois in the effort and eventually gained the lion's share of business. Brisbois lived to see the day when his competitor dominated the trade market in the pioneer post and empowered control over the upper Mississippi Valley Indians.

Legend has it that near his death, Brisbois requested to be buried on a hilltop so that in death he might look down upon his hated rival. Whether or not there is any truth to the legend, Brisbois' grave is on a hilltop overlooking Rolette's burial site in the old French cemetery not far from the foot of the Prairie du Chien bluffs.

Both marble tombstones are forever a reminder of the pioneer days when the water at Fisher's Coulee turned the wheel at Shaw's Mill – the first flourmill of the Old Northwest.

The Mississippi River Becomes a Great Highway

Canoes and keelboats, the only vessels to ply northward from Fort Crawford at Prairie du Chien, had transported troops and supplies to the far-reaching Minnesota site of Fort St. Anthony, now Fort Snelling near present-day St. Paul.

But in May 1823, on the high springtime water level, the simple but spunky *Virginia*, under the command of Captain Crawford, puffed its important way up the Mississippi beyond Prairie du Chien and arrived at Ft. St. Anthony, laden with supplies and passengers. This stern wheel boat was built at Pittsburgh, fitted with the intimidating high-pressure engines. (One writer of the day described them as "ones that blow off steam like unbottling an earthquake.") The United States government chartered the boat for this trip. Exact dates for its departure from St. Louis and its arrival at the Minnesota Military post are uncertain, as no two records of the event agree, but according to historian Captain Fred A. Bill in his report to the La Crosse Tribune, May 1923, "May 10 should be celebrated as the centenary of the arrival of the first steamboat and the opening up of steamboat traffic on the upper Mississippi River."

This was 18 years before Nathan Myrick landed his canoe at the site of La Crosse and erected the first log cabin there to establish the official beginning of the city. When the *Virginia* steamed past, the site was no more than a vacant stretch of prairie known only to the natives as their ceremonial grounds. Those terrified natives watched in awe as the smoke spewing, 118-feet-long vessel chugged up the river, appearing to them as some huge monster coughing and spouting water and steam in every direction. Various accounts of the trip indicate the *Virginia* had been aground five times, encountered several snags (fallen trees lying beneath the water surface) and bore the marks of battle with the river and the elements. Nearly a month-long voyage marked the triumphant inauguration of steam navigation and ushered in long-lived freight and passenger traffic on the upper Mississippi. In the many years to follow, such majestic names as *War Eagle, Blackhawk, Orion, Far West, Enterprise, North Star, Trident, Diamond Jo, Delta Queen, Sultana* – just to list a few – graced the magnificent paddle wheelers churning the Father of Waters. Time cannot shadow the romance of the old days on the river, when every boat brought letters and farm implements, food, new dresses and adventure into the lives of the pioneers.

As more settlements sprang up throughout the territory and their populations grew, the lack of access to them hindered economic growth. More people meant the need for larger quantities of supplies delivered to the settlements. The rivers were still the primary source of communication, as much of Wisconsin flourished dense forest, making overland travel difficult.

The Need For Overland Routes

Before the Wisconsin Territory neared statehood, the journey between Green Bay and Prairie du Chien followed the waterways. Most settlements, consisting of nothing more than a single log cabin housing a trading post, sparsely dotted the banks along the Fox, Eau Claire, Wolf, Chippewa and Wisconsin Rivers. It wasn't until the late 1820s that the first mail was carried on foot via an overland route following trails used by the Indians to reach hunting grounds. This same route in 1829 felt the white man's footfalls when Henry Baird, Morgan Martin, James Doty and an Indian guide set out from Green Bay to make the first land journey all the way to the Mississippi River. A short time later, that route established an avenue of overland travel across the territory, and would eventually become known as the Military Road.

The need arose for an improved road connecting the three established military posts at Green Bay, Portage and Prairie du Chien, as it became impossible to transport supplies between them via the water routes in winter. At a public meeting in Green Bay, Congress was petitioned for roads to Chicago and to Fort Crawford at Prairie du Chien. Congress responded with an appropriation for the survey.

Judge Doty and US Army Lieutenant Alexander Center completed the original survey in 1832. Most of the 235-mile route was traced along the heavily traveled Indian trails, zigzagging across the territory. From Fort Howard at Green Bay it followed along the Fox River southwestward to the eastern shore of Lake Winnebago, south to Fond du Lac, then turned abruptly westward through Brandon to Fort Winnebago at Portage where it again made a southerly turn to the northern tip of Lake Mendota. From there it turned westward again through Cross Plains, Blue Mounds, Dodgeville, Fennimore, crossed the Wisconsin River at Bridgeport and ended on the bank of the Mississippi River at Prairie du Chien's Fort Crawford.

Even before the Indians used them, as the old settlers would tell, the buffalo had pounded the trails smooth. This fact can be substantiated: often they were in key positions near feeding grounds and water supply. Many highways, just as the old settlers told, started as buffalo paths, then Indian trails and eventually were improved upon by the white pioneers and made into wagon roads.

Actual construction of the Military Road began in 1835. Regular Army soldiers, given the task of clearing a 30-feet-wide path through the heavily forested areas, often left tree stumps protruding in the middle of the roadway. Across the open prairies the trail was simply marked with wooden stakes and an occasional mound of rocks. Tree blazes (patches of bark removed with an ax) indicated the route through light timber. Corduroy roads (small logs laid side-by-side) provided passage across marshlands but were not always entirely effective. Eventually, ferry service was established at river crossings.

As early as 1825 a mail route was established between Chicago and Green Bay by way of Milwaukee, although but one white inhabitant, Solomon Juneau, lived there at that time. The mail carrier, accompanied by an Indian guide is given credit for blazing that first connecting trail between those settlements.

He was clad in smoke tanned buckskin hunting shirt and leggings, a wolf skin chapeau, and elk hide moccasins. He carried a heavy mountaineer's rifle attached to a strap so that it could be slung over his back. A powder horn hung by a lanyard from his shoulder, and a belt around his waist held a sheathed knife, a pair of pistols, a short handled axe, and a mink skin bullet pouch. Tied to his powder horn were several charms, believed to protect the wearer from danger. A flat tin canister contained the mail.

If one had traveled over the trail from Green Bay to Chicago or to Prairie du Chien in 1826, this was the only person he might encounter along the way. It may be hard to imagine, in this day and age of familiar red, white, and blue postal vehicles scooting from mailbox to mailbox on our city streets, that such an extraordinary transformation has evolved. We take for granted the expediency of present-day mail delivery to our doors – a luxury not commonly afforded to the pioneers. It was not unusual for an early settler to trudge twenty or thirty miles through the wilderness to a town where a letter carrier might stop, only to be disappointed when there was nothing for him in the mail pouch.

The first roads traversing Wisconsin's wilderness could hardly be called roads by today's standards. They were simply Indian trails cleared of the biggest trees in the heavily wooded regions, and across open plains were sparsely marked with wooden stakes. Used primarily to move troops and supplies between Fort Howard at Green Bay, Fort Winnebago at Portage, Fort Crawford at Prairie du Chien, and Fort Dearborn at Chicago, these trails also served as "post roads" – the routes taken by men on foot who carried the mail between these securely established settlements. But before the roads were blazed in the 1830's, the letter carrier, usually a soldier detailed from one of the military installations, found his way accompanied by an Indian guide. The companion was necessary, too, for the trips were not without danger from cold, starvation, accident, wild beasts, illness, and unfriendly Indians. A round trip between Green Bay and Chicago required a month, or longer if the weather was exceptionally bad or if the snow unusually deep. For food, the carriers relied on the game they might shoot, but in reserve they toted a bag of parched corn. The nights were sometimes spent in an Indian village, but more commonly, wherever darkness overtook them, on the ground in the woods. One carrier told his experiences of camping beside a flowing stream, and discovered, to his pleasure, that the water was literally alive with trout. He took a light kettle from his pack and effortlessly dipped out as many as he and his guide could consume, and fried them over an open campfire.

As the period of transformation of trails to roads approached, almost everyone looked to the future when the government would send out engineers to judge the necessity and feasibility of road improvements. Congress did take the first steps by appropriating funds to survey the routes, and then employed the use of military personnel to clear the trails, however, little of the distances were actually negotiable with horse or oxen-drawn vehicles. The mail was still relegated to man on foot.

The Milwaukee-Green Bay Road was surveyed in 1833 and laid out along the original mail route. Stakes were driven, 30-feet-wide paths were cut through the heavy timber and crude log bridges were constructed across difficult creeks and streams. The southern extension of this route was improved too, across Kenosha County and followed along the west bank of the Des Plaines River to Chicago. The entire distance remained for many years as merely a blazed wagon path providing good travel in dry weather, but during rainy seasons presented travelers with burdensome deep mud.

More trails were discovered, used and improved in the years to follow, and with them came an increasingly steady flow of settlers into this vast wilderness. It's no wonder that so many people were drawn to this utopia. The southern portion of the territory populated first, perhaps because it was the nearest and easiest to reach for the newcomers arriving by way of overland routes from the east and south, or perhaps because the terrain was more suitable for farming. Fertile soil and pure water made this land an agricultural paradise.

Wisconsin's Gray Gold

Not all the new arrivals came with intentions of planting crops or raising livestock. The southwest regions drew interest in mining, as lead deposits had been discovered and proved to be plentiful, and extended a fresh opportunity of hope and speculation. Countless lead mining settlements sprang to life and that industry quickly gained a foothold and prospered.

Lead had been mined in Wisconsin for hundreds of years before white men came to America. Evidence of Indian lead mines was revealed in the journals of some of the early explorers as they journeyed down the Wisconsin River. Nicholas Perrot, the first fur trader in Wisconsin, told in his journal of a Miami chief giving him a piece of lead ore in 1690. It had come from a "very rich mine" situated on the banks of a stream that emptied into the Mississippi River. And in 1687, a map created by Louis Hennepin, a member of La Salle's expedition in 1679, was published noting lead mines in the area of the Wisconsin-Illinois border along the Fever River. Julien Dubuque traded with the Indians who obtained lead from both sides of the Mississippi, and in 1788 they granted him permission to work mines in Iowa.

Prospectors from Missouri, Illinois, and Kentucky were drawn to southwestern Wisconsin in the 1820s when they learned of the Native Americans using lead – "gray gold"—that they had "mined" from the area hillside surfaces to make jewelry and other ornaments. Though the Indians were aware of lead, mined it, and did make use of it, it was in small quantities, and to them, lead was not a significant commodity. But to the white men, the mineral used primarily for lead shot was a valuable commodity, and continued to bring Wisconsinites considerable wealth, at least until the close of the Civil War.

These early prospectors dug the ore from surface mines, and due to the absence of readily available timber in that area, many of the early miners dug living quarters into the sides of hills or erected sod huts on the prairie. This makeshift housing, some people say, gave rise to the nickname "Badgers" for Wisconsin residents, for the homes and diggings of the first settlers resembled den holes of badgers.

There was no local production of food, and since almost all food had to be brought up river from St. Louis or overland from Chicago, it was extremely expensive. To buy adequate provisions and equipment, it was essential to produce large quantities of ore.

The miners soon learned that the ancient Indian digging sites were sure indicators of the presence of ore. Where erosion exposed the lead ore, chemical changes stabilized the lead that concentrated at the surface as surrounding soils were eroded away. This material was called "float" lead, as it had apparently "floated to the surface." This was probably the first ore to be mined, and had only to be picked up. The miners soon realized that, in most cases, when they found float mineral, there was more ore directly beneath the surface or nearby. Here the miners dug down to work ore deposited in the cracks between the rocks. Where the ore justified the effort, they dug shafts more than 30 or 40 feet deep. Here a windlass and tub or bucket was used to raise the ore. One or more men went down into the shaft to loosen the ore where it was loaded into the tub. One or two men operating the windlass raised the ore to the surface.

Blasting powder was extensively used, too, to open up deposits under ground. The veins of ore tended to follow horizontally along the cracks in the rock, and the miners tunneled in along the vein as far as possible before ground water or a threatened cave-in made them halt, or the vein petered out. Their only tools were shovels, picks, and gads (pointed steel pry bars). Candles provided their only light as they trundled the loosened ore along the drift in a wheelbarrow to the base of the shaft. Seepage of ground water into the mines was a constant problem. Hand pumps were used, but in many cases they could not keep up with the seepage and the mine would flood, causing its abandonment.

In 1823, William Hamilton, son of Alexander Hamilton, was prospecting east of present-day Darlington and came across a heavily timbered tract where there were strong indications of ore. He made test digs and found an ample quantity of lead. Hamilton hurried back to Galena, where he secured a lease. (Prior to 1847, the Federal government leased mineral lands in this area, rather than selling land to settlers.) "William Stephen Hamilton is hereby permitted to dig and mine on the United States land. He is not to set fire to the prairie grass or woods and must deliver his mineral to a licensed smelter and comply with all regulation" – thus read Hamilton's permit.

Hamilton hired several men and the mining began immediately. The most remarkable strike in the Wisconsin lead mines occurred at Hamilton's diggings, located in the present-day village of Wiota. The largest known mineral float to exist was discovered, measuring 30 feet long, 15 feet deep, and 5 feet wide. The site yielded 250,000 tons of pure ore. Ox carts plying between Hamilton's diggings and the smelter at Galena soon had created a well-traveled road, which was used by stages and wagons carrying lead to Chicago, Milwaukee, and other points along the Lake Michigan shore.

Hauling the ore overland to Galena, 50 miles distant, was expensive and time-consuming. Hamilton envisioned a city on the East Pecatonica River, about five miles from his diggings, that he hoped one day could rival Galena. When the sale of land by the United States began in Mineral Point in 1835, he approached some wealthy Easterners as potential investors in his proposed city. They formed a partnership and purchased 1,000 acres of land in 1836, platted 250 acres of it as the town they called Wiota, sold lots and soon the construction of several buildings was under way.

Unfortunately, the river flooded that year, leaving the infant town in a mosquito-infested swamp. The Pecatonica was found to be un-navigable, and the town's remoteness offered little or no reasonable means for a tolerable lifestyle, so the few settlers that had started building there moved away. Hamilton's dream of founding his own town faded away, as well.

Hamilton's Diggings, though, began to grow and prosper as more miners – single men and families – located there in search of their own mining opportunities. The new residents constructed more and better homes, and soon a post office was established with William Hamilton as postmaster. He renamed the settlement after his original dream town that had failed – Wiota – and the more settled, civilized community survived, and remains today.

Population in the mining district rose drastically from an estimated

200 in 1825 to over 10,000 by 1829. The tiny settlements of Hazel Green (originally known as Hardscrabble) and New Diggings had been established in 1824 when large deposits of lead were discovered there. Mineral Point followed in 1827 and grew to be the primary commercial center of the district. Many other towns came to life as well: Cuba City, Dodgeville, Platteville, Linden, Benton, Shullsburg, Beetown, Potosi, and Mifflin, to name just a few.

The year 1829 saw the first log house constructed at the village of Helena on the south bank of the Wisconsin River, across from present-day Spring Green. Soon another house was built nearby, and the government erected a storage shed and stationed an agent there. A store was opened the next year and it appeared that the town would grow and flourish. Some businessmen from Green Bay who had seen the success of the lead shot business in Missouri decided to have a shot tower built on a sandstone bluff behind the town of Helena. Work began in 1831. On top of the bluff were constructed buildings where the lead could be melted, and at the base, facilities for grading, polishing, and packaging the shot for shipment. Lead from the various mines in the immediate neighborhood (especially from Dodgeville and Highland) was used for production of shot. Transported by wagon to the tower, the lead was melted and passed through perforated ladles to produce shot of uniform size. As the molten lead fell down the shaft, it assumed a spherical shape and cooled, falling into cold water at the base of the shaft.

Much of the lead shot was taken up the river by boat to Fort Winnebago, portaged to the Fox River, and then boated to Green Bay for shipment to eastern ports. During the Black Hawk War in 1832, while the fleeing Indians escaped down the river in canoes, the pursuing militia came through Helena, and razed the log structures to make rafts to cross the river. In time, Helena would be rebuilt, and would become a thriving village for a few short years, and the shot tower worked until 1861, when the buildings and machinery were finally sold.

By the 1830s, word had reached Cornwall, England of the mining opportunities, and soon streams of Cornish immigrants flowed into the area where Mineral Point is now a thriving city. They brought with them their deep shaft mining techniques, and further boosted production. The Cornish were also proficient builders with stone, and their heritage still remains today in the

The Galena Lead District
(Created from David Dale Owen's map, 1839)

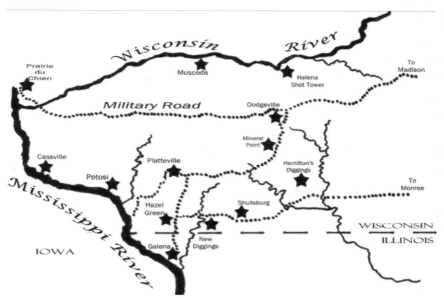

many limestone and sandstone structures they built for homes and shops in Mineral Point and other locations in southwestern Wisconsin and northwestern Illinois. Lead mining had reached grand proportions long before the railroad reached Mineral Point. During the earliest years, Milwaukee was the nearest shipping facility, and with no water route, and no railroad until 1857, the ore had to be transported by wagon and teams overland. Such an undertaking required extensive preparation for a wagon train. Teamsters faced a 125-mile journey through sparsely settled country, nearly void of any roads other than blazed trails that were almost impassible during prolonged rains.

To the infant city of Madison was only one-third the total distance to their destination, and there the wagon train stopped to rest the oxen teams and to obtain provisions for the remainder of the trip. Upon departing, the wagons crossed a rickety bridge over the Yahara River that was barely adequate for such heavy loads, making the entire endeavor for the lead train teamsters even more harrowing. But their freight must reach Milwaukee, and fellow miners back in Mineral Point were counting on them to return with much needed supplies.

The thirty-day round trip always proved labor-intense, and although the teamsters accomplished what they set out to do, their efforts could hardly be considered a first class financial success. That situation improved, though, as navigation on the closer Mississippi River steadily increased.

The successful journey of the steamboat *Virginia* to Fort St. Anthony (now Fort Snelling) in 1823 established a practical transportation route into the northern reaches of the new territory. Soon, advocates began promoting their ideas of improving the navigability on the great river by eliminating the rapids with several canals and locks. Although their principle interest leaned toward more favorable shipping conditions for the mining district, their recommendations to the Secretary of War (who maintained jurisdiction over the rivers) carefully included the benefits of a more efficient means to transport troops and military supplies. The advice was well received and its consideration would not be dismissed, but the river improvement project was not immediately started.

Because of the dangerous risks on the Mississippi, and with the high and fluctuating freight rates that were greatly influenced by the river's frequently changing water stage, alternate shipping routes were considered and tried. Great Lakes cities wanted the mining trade routed through their ports so they might reap the handsome profits already claimed by St. Louis and New Orleans merchants. Needless to say, rivalry developed.

Some lead was conveyed up the Wisconsin River to Fort Winnebago, hauled across the portage and then taken down the Fox River to Green Bay. There it was loaded onto Great Lakes steamers destined for New York. The Wisconsin/Fox Rivers route, however, was looked upon with greater uncertainty. Full of sandbars and a frequently shifting channel, the Wisconsin presented difficult navigation and was deemed unfavorable for the lead trade. Although some shipments did continue for a while, they constituted a very small percentage of the total output.

Although Galena, Illinois is situated five miles east of the Mississippi River, it was a major port for the Mississippi packets from the early 1820s through the 1840s, as the Fever River, (now known as the Galena River) a tributary of the Mississippi flows through the city, and at that time supported heavy riverboat passage. Galena was second only to St. Louis in steamboat traffic, and before the Civil War, more steamboats navigated the Fever River to Galena than arrived at St. Paul.

Even before Illinois achieved statehood in 1818, frontiersmen flocked into the area around Galena to mine the rich lead deposits. Galena soon became a widely known and popular town. Homes were notched into the steep bluffs of the narrow river valley, and steamboat owners, shopkeepers, and miners built magnificent brick and stone places of business in the fashionable Classic, Gothic, and Italianate styles of the times.

Lead mining declined after the discovery of gold in the far western territories, and the few people who did not leave for the western gold mines took up farming. The Fever River became obstructed by sediment from area farmland cultivation, and eventually, the steamboat pilots encountered difficulty, and no longer deemed navigation of the shallow river to Galena profitable or practical. The once popular river town was becoming isolated.

Then in 1890, Congress authorized the city of Galena to improve the river for navigation once again, with dredging and the construction of a lock and dam. The dam was built near the Mississippi River where the Fever branched into three sloughs. With the lock and the channel improvement, navigation was restored, and Galena was a Mississippi River port again.

The federal government purchased the Galena lock and dam in 1894 and the Corp of Engineers assumed control. But river traffic gradually declined again, and its operation was abandoned in 1925.

Land routes over poor trails and rough corduroy roads to Milwaukee provided another tried alternate. But even though the overall lead ore shipping cost was a little less per ton, the oxcarts and wagons were slow and could not handle the tremendous volume of the heavy cargo. Chicago, too, was making its bid for a share of the lead trade with plans of railroad construction to Galena. But that would not materialize until the mid-1850s, and until then, no overland route won any favorable advantage over the Mississippi River. All of the best efforts by the lake cities to divert the trade routes could not turn the tide. Wisconsin Governor James Doty succeeded in getting Erie Canal tolls reduced to encourage more shipments over that route. But a Buffalo newspaper reported in 1846 that lead shipments received there amounted to only one-fourth of what had arrived in 1844. Until the advent of the railroad, over 95 percent of the lead mined in southwestern Wisconsin and northwestern Illinois made its way down the Mississippi to New Orleans, and was loaded on ocean vessels destined for the eastern seaboard markets.

Sinipee

It wouldn't seem likely that a Mississippi River town that had raised to the status of a regular port of call for many steamboats, and that had become a popular shipping and commercial center, could just vanish with hardly a trace. The story of Sinipee, though, reveals the remarkable rise and fall of such a town.

Miners in southwestern Wisconsin Territory found themselves at the mercy of shippers and merchants in Galena, Illinois, the dominant shipping port in the region. No competition meant high prices for supplies and shipment of their only product – lead – that was in high demand in the eastern markets. But the Mineral Point miners thought the businessmen of Galena seemed to be taking a little more than their fair share, so they began searching for an alternate shipping port. They found their answer on the bank of the Mississippi just four miles north of

Dubuque where there was an excellent landing, easily accessible for the largest boats. Here they would establish a shipping depot for the lead mining district, and they would call it Port Sinepee. (Sinipee is derived from the Sauk words assini, for "rock" and nipee, for "water." Combined, their meaning becomes "the place of the rock by the water," which accurately describes the towering limestone bluff with its base at the river.)

Twenty-three Mineral Point investors formed the "Louisiana Company" in 1838 and for the sum of $12,000 purchased the riverfront land from Payton Vaughn, who had settled with his new wife in the shadow of the bluffs at the mouth of the Sinipee Creek in 1831, built a log cabin, and operated a cable ferry. Part of the agreement they made with Vaughn obligated him to build a substantially adequate hotel to accommodate travelers at the new village. The company then hired civil engineer, John Plumbe, Jr., to survey the site and act as agent to sell building lots. Plumbe had recently come to the Wisconsin Territory from the east where he had been instrumental in building the first interstate railroad from Petersburg, Virginia to Roanoke Rapids in North Carolina.

Construction began, and by early spring of 1839 about twenty-five commercial buildings had been erected at Sinipee, housing blacksmith shops, warehouses, several stores, a bank, a church, a post office and residences. Payton Vaughn's large hotel, appropriately known as "Stone House," was completed in grand style, constructed with local stone, finished with elegance uncommon to the Wisconsin frontier, fireplaces in every room, and a ballroom occupying most of the second story that served as the social gathering place for the entire community.

It was at Stone House in December 1838, where John Plumbe presented to the Sinipee citizens gathered there his idea to petition Congress to fund the building of a railroad from Lake Michigan to the Mississippi River. He possessed the far-sighted reasoning that a railroad would someday stretch to the California coast, and his road across Wisconsin to Sinipee would be the first link of that transcontinental system. His presentation drew unanimous support, and the proposal was drafted and introduced to Congress by Territorial Delegate G.W. Jones. It received favorable consideration, and the funds were appropriated for the survey. Although it would be many years before the railroad was actually built, it is quite conceivable that the initialization of the United States transcontinental railroad was born at Stone House in Sinipee, Wisconsin.

Large quantities of lead began arriving at Sinipee for shipment down the Mississippi, and a number of St. Louis steamboats made the port a scheduled landing. Real estate values soared as the business traffic increased and more people took watchful interest in the new settlement. It appeared that Sinipee's prosperity was assured, and that it could easily rival Galena, and even Dubuque as a major river port.

Drawing of the Old Stone House at Sinipee as it appeared in the Fennimore Times, September 1927

Expansion and further development of Sinipee's residential and business areas was planned and in progress when disaster struck the little town of about 200 population in the spring of 1839. The Mississippi swelled with the spring thaw and unusually heavy rains. Most of the village flooded, and although the immediate property damage was not great, the receding floodwaters left behind stagnant pools of slime. Warm summer temperatures followed, and within a short time uncontrollable swarms of malaria-carrying mosquitoes infested the town. At that time, treatment of the disease was unknown, and most of the citizens became ill, and many died. The only hope of survival for those remaining was to vacate the settlement, and after such a short existence, Sinipee was a ghost town.

When the C B & Q Railroad built through the area in the 1880s all the wooden buildings had long ago been dismantled for their valuable lumber or moved on sleds across the Mississippi ice to Dubuque. Its tracks were laid within a few feet of the only remaining structure – the old Stone House hotel. It survived until 1904 when it was consumed by an accidental fire. Eventually, a contractor demolished the remains and used the rock from the walls as fill for a Mississippi dam. In October 1934, Lock and Dam Number 11 was completed, raising the water level behind it. Water now covers most of the land where once stood the incredible little river town, Port Sinipee.

Dry Bone Fortune

The California Gold Rush of 1849 lured a vast number of Wisconsin miners – as well as people of nearly every profession – with promises of greater riches. In time, many returned, their hopes and dreams shattered as the result of failed gold prospecting attempts.

It had been known for years that there were large quantities of zinc in the lead district, but zinc was not mined because there was little demand for it and smelting it was expensive. But in the 1860s, zinc mining and processing became more prevalent, as galvanizing steel with a zinc coating to prevent rust and corrosion was discovered to be useful and necessary, and when brass and other alloys that require zinc came into demand, the call went out for the mining of zinc. Earliest mining of "Dry Bone," as the miners called it, was quite simple. It had been considered an annoying waste product by the lead miners and was merely thrown out on the tailing heaps. It took many years to reclaim all the zinc that had already been taken out of the ground.

During this time, too, the Mineral Point Railroad was completed, connecting to the Chicago & Galena Railroad and the Illinois Central. Mineral Point had now become a shipping and supply center. A second railroad, the Mineral Point & Northern followed in 1904. The demand for lead and zinc diminished after World War I, however, and the once profitable industry gradually faded out of existence in southwestern Wisconsin.

But in its heyday, the lead mining industry in southwestern Wisconsin played largely in the influence on transportation priorities of the new territory. Not only did it create a product that demanded high-level needs for transport. It encouraged thousands of emigrants – adventurous and industrious settlers who built cities and formed society – an influx that in turn demanded ever increasing supplies to a region that was not yet

self sufficient. New arrivals continually pushed the frontier beyond the frontier. The steadily rising number of steamboats required on the Mississippi and its tributaries to support all this, prepared the transport companies for even greater demands as the coming waves of emigrants flooded into the Upper Mississippi Valley after the Minnesota Territory opened up for settlement. Meeting the transportation needs of the mining district provided valuable experience to help develop the northward movement of settlers and commodities, and eventually for the vast quantities of agricultural and forest products that would soon flow down the Mississippi from the northern regions.

Mineral Point Railroad freight depot as it appears today. The depot was built in 1856 from local materials, and is the oldest surviving depot in Wisconsin. The Mineral Point Railroad Society was formed in 2000 to further the restoration of the historic depot, and to promote preservation. The restoration was completed and the depot reopened to the public as a museum in 2004. (Photo by author)

More Settlers, More Roads

Just as the Cornish were enticed by the prosperous mining in the southwest, Norwegians began settling father north in the fertile agricultural region that is now La Crosse and Vernon counties. This area had been untouched by the ice age glaciers; streams and rivers had cut deep valleys leaving ridges and sheer rock bluffs, much the same landscape of the Norwegians' homeland. Settlement in that area began in the 1840s when Norwegians arrived via river steamboats at Prairie du Chien and then walked some 70 miles northward into the region occupied only by the Winnebago Indians. Several small communities born of this era grew and remain today, but many withered away, lost to time and now only memories to a few.

Evan Gullord, a Norwegian, was the first known white man to explore and settle on the Coon Prairie in Vernon County (known then as Bad Ax County) in 1848. He walked from Galena, Illinois on the main trail to Platteville, Wisconsin, to Prairie du Chien and then followed the old Indian trail into Vernon County. The next year, 1849, another Norwegian, Helge Gulbrandson migrated to this area from Muskego, an established Scandinavian settlement near Milwaukee, and made the first settlement in "Helgedalen," the location that is now the village of Coon Valley. He shared that valley with only the friendly Winnebago Indians and an overabundance of raccoons for two years before others followed.

La Crosse was merely a dozen log homes, a land office, one hotel, and two general stores; Prairie du Chien was still the closest center of commerce, but the 70-mile journey through the wilderness proved difficult and treacherous. Indian trails provided passage; the Hudson-Prairie du Chien Road had been surveyed in 1838 by Jefferson Davis, but was not yet improved.

By that time, with the advent of a growing population, many more roads had been developed after the Territorial Assembly of 1845 appointed a commission to survey them. Of this next wave of settlement links, Milwaukee served as its hub, connecting that city to Fort

Winnebago, Fox Lake, Watertown and Madison via Janesville, all instrumental in the state's vital transportation network.

Likewise, trails leading from Prairie du Chien northward to the Coon Prairie in Vernon County and eastward to Madison and Janesville became heavily traveled routes connecting and intersecting with those from Milwaukee. The shipping port on Lake Michigan was now linked overland with the Mississippi River.

Early in the 1850s great interest was taken in a new method of road building. Two-inch-thick, eight feet long wooden planks nailed to four-inch square stringers made for a smooth, dry traveling surface. The first of these plank roads was built from Milwaukee to West Bend and Fond du Lac, and from Fond du Lac to Sheboygan. Another plank road was built linking Milwaukee and Watertown, and the planked route to Janesville, which had begun as early as 1844 was completed. About every three miles, travelers encountered a tollgate where they were charged a cent per mile for each animal and vehicle.

The abundance of standing timber seemed to offer plank roads as a solution to the transportation problem. The construction work was simple, although the methods employed were rather crude. The giant oaks standing within reasonable distance from the trail were felled and sawed into planks and heavier stringers by means of portable sawmills. The stringers were laid in shallow trenches to prevent movement, and the planks securely spiked to them. Progress was necessarily slow, but the decay resistant qualities of the oak timber gave promise of a durable and permanent highway. Had the timbers been seasoned before they were laid, the expectation of long life would have been more fully realized.

Heavy traffic over the years caused the planks and timbers to warp, dislodge and decay, creating more of an obstacle course than safe and comfortable travel. This problem with all the plank roads brought about a steady decline in their popularity.

One such instance of premature deterioration of the plank road between Sheboygan and Fond du Lac could not have been foreseen at the time it was built. Railroad construction was in progress southward from Fond du Lac. A locomotive had been shipped to Sheboygan via a Great Lakes steamer; however, getting it to the inland town posed a serious problem. The only solution was transporting it over the plank road. It was represented that by laying timbers lengthwise on the planks, the roadway would be adequately protected from cutting by the wheel flanges on the 46,000-pound engine. The highway promoters objected strenuously to this abuse of their pet project, but it was found that their charter allowed any horse or oxen drawn wheeled vehicle to pass over the highway, and they could not deny the use of the road for this purpose, as the locomotive was a wheeled vehicle to be towed by as many as forty horses and oxen. Although the long timbers were placed under the wheels, and replaced as the locomotive moved forward, they did not stay there, and the roadway suffered heavy damage in many places. After a series of expensive repairs, a second locomotive was brought over the plank road from Sheboygan to Fond du Lac, and the damage was even greater than the first.

The state purchased the deteriorating Janesville road from its owners in 1908 for $10,000 and later it became the first paved road in Milwaukee County.

By this time the southeast was booming, but the lesser-populated Mississippi River Valley still utilized the undeveloped Indian trails for overland travel. Steep hills and bluffs surrounding the valleys presented more difficulty in road improvement, not to mention the greater travel distances over the less-direct routes to reach any destination.

No one had ever attempted to traverse the distance from Prairie du Chien to La Crosse by a land route until November 1845. Prior to that time the Mississippi River provided the only means of conveyance between the two settlements.

Samuel Snaugh, (pronounced Snow) a merchant, visited trader John M. Levy at Prairie du Chien in the fall of 1845 with the intention of obtaining a supply of goods for his La Crosse store. While there, he convinced Mr. Levy of the bountiful opportunities waiting at La Crosse, and as an added incentive offered a partnership in the business there. Levy, somewhat discontented with his position in Prairie du Chien, consented to the deal. They procured a team of oxen and wagon, loaded it with a store of merchandise and embarked on the overland trip that had never before been attempted. There were no paths or trails through most of the heavily wooded eastern bank of the river, but eight days later Snaugh and Levy arrived in La Crosse with their goods, leaving behind a newly blazed trail that would become a popular route in the following years.

The need for roads had been realized. In 1850 and 1851 the state legislature took an active role in the advancement of more overland communication. Commissioners were appointed to lay out and establish a network of state roads linking many of the growing towns. The most feasible and direct routes were to be chosen between Adams (Baraboo) and the Dells on the Wisconsin River, and from there to Prairie La Crosse on the Mississippi River; from Reedsburg to Stevens Point; from Wyocena in Columbia County across the Portage Canal to the Dells; from Black River Falls to Wisconsin Rapids. Although the state legislature encouraged the development of the roads and even appointed the commissioners to establish them, no state funding was appropriated to maintain them.

About the same time, Frank Petit is given the distinction of being the first white man to settle in the La Crosse River Valley; he built a log cabin near Castle Rock. His brother, William Petit built the first log house in 1851 at the site that is now Sparta.

Sparta's significance was soon recognized, located at the very intersection of the two main thoroughfares of the time. The route from Black River Falls to Prairie du Chien ran north and south past Petit's cabin, and not far away, the east-west route between La Crosse and Baraboo. By 1855, Petit's cabin had been converted to an inn, sold to new owner Hiram Foster, expanded with additions and renamed "Globe Hotel." By no means was it the first hotel in Sparta: preceding it, the Monroe House, the Allen House and the Sparta, another tavern, were situated among only fifteen dwellings. Four hotels near the crossroads boosted Sparta into popularity as a good stopping place for travelers. Located not only in the center of the settlement but also at the road crossing, the Globe Hotel enjoyed the greatest success for the next three years.

To the north, Black River Falls had a much earlier beginning. An old diary written by Willard Keyes and received at the Wisconsin State

Historical Society about 1919 indicates that he was a member of the Rolette expedition in 1818-1819 to journey north from Prairie du Chien. At the location that is now Black River Falls on the Black River they recognized an ample waterpower supply and constructed a sawmill. It is not clear whether they intended, at that time, for this to be a permanent settlement as there are no indications as such. Their efforts were short lived, however, as the Indians burned the mill and drove these first industrialists out of the region soon after the sawing began.

Twenty years later, 1839, another expedition, perhaps originating at Prairie du Chien, and this time equipped with adequate provisions, set out on the Indian trails northward. Jacob Spaulding led the party of settlers to the same location and by the spring of 1840 was successful in building another sawmill and several houses. Although the road to Black River Falls had been surveyed in 1838, it was not improved until 1849. But many settlers arrived in that area long before the road was opened. They came in pursuit of the abundant pine forests and the logging and lumber industry. As a result, vast acres of land were cleared for farming and by 1851 Black River Falls had boomed into existence. The road southward now supported frequent traffic, connecting the settlement with the rest of the more populated regions of the state.

Sixty miles south along this road, another settlement had already sprung to life. By 1851, the site that is now Viroqua embraced permanent residence of three families, Moses Decker being the first to arrive in 1846. This community grew slowly as a town, although settlers coming mostly from Southeastern Ohio and other points east sought the surrounding rich farmland soil. A few years later, Viroqua would boast many businesses. Jeremiah Rusk, born in a log cabin in Ohio, 1830, began his stage-driving era at the age of sixteen in his native state. He migrated to Viroqua, Wisconsin with a new wife in 1853, where he built and proudly named a popular hostelry the "Buckeye Hotel" in honor of his homeland, and it would become a popular stopping place for travelers on the north-south road. Rusk continued his stagecoach driving, too, acquiring a stage line between Prairie du Chien and Black River Falls. He ran that route until the Civil War called him to the south. It may be said that as a result of his stagecoach experience, Rusk rode into military distinction, the governorship, and the cabinet.

Just seven miles north of Viroqua, what is now the center of Westby, this road crossed an Indian trail. For centuries it had been the route used by the Winnebago tribe living in the Kickapoo Valley to reach their ceremonial grounds at Prairie La Crosse. It passed over the Coon Prairie, through the valley that is now the village of Coon Valley, ascended the steep hills west of that settlement, progressed atop the ridge and then down into Mormon Coulee and on to the prairie that is now La Crosse.

This trail was not used by the settlers of Coon Valley until after the advent of the railroad extending to La Crosse in 1858. By that time La Crosse had expanded to a larger commercial center. The railroad provided a great boon to its progress, and now the settlers of Coon Valley could market their produce at the much nearer river town rather than making the difficult 70-mile trek to Prairie du Chien. The settlers of the area considered this a giant leap forward. But it was, at that time, still a dangerous 35-40 mile journey due to the lack of an adequate road. The long and tedious route led their oxen-drawn wagons up what is now known as Timber Coulee to Hazen Corners (now Cashton), westward across St. Joseph Ridge and down a treacherously steep hill into La Crosse.

A shorter, better route to La Crosse became the order of the day; the old Indian trail was observed, explored and determined to be only half the distance of the previously used route to La Crosse. A few trees were cut and the most intimidating holes filled with rocks, transforming a nearly unknown trail into a useable wagon path.

Although the pioneers were quite pleased with such a marvelous improvement, journeying over the hills to La Crosse with a wagonload of wheat still presented a laborious task. Reaching 500 feet above the valley floor, the hill just to the west of the Coon Valley settlement ascended at such a steep angle in places that teams of oxen or horses could not manage the loads. Undaunted by the inconvenience, wagon men hand carried the sacks of grain, one by one, to the top where they were once again reloaded into the empty wagons that had been more easily negotiated up the remainder of the hill by the teams.

Eventually a narrow wooden wagon bridge spanned the creek at the west end of the village; the development of this route became a popular one for all the settlements to the east. By the 1870s it saw heavy farm-to-market traffic and eventually evolved to become part of the main highway between Minneapolis and Chicago. (It is also interesting to note that this highway, a once-isolated Indian trail served as a navigational aid to air traffic between those cities in the 1920s and '30s.)

Farmers Hauled
Wheat to the Mississippi River

Lars P. Larson – now there's a name that could come from only one place – Norway. When Lars was a lad of 10 in 1847, his father decided it was time to leave behind their impoverished life in Biri, Norway, and go to the "new country" across the sea. Together with several other families, Peter Larson, his wife and their two children spent seven weeks aboard the sailing ship *Nordlyse*. The boat was far from being seaworthy. It was overloaded with 400 passengers packed aboard, and when it reached Quebec, the captain narrowly escaped prosecution.

At Quebec, the Larsons took passage on another boat bound for Wisconsin via the lake route, and finally ended their journey near Coon Valley (Vernon County) not far from the Mississippi River. There they remained until 1851, when they set out for Trempealeau County with ox team and covered wagon. They crossed Black River on a ferryboat operated at a point that later became the site of the first Hunter's Bridge. From there they drove across prairie and over hills to a homestead near present-day Ettrick. They built a log cabin, and then the work of clearing the land began, and that kept the family busy for several years to come. They didn't have much in those early years, but they were happy. The territory was thinly populated, and the land was wild but fertile. There was little timber, but game was plentiful, so they always had food. And, of course, there were Indians. They hunted, trapped, and camped everywhere, but they always seemed peaceful and never caused any threats.

Lars was 14 by then, capable of doing a man's work. He learned and became proficient at driving teams of oxen and managing a breaking plow. In the pioneer days in Wisconsin, the ox was the motive force, and to them the fertile farms of today owe much, as this slow but sure beast first turned the virgin soil. Following a plow hitched to a half-dozen oxen was a task in itself, requiring headwork and cleverness. Although a sulking oxen may not do much thinking, it's a sure bet that a half-dozen would never think alike, and it was the driver's business to make them perform as one.

When he could be spared from home, Lars worked for other neighbors with more land to plow. They all knew he could handle three or four yoke of oxen as expertly as any of the adults. As a youngster, he hauled the lumber from a mill at North Bend for the first frame barn in the community, and for the Larson's new house that replaced their tiny log cabin.

Hauling wheat to Trempealeau was another job for the boy. Trempealeau was twenty-one miles from the Larson farm – a two-day trip with oxen. There were always several teams that would travel together, starting out before daybreak, making camp that night at some midway point. They picketed the oxen to graze in the prairie grass for the night, and then they would build a campfire. After supper, and before rolling up in their blankets, there would be songs and story telling, although one story they probably avoided was the very reason they traveled in a group: marketing their wheat was not without danger. Sometime previously, a lone wheat hauler on this route had been robbed and killed. (The story circulated many years later that the murderer confessed the crime on his deathbed.) Lars never encountered such problems, as there were usually too many in his caravans to allow an attacker any degree of success.

Sometimes the wheat haulers would stop at the old Four Mile House, halfway between Galesville and Trempealeau. Ox teams and wagons lined both sides of the road for the overnight stay at the popular inn run by Mrs. C. Schmitz.

The next day the caravan would reach its destination – Trempealeau – to deliver the wheat loads at the docks. During the peak wheat seasons, wagons would be lined up a half-mile or more waiting their turn to unload, and at night, fires could be seen out across the prairie where the haulers were camped. Every idle man in Trempealeau could find employment loading wheat on the steamboats. Two or three boats would be loading at a time, and steamboat men would be scouring the town for more help.

Left –The Melchior House at Trempealeau in the 1800s. This inn was built with a brewery at one end. (From *Stagecoach and Tavern Tales by Harry E. Cole*) Right – The only remains of the building today, located along the road between downtown Trempealeau and Perrot State Park. (Photo by author)

Trempealeau was a lively town then. The long riverfront streets lined with buildings on both sides were so crowded that sometimes it was difficult to maneuver the teams and wagons to one of the four big grain warehouses. And when the work was done, it was time to enjoy a night on the town. If overnight lodging was necessary, Lars checked into the Melchior House, another popular inn at Trempealeau. Watching the "floating palace" steamboats coming and going at the levee always proved exciting, and for a teen-aged farm boy the rest of Trempealeau was sure to provide plenty of entertainment.

Some farmers would put their loads aboard a ferryboat destined for the Pickwick flourmill on the Minnesota side of the river. The six-story mill constructed of locally quarried limestone was built by one of the first settlers in that valley, George W.T. Grant and his associates, Wilson and Timothy Davis. Recognizing a good source of waterpower in Big Trout Creek, they began construction in 1856, and the mill was in operation two years later. It was a very large mill for its time, producing as much as 100 barrels of flour per day. The region was part of the wheat belt at that time, and farmers of a large area, including many on the Wisconsin side of the river, depended on the Pickwick Mill for their services. Sometimes wagons lined the road for a mile, waiting their turn to unload the wheat. A hotel soon appeared next to the mill to provide overnight lodging for the farmers. During the Civil War, the mill operated around the clock to supply flour to the Union Army as well as the domestic and foreign trades. Flour was hauled by wagon to the La Moille landing, where it was loaded onto steamboats, and later onto railroad cars.

The mill at Pickwick remained in operation until 1978. After a devastating flood in 1980 that nearly wiped out the entire town and caused considerable damage to the mill, local citizens bought it and formed an organization to give new life to this magnificent historic landmark. The dam, gates and millpond were restored, as well as the mill brought back into operating condition. A tour of the site today is like a wonderful journey back through time.

Nestled in a picturesque valley on a tributary stream two miles from the Mississippi River, the imposing stone structure of the Pickwick Mill still stands, and its machinery still operational, driven by an "overshot" water wheel. The building is open to the public for self-guided tours. (Photo by author)

Bread for the Children

It is difficult for us to imagine the obstacles the pioneers faced just to survive. We take for granted our ability to reach a nearby store within a few minutes to purchase a loaf of bread or a gallon of milk, or any other commodity we might desire. It wasn't so easy for the pioneers. The lack of roads and bridges commonly restricted the convenience that we enjoy today.

The following is a true story, recreated from the account of an early pioneer family in the town of Lowell, Dodge County. It illustrates quite well how, without the luxury of a road, a short distance (in terms that we consider today) presented the traveler with a significant degree of challenge. It also illustrates the courage, the ingenuity, the faith, and the never-give-up attitudes that allowed the settlers to succeed and to prosper.

The year: 1844. Settlement in this part of the state was sparse. Dr. Eldred and his family had managed to successfully raise and harvest a crop of wheat that summer, and after the tedious task of flail threshing, they had six bushels of grain. It was just in time, too, for their supply of flour was depleted, and none other available. The younger children were hungry and begging for bread.

The nearest gristmill was at Watertown, some thirty-five miles distant. Dr. Eldred's oldest son, Daniel, was the most capable of making that journey with a wagon and a team of oxen. There was no road leading east from Lowell, but the best route was to reach Oak Grove, where a road did lead to Watertown. Daniel started early the next morning.

Over hills and through marshes he trudged the oxen along, until he encountered the most demanding obstacle on his way to Oak Grove. Pratt Creek lay between him and the road to Watertown. The stream was too deep and too wide for the wagon, especially with the precious cargo of wheat.

Daniel knew what he had to do. He carried the necessary tools in the wagon. His little siblings were counting on his success, and Pratt Creek would not stop him from completing the journey.

Nearby trees were felled with his axe and drug to the creek. The cut poles would not reach across the breadth to make a bridge, but enough of them lashed together would serve as a raft to float the wagon over. The oxen swam across, towing the raft, and on the opposite bank, with the use of chains, they landed the wagon.

Main Street, present-day Lowell, Dodge County, Wisconsin. (Photo by author)

Daniel tied the raft securely to the bank, hoping it would still be there for the return trip. He hitched the oxen to the wagon again, and continued his quest for the road to Watertown.

The north-south road between Watertown and Oak Grove had been somewhat improved, and more wagons and stagecoach traffic had pounded it smooth. The going was a little easier the rest of the way, but it was sundown by the time Daniel arrived at the Watertown mill, exhausted from the grueling trip.

"How soon can you grind my wheat into flour?" Daniel asked the miller.

"In about six weeks and no sooner," the miller replied.

Daniel thought about the little children at home crying and hungry, and he desperately pleaded with the miller, hoping to gain his sympathy in this dire situation.

"It's just not possible," the miller said. "My mill is broken down and cannot operate," but he explained that he understood Daniel's desperation.

"Could you give me some flour, or exchange it for my wheat?" Daniel wasn't going to give up.

"We haven't any flour at all."

Daniel couldn't return home without something to help feed the children. "Then, how about some bran? Could you give me some bran?"

His persistent pleading had finally convinced the miller to help him. "Perhaps I can let you have some bran in the morning." He offered to let Daniel sleep overnight on some bags in the mill, but Daniel did not rest easy. He worried about what his mother would say if he returned without any flour.

True to his promise, the next morning the miller presented Daniel with two bags of bran he had filled sometime during the night, and without further ado, sent Daniel on this way home just after sunrise.

It was another long, tedious journey back to Lowell. His raft was still in tact at Pratt Creek, but it required the same laborious task to get across. He arrived at home about sundown, met at the gate by his mother, who excitedly asked, "Daniel, have you got the flour?" She sobbed when he told her the mill could not grind the wheat. "It is too bad that we brought our little children out into the wilderness to starve."

"But Mother," Daniel said. "I have two sacks of bran in the wagon. You can sift out the finest part, and bake bread for the children."

Daniel had saved the day, even if he didn't get the flour, for in due time, a loaf of bread was baking, and the children were happy.

Later that evening, Daniel heard voices in the nearby woods; someone was coming with a team of oxen and a wagon. Three gentlemen and two ladies requested of Dr. Eldred a place to stay for the night. Mrs. Eldred agreed, but she informed the strangers there was no bread for them to eat for supper.

"We have three bags of flour in our wagon," one of the travelers replied, "and we will give you one of them."

At the supper table, the strangers decided they had traveled far enough. They would settle at Lowell, and the Eldred family was glad to have such good neighbors.

Early Iowa Settlement

Julien Dubuque was the first known white man to settle within the limits of Iowa. Well-educated and knowledgeable in mineralogy and mining, he came to the "west" from Quebec, eager and determined to procure an interest in the mining region. He was but twenty-one years of age when he arrived at Prairie du Chien in 1784. He soon gained the confidence of the Mesquakie Indian chief whose tribe then occupied the northeastern portion of Iowa and thus began an extraordinary relationship. He proceeded to prospect the land in that vicinity, and discovered considerable quantities of lead ore existing there. Negotiations with the Indian chief resulted in the exclusive rights to work the mines. Dubuque established a trading post, and hired Indians and French laborers to extract the lead, which he periodically transported to St. Louis and exchanged for trade merchandise. A city bearing his name would get its start in the 1830s.

The next white settlement was that of Basil Giard, a French American who, in 1795, obtained a land grant from the Lieutenant-Governor of Louisiana Territory. The tract occupied a portion of present-day Clayton County in Iowa, directly across the Mississippi River from Prairie du Chien. When the United States acquired the Louisiana Territory in 1803, the government issued Giard a patent, which was the first legal land title obtained in the limits of Iowa. On this land would eventually stand the village of North McGregor, later being renamed Marquette.

Louis Honore Tesson, a French Canadian, made the third settlement in 1799. The Louisiana Lieutenant-Governor authorized Tesson to establish a trading post at the head of the Des Moines Rapids of the Mississippi River. He selected a site that is now the location of Montrose in Lee County, in the extreme southeast corner of Iowa. Once the trading post was erected, Tesson enclosed his farm with a rail fence and planted crops of corn and potatoes, and a hundred apple tree seedlings that he had brought from St. Charles, Missouri. The trees adapted well to the country and climate; it was the first orchard planted on Iowa soil.

From those beginnings, a flow of emigrants found their way across the Mississippi into Iowa, and by the 1830s and '40s, land seekers – farmers, millers, tradesmen, entrepreneurs of all varieties – were arriving at an alarming rate. The population of Clayton County was only 275 in 1840; by 1850 that number had grown to 3,875. People from New York, Massachusetts, and Pennsylvania were rapidly taking advantage of the land offered by the government for $1.25 per acre.

Many of the earliest towns were established on or near the banks of the Mississippi River, where there was easy access by boats to deliver supplies from distant sources. Most of these towns derived their business directly or indirectly from the agricultural activity of the surrounding country, and that resource steadily increased. Flour milling became an important industry, and with the ever-expanding population, the demand for lumber was high. Much of Iowa did not have the abundant timber, as found in Wisconsin and Minnesota, so logs were rafted down the Mississippi to supply the sawmills.

And because the river served as the main avenue for the arrival of newcomers, the river towns were the portals to the inland prairies, where awaited the tracts of fertile soil. But at least one night of rest in the town would be sought before continuing the journey; hotels did a booming business. Aside from a trading post or, perhaps, a general store, a tavern or hotel was among the first of the commercial buildings to appear. They provided lodging and meals for the traveler, and temporary shelter for those constructing other homes in the community. As the villages developed, the hostelries served as popular gathering spots for everything from church services conducted by an itinerant preacher, to dances with a single fiddle player providing the music, or any other social celebrations.

A trading post was established at present-day Muscatine in 1833 under the direction of Col. George Davenport of Rock Island, Illinois. That same year, James Casey and John Vanatta arrived, and soon their wood yard supplied fuel to the steamboats in route up the Mississippi. The little settlement became known first as "Casey's Woodpile," but when the town was surveyed and platted in 1836, the name Newburg appeared, and that name was soon discarded and replaced with "Bloomington." The population was then 71.

Robert Kinney built a 16 x 30 feet, story and a half frame structure and became the first landlord in the town with his hostelry, the Iowa House that contained six rooms. The steady arrival of emigrants into the new territory meant steady business for Kinney, and within two years he enlarged the tavern with a 30 x 40 feet, two-story addition. The two-story veranda across the front became a popular loafing place – it offered a clear view of the river and the boat landing, and there seemed to always be a cool breeze on hot summer days. The men usually occupied the lower level, smoked and traded stories, while the women gathered and gossiped on the upper floor.

Even in a tiny village such as this, the Iowa House soon had competition. John Vanatta contributed to the community the Lawson House, a pretentious 20 x 40, two-story tavern, and offered the best accommodations available for the time. The house was constructed with oak lumber hand-hewn from timber cut at or near the building site. A square post next to the street supported a whale oil lamp, lighting the way to the Lawson House for weary travelers. But even with a successful business, Vanatta tired of it, and in 1839 Josiah Parvin took over.

Parvin provided for his guests the most hospitable accommodations and the best food the times had to offer. His reputation gained him added success, and after just one year it became necessary for him to build a larger structure to accommodate the growing number of guests.

A third hostelry in the early days of the small village was that of James Palmer, which became known as "Captain Jim's." A stonemason, Suel Foster, had started its construction in 1838. Judge Joseph Williams, seeking a home after arriving at Bloomington, purchased the unfinished structure and hired a wood craftsman to complete the work on the commodious dwelling. Eventually, James Palmer came into its possession and engaged in the hotel business. He advertised in the local newspaper, the *Bloomington Herald*, single meals for twenty-five cents, lodging per day with meals for seventy-five cents, and a horse fed and stabled overnight for twenty-five cents.

Bloomington was incorporated in 1839, and had become the Muscatine county seat. But there was confusion at the post office: many letters were misdirected to towns with the same name in several other states, and after struggling with the circumstance for several years, the town's name was finally changed to Muscatine. The name is derived from the Mascoutin Indians, a tribe that had been driven across the Mississippi and settled near the present city.

Muscatine, a popular stopping place on the Mississippi River, became a major lumbering center and remained so for many years. Then in 1890, pearl button manufacturing began stealing the limelight. Freshwater clamshells, plentiful in the Mississippi, made stronger buttons than those made of animal horns, and more closely resembled the fashionable, expensive imports. By the turn of the Twentieth Century, half of Muscatine's workforce was employed in the button industry, and the town earned the title of "Pearl Button Capital of the World."

A hotel has occupied the corner of 2nd and Main Streets in Dubuque since 1839. The original four-story structure stood as a sentinel and gave first greeting to travelers as they entered the city. It received a major reconstruction in 1854 when it was doubled in size to 80 rooms, and at that time it was renamed the Julien House, in honor of Julien Dubuque, the first Iowa settler and the founder of the city.

By the late 1800s, the city of Dubuque nearly equaled Chicago in size, and its strategic shipping location on the Mississippi quickly registered the town as an important center of trade and commerce. Throughout the economic crescendo of the later 19th Century, the Julien House remained the focal point of the town, and was an all-important gathering place. It entertained such notable guests as Abraham Lincoln, Ulysses S. Grant, Mark Twain, and William "Buffalo Bill" Cody.

In 1839 Congress appropriated the funding to survey, grade and bridge a military route from Dubuque to the newly located territorial capital at Iowa City. Although it was labeled as the "Military Road," the incoming droves of settlers using the thoroughfare outnumbered by far the soldiers passing over it. During prior years, the Mississippi River towns had filled with men eager to venture out into the wilderness. They followed the old Indian trails, and subsequently many found the spots of their desire. But it was along the roads, after they were developed and became more heavily used, where settlements started appearing. Transportation was that magic element that helped the towns to prosper, and to become great cities. During the time of

Conestogas and stagecoaches, the territorial road from Dubuque to the capital at Iowa City was the main route of commerce. At harvest time, ox and horse-drawn wagons loaded with grain and other produce rumbled and creaked over the road to reach a market. Upon return, they hauled the family's supplies for an entire winter.

Just like the towns developing along the Mississippi River for the sake of good transportation, so did the settlers choose their claims along the road. Mail routes were set up and the cabin of one prominent settler was selected for a post office. Then someone would come along and establish a general store, and likely, a blacksmith would set up shop. Those amenities would attract more settlers, and growing populations attracted more craftsmen. Before long, there were the makings of a successful town.

Natural and logical locations that were selected wherever the highway intersected a river, those early settlements grew, prospered, and with few exceptions survive yet today.

Nicholas Delong arrived at the cascading waterfall on the North Branch of the Maquoketa River in 1834, long before the Military Road was constructed. He staked his claim, broke ground and planted a field of corn. Two years later he brought his wife, five sons and a daughter to their new home. More settlers followed, and Delong soon sold the land with the waterpower to John Sherman and Arthur Thomas who built the first flouring mill, the first hotel, and the first store, all in 1837. The following year, 1838, the Delongs built a sawmill.

Then the Military Road came, and due to the heavy traffic, after 1839 the settlement made extensive advancements. Caleb Bucknam bought out the Delongs, and in 1842 platted the village of Cascade, the name owing to the waterpower on the adjacent Maquoketa River. A post office was established that year, and in the years to follow Cascade became a bustling community. By 1856 its population had reached 450; just two years later, nearly 1,000. When the stagecoaches stopped at the tavern, and the passengers disembarked for a brief rest, enterprising young real estate agents pitched their best deals to the prospective investors. In 1858, seventy-five new buildings were erected on both sides of the river, and in addition to the mills grinding flour and sawing lumber, Cascade had Frank May's brewery that produced 2,500 barrels of beer annually, Heitchew & Murphy's furniture factory, and Charles

Huntington's wagon factory. By 1880 there were seven general stores, four carriage and blacksmith shops, three restaurants, two hotels, six boarding houses, a cabinet manufactory, twelve saloons, five boot and shoemakers, and a wide variety of other craftsmen and merchants ranging from carpet weavers to toy stores. And because the railroad had been extended from Bellevue to Cascade in 1878-79, the town had a busy railway depot.

Three years before the Military Road was established, Daniel Varvel, an adventurous native of Kentucky, came to the mouth of Kitty Creek on the South Fork of the Maquoketa River. The wooded hillsides had not been disturbed by any lumberman's axe, nor had the fertile prairie that rolled beyond the horizon been turned by any plow. Varvel liked what he saw, and without further hesitation, he decided this would be his new home.

His log cabin became a landmark for the weary traveler seeking overnight shelter, served as headquarters for the men who laid out the road, and mail that came once a week for settlers in the surrounding area was thrown off there. And then the traffic started pouring over the Military Road; soon there were more cabins, and a two-story hotel was constructed. The little settlement continued to expand, and became known as Monticello, soon to be a flourishing city.

Old Mission Road

The government had built Fort Atkinson inland in northeastern Iowa and a road leading to it from the west bank of the Mississippi at Dubuque. Fort Crawford at Prairie du Chien was looking after Fort Atkinson, furnishing it with soldiers and supplies, and patrolling the Old Mission Road, as it was popularly known, keeping it safe from the possible threat of hostile Indians.

The road, merely a path marked with wooden stakes indicating the miles, was laid out within a 40-mile-wide strip of land 200 miles long that had been established to separate the Fox and Sac tribes from the Sioux and Dakotas, and to protect the more peaceful Winnebago from the hostile tribes. Hunting and fishing was allowed in the "neutral ground," but no warring. Fort Atkinson was the only fort built to protect Indians from other Indians. It existed for nine years, and then was abandoned, with never an angry shot fired.

Although no settlements existed on this route at the time of its conception, it quickly became a popular and heavily traveled road used by the settlers seeking northern Iowa and southern Minnesota, and as a result, several villages evolved.

Strawberry Point is one of those towns. About midway between Dubuque and Fort Atkinson, a spring located within a tract of timber that came to a point became favorite campgrounds for military troops while moving a large number of Winnebago Indians from Wisconsin to their new home at Fort Atkinson. Abundant wild strawberries grew in the area, and on the mile marker placed along the road was inscribed "Strawberry Point." By 1851 many families had located claims in the near vicinity, and a post office was established as well as blacksmith shops, sawmills, and stores.

When the town was platted and the chosen name of "Franklin" was submitted on the post office application, it was discovered that the name had already been used in Lee County. The application was changed to Strawberry Point, and the name was adopted. But the name issue was not quite over. The Davenport and St. Paul Railroad, in 1872 located a depot there; railroad officials didn't think Strawberry Point was appropriate, and consequently named the station "Endfield." Eventually, the State Legislature stepped in and passed a law requiring that station names must correspond with the original town names. Strawberry Point was official and permanent, once and for all.

Until the railroad rendered them obsolete, stagecoaches ran between Dubuque and Fort Atkinson. Even though the fort had been abandoned, a city continued there. At Strawberry Point the Franklin Hotel served as an overnight stop.

McGregor, Iowa

An ambitious young fellow from New York, Alexander MacGregor arrived at Prairie du Chien in 1835. By trading off what he considered to be a bad real estate investment in Chicago (the area that is now the "Loop") he bought up some land on the Iowa bank of the river, and with partner Thomas Burnett, he procured a flatboat, arranged a treadmill and paddlewheels, and acquired a strong, steady mule to propel the craft. With this outfit he went into the ferry business, primarily to serve the fur traders between Prairie du Chien and the landing on the Iowa bank, which naturally became known as MacGregor's Landing. The following year, MacGregor bought out Burnett's share of the business.

Patronage of MacGregor's ferry soon included a stream of emigrants seeking passage across the river to the Iowa Territory, and the movement of troops from Fort Crawford on their way to Fort Atkinson over the Old Mission Road with supplies and patrol personnel. Besides transporting settlers' wagons and teams, the freight business was particularly good, and MacGregor soon realized the need for some sort of building at the Iowa landing where supplies could be stored while waiting for the overland freighters to Fort Atkinson. He constructed the first frame warehouse of its kind that far north on the west bank, and before long the steamers bringing supply goods destined for Fort Atkinson were landing at his front door.

Authentic 1850s log cabin located at the McGregor landing. (Photo by author)

A great surge of immigration into northern Iowa and southern Minnesota began channeling into Prairie du Chien, probably because of a good river crossing to MacGregor's Landing. The ferrying and freight business had grown to such immense proportions by that time, that MacGregor was on the lookout for a new partner. Among the waves of incoming settlers at the Landing came Mr. and Mrs. Joseph McHose. An offer was made, and young McHose joined fortunes with MacGregor, moved his family into the upper story of the warehouse, rolled up his sleeves and went to work on the lower level, which had become one of the busiest spots on the Upper Mississippi.

Present-day Main Street, McGregor, Iowa. The 19th Century charm remains throughout this beautifully maintained historic district on the bank of the Mississippi River. (Photo by author)

His first order of business involved mostly incoming freight, but after a season or two of Iowa settlement, loads of wheat started coming in over the Old Mission Road. Because McHose had the only warehouse on the west bank, he did a booming business, and within a few years there were as many as fourteen warehouses along the bank taking in grain and spouting it out into steamers on the river.

MacGregor and his wife moved from their home in Prairie du Chien and occupied a log house at the Landing in 1847. That year he had a six-block area near the river surveyed and platted. (He would eventually allow the "a" to be dropped in the spelling of the town's name.) H.D. Evans opened the first retail business, a dry goods store, and during the next twenty years, the population would reach over 5,500 people, the growth owing greatly to the tremendous grain shipping business carried on with the Mississippi riverboats and the railroad.

As for the McHose Forwarding and Commission concern, business continued to be good. According to Mrs. McHose, who was the subject of an interview by a La Crosse (Wis.) Tribune reporter in December 1919, told of a thrilling life that went on about the warehouse, and of the interesting activities she witnessed from her upstairs parlor window.

"Farmers used to come from 150 and 200 miles with their wheat," she said, and went on to explain how the wagons and teams would be lined up for a mile back from the levee, waiting their turn at the city scales. All around the scales were the buyers from each of the warehouses, and even representatives from Milwaukee and St. Louis firms. They would inspect the loads, test the wheat by biting into a few kernels, and call out their bids. When a deal was closed, the farmer drove his wagon to the levee and unloaded at the warehouse. Steamers arrived regularly – many per day – and each warehouse competed for shipping space. The storage facilities were situated such that the boats could navigate right to them, and the grain was run down chutes onto the steamers and their barges. Mrs. McHose remembered "watching one day a steamer back away from the levee, its hold and deck piled with sacks of grain and five barges in tow loaded so heavily with unsacked grain that they almost dipped water."

Large numbers of passengers passed through McGregor from the many steamers landing there. Throngs of Scandinavians in their unique native dress knew but one English word: "Minn-e-so-ty." A sign over the doorway at a tavern near the levee where most of them stayed the first night read: "Father's House, Eat, Drink and be Merry for Tomorrow You Go to Minnesota."

Mrs. McHose told of the exciting races between the boats, the steamboat companies all attempting to make records for fast time. "But of all the fascinating life of the river none compared in interest with the [log] rafts. The river was full of them. There was hardly a time during the summer when I could not see from my window at least one of these drifting down, with their red-shirted crew pulling at the long oars to keep the rafts in the channel. One night I was awakened by singing and the sound of a fiddle. The river was bright as day almost with the light of a full moon. I looked out of the window and found the singing was coming from a raft, which was drifting past in the moonlight. The crew was dancing and singing around the fiddler. The fiddler stopped. One of the crew scrambled up on top of the little shanty on the float, struck the attitude of an old-time Methodist preacher and launched into an exhortation to righteous ways. His derisive harangue was greeted with boisterous laughter. As the laughing stopped the voice of a man at the oars suddenly sang out clear over the water, above the preaching, "Go, tell Aunt Rhody her old gray goose is dead." The preacher stopped and he and the whole crew took up the refrain. The song sounded lovely coming over the water and I listened as long as I could see them and hear the singing for the music and the beauty of the moonlit river fascinated me."

Mrs. McHose remembered other times not so romantic, when the rafts tied up at shore during a fog or storm and the crew broke loose in the town. There were wild doings then, as there was when the town was packed with teamsters, too. A number of saloons stretched up the street, and fighting was a common occurrence among the crowds that frequented them.

As a wheat buyer, Joseph McHose became quite prosperous in those days. Besides buying independently, he was an agent for Diamond Jo Reynolds. The old frame warehouse served its days of usefulness, and a substantial brick structure replaced it in later years. When Joseph McHose died, his wife continued to live in the river town, and for many years enjoyed the wealth acquired back in the days when the old Warehouse No. 1 was in its glory.

The decline in steamboat and railroad traffic in later years drastically reduced McGregor's population, but it has survived and remains today as a bustling little river town with its nicely preserved original Nineteenth Century Main Street. A visitor can still stand in the very spot in the brick building from which Diamond Jo Reynolds commanded his fleet of steamboats.

Poised near the river landing in downtown McGregor, the Diamond Jo Reynolds building is one of many structures of the town listed on the National Register of Historic Places. Built in 1880 by Diamond Jo Reynolds, one of McGregor's most prosperous businessmen, the first floor of this building served as the headquarters for his steamboat business, while his residence was on the second floor. Over the years it has housed the post office, a gentlemen's billiard parlor, a restaurant, a number of gift and antique shops, and a winery. (Photo taken by author during Grand Excursion 2004.)

Lansing, Iowa

About twenty-five miles upriver is the old river town of Lansing, Iowa, first settled in 1848 by William Garrison, John Haney, and H.H. Houghton of Galena, Illinois. They recognized the location as being ideal for a farm market and a good steamboat landing for shipping purposes. A year later, a post office was established at Lansing (named for Garrison's hometown in Michigan) and in 1851, Haney and Houghton bought Garrison's land rights and platted the new town. Lansing was incorporated in 1864.

Located on the main channel of the Mississippi River, Lansing boomed right from the start. It became a significant grain-shipping terminal, and a popular port of call for many steamboats. Lumber mills kept busy with logs rafted down the river from northern Wisconsin and Minnesota, and in 1899, J.M. Turner opened the first pearl button factory. That industry grew to employ hundreds.

Minnesota Beginnings

Until about 1840, the chief business in Minnesota was the fur trade. The fertile soil was not yet discovered, so agricultural practices were non-existent, and the lumber industry wouldn't take hold until 1850. Fort St. Anthony (now Ft. Snelling) was established at the confluence of the Minnesota and Mississippi Rivers in 1819. Long, bitter winters recorded and reported by the soldiers at this outpost in Indian Territory had discouraged many would-be settlers. Indians, trappers, and traders populated the region only sparsely.

A French-Canadian trader nicknamed Pig's Eye established a lucrative business in a shantytown that sprang up when squatters at Ft. St. Anthony were evicted for selling whiskey to the Indians. He gave the town its first name: Pig's Eye. In later years, more respectable settlers changed the name of the growing community to a more appealing St. Paul.

The fur trade gave St. Paul its initial expansion boost. All business there centered around the fur market. Valuable pelts came in by canoe down the Minnesota and Mississippi Rivers, and in backpacks of the weather-beaten trappers who brought their winter's harvest to exchange it for supplies that would sustain them for another hunting and trapping season. Millions of dollars worth of furs passed through St. Paul, and that money earned by the hunters and trappers was spent in the city on clothing, guns, ammunition, tobacco, foodstuffs, and all other needed supplies.

St. Paul supplied all these goods, but none of it was produced within its own neighborhood. Everything was shipped in from downriver. In early times, most of the supplies came from St. Louis, although much of it originated in eastern cities.

As the steamboats began puffing their way farther upstream, and the merchandise became more readily available as far north as St. Paul, immigrants – mostly Germans and Scandinavians – started pushing into the territory populating the mining towns, army posts, fur-trading villages, and sawmill settlements. Thousands of pioneers blazed into the wilderness in search of prairie farmland.

But many of the new arrivals kept close to the timberland where the needed fuel for the severe winters could be easily obtained. And many remained in the security of the populated cities. At St. Paul, with no area agriculture started and a population of 6,000 by 1854, importing food to sustain its people was big business. Even hay to feed the horses in St. Paul was brought in from Iowa, although thousands of acres of prime prairie grasses grew just to the west of the city.

The territory went wild with speculation. As the population increased, so did the price of land, reaching extravagant levels with the anticipation of future railroad development.

Then the panic of 1857, caused by big business failures in the east, struck Minnesota in disastrous proportions. St. Paul suddenly lost half of its population. Those who were left turned bitterly against speculation and toward the development of the vast natural resources. Thousands of farms were opened, cultivation begun, and there was work for everyone. What had first appeared as a dreadful situation turned into a blessing in disguise, for it jump-started agriculture in Minnesota. The new farmers experimented with crops of wheat and were pleasantly surprised with the success. By 1859, Minnesota farmers were producing an astounding surplus, and their success was drawing even greater farm population growth.

After a few years, though, due to the lack of technology and the yet unlearned knowledge of crop rotation practices, the soil was exhausted, and raising wheat in southern Minnesota became an unprofitable endeavor. Farmers of the region abandoned wheat and turned to corn and hogs. But about that same time, the northern region of the Red River Valley was discovered to be the most ideal land for raising wheat, and the cheaply obtained land drew much attention. This area – larger than all the Great Lakes combined – some 11,000,000 acres that occupied Canada, Dakota, and Minnesota – is actually a flat plain left after the receding waters of a huge lake formed from melting glaciers during the Ice Age. Fine earthy and mineral material settled in this great basin and slowly mixed with decayed vegetation, eventually producing a rich loam many inches deep. After the waters disappeared, superb grasses sprang to life, and for countless years, this prairie land was an extraordinary feeding ground for immense buffalo herds. Thus, the fertile soil was further enriched.

President Lincoln confirmed a treaty with the Indians in 1864 that opened this region to settlement. Soon, convoys of prairie schooners carried immigrants, their families, and everything they owned across the state to these northern reaches – many were experienced wheat farmers from southeastern Minnesota; some were from neighboring states; others came directly from Europe.

The Red River Valley was incredibly smooth and flat, allowing farmers to till, plant, and harvest crops with remarkable ease. By 1885 Minnesota had suddenly become one of the principal granaries of the world. Development on such an enormous scale was made possible by three reasons: first, the labor saving machinery – the reapers and threshers – that came into general use during the time when Minnesota was being settled. These new implements permitted farmers to harvest larger crops in a shorter time and with less manpower, thus protecting them from suffering losses due to storms before the crops were brought under cover. All this helped generate greater profits.

The second reason for Minnesota's rapid advancement in food production was the introduction of an improved method of milling. A Frenchman named La Croix came to Minnesota in 1870 with a European milling concept that utilized a machine called the "middlings purifier." This machine effectively separated the bran covering of the wheat kernel and largely saved the gluten, avoiding discoloration of the flour.

Soon after, the mills of Minneapolis sent a representative to Europe to study the milling methods. As a result, in 1874 the Minnesota flourmills adopted the Hungarian design using iron or porcelain rollers instead of millstones.

The roller mill proved to be a more efficient method of producing flour with less waste and higher quality, and commanding higher prices. By 1878, Minnesota mills were exporting their high-grade "Minnesota

Patent" flour to foreign countries as the state's wheat crop doubled, and farming in Minnesota had become a recognized profession.

The third and perhaps the most significant cause for increased farm production in Minnesota was improved transportation. The coming of the railroad enabled farmers to expand into areas that were not necessarily close to a navigable waterway. The freight charges earned by the railroads for carrying agricultural products to market were the key factor in their support. It is easy to understand that the development of railroads and new farmland kept pace with each other in Minnesota's early years.

Railroads in Wisconsin had already been doing a booming business by the time the first locomotive chugged along rails in Minnesota in 1862. That locomotive, named the William Crooks in honor of the first engineer, had been brought up the river via barge and landed at St. Paul the previous year for the St. Paul & Pacific Railroad, the company that built and operated the first ten miles of track between St. Paul and St. Anthony, and eventually developed into the Great Northern Railway in 1889. (The William Crooks engine is one of the only Civil War era locomotives to survive to present-day. It is currently on display at the Lake Superior Railroad Museum in Duluth, Minnesota.)

In areas other than the southeast that was unaffected by the Ice Age glaciers, Minnesota enjoyed natural advantages that aided in rapid expansion of the railroads there. The terrain was mostly flat, requiring much less grading, and the presence of ample forests provided ties. Both conditions greatly reduced the construction cost and the amount of time required. With a relatively short period, numerous commercial routes were established. Minnesota was no longer dependent on ox carts and steamboats, and just as in previous times and locales, settlements through which the rails did not pass, moved houses and commercial structures to be close to the railroad in order to have the advantages and benefits equal to newer towns located on the line. And just as important as the depot itself, at every station in the Minnesota wheat regions there appeared the tall, awkward grain elevator buildings that were essential in storing the valuable product and transferring it into railcars for shipment to distant markets.

Industry Trends Change

Very necessary to the survival of the pioneer were the resources of the forest. There he found the materials with which to build his home, and the fuel to cook his food and to keep him warm during the cold, harsh winters. By hunting and trapping the animals that thrived in the Minnesota wilderness, he obtained not only a major portion of his food, but furs as well. Thus the forest supplied his basic needs for food, clothing, and shelter. From this grew the first and primary industry of the territory – the fur trade – that derived the only income for its inhabitants for many years.

But with the influx of more settlers, the fur bearing animals diminished, and the fur trade rapidly became less profitable. It was only natural that the people would turn their attention to the next close resource – the trees. By 1850, lumbering had displaced the fur trade as the leading industry in the Minnesota Territory, and would remain so for more than half a century.

More than half the state was covered with magnificent forest: the great pine regions of the north and east, and the hardwoods that bordered them to the south and west. Some of the most extensive white pine forests in the world were once found in the St. Croix and Mississippi River valleys of Minnesota.

Lumbering in Minnesota began with the early days of Ft. Snelling, but the treaties with the Chippewa and the Sioux in 1837 that first opened the territory for settlement was when the industry launched into serious involvement and buzzing sawmills started appearing along the streams. The first commercial lumber was sawed in a mill at Marine on the St. Croix River in 1839.

About that same time, Franklin Steele, who became a prominent figure of the Minnesota lumber industry, established the St. Croix Lumber Company, locating a large logging camp at St. Croix Falls where there was ample waterpower to run a busy sawmill.

Most of the early lumbermen came from eastern states where the forests had already been depleted. And just as would also happen in Wisconsin, these pioneers used reckless logging methods, unregulated by any public or governmental control. For many years it was believed that the vast supply of timber could never be exhausted, and the glowing reports to that effect sent by lumbermen to their friends in the East drew more settlers and more lumbermen.

Stillwater quickly developed into the leading lumber town of Minnesota when its first sawmill opened in 1844. With its advantageous location near the pine forests, and built on the banks of the St. Croix River, the town grew rapidly; at one time it had twelve operating sawmills, and its population exceeded that of St. Paul. Because of the logging and lumber industry, Stillwater was expected to become the largest city in this part of the country that was known then as the Northwest.

Most of the Minnesota lumberjacks, at first, were French-Canadians from Maine, who brought with them the methods used there. The logging was done during the cold winter months when logs could be easily hauled on sleds over iced roads from deep in the forests to the nearest stream. Then the springtime floods floated the logs downriver to the mills. There they were collected in the booms – a chain of heavy timbers connected end-to-end and extended from bank to bank. In this corral, the logs were sorted according to the branding marks stamped on them by the owners at the time of cutting.

The relatively small population of Minnesota could not possibly create a market large enough to consume the amount of lumber being produced. A ready market, though, laid waiting in the treeless plains to the south, east, and west. Combined with equally enormous quantities of Wisconsin forest product, Minnesota lumber proved a significant factor in the settlement and development of the prairie regions.

Several years after logging was established on the St. Croix, Franklin Steele sent out a scout who discovered the abundant white pine forests adjacent to the Mississippi River valley some distance above the Falls of St. Anthony. Steele had considered making use of the waterpower at the falls, but dismissed the idea for fear of not finding enough logs upriver to make a mill there worthwhile. But with the new discovery, St. Paul would soon join the ranks among the lumber industry.

After some delays, Steele built this first commercial sawmill on the Mississippi River. The logs intended for constructing the mill were lost in an uncontrollable drive during extremely high water in 1847.

Consequently, Steele was obliged to build his mill with hardwood cut from nearby Nicolet Island. Then the new machinery that had been ordered was lost during shipment in the Erie Canal. But after all the delays were overcome, logging and the lumber industry in this region expanded and developed rapidly.

By 1850 lumbering had established a foothold as the number one industry in Minnesota, and it attracted rapid population growth during the next few years (From 6,000 in 1850 to 100,000 in 1856) as immigrants steadily flowed in.

As successful as this industry had become, it was restricted to a seasonal market. Most of Minnesota depended on the Mississippi River as the cardinal course of commerce. When the river froze during the winter months, Minnesota was shut off from the rest of the country as far as any substantial shipping was concerned. The lack of railroads presented a handicap until 1867 when Minneapolis was finally connected to Prairie du Chien by rail.

Until that time, the logging crews had only worked where they could easily access the waterways. Then, the wealthy lumber giants who owned vast tracts of forest began building their own railroads, making it possible for their crews to penetrate deeper into remote timberland.

At the close of the Nineteenth Century, Minnesota ranked first as the nation's lumber producer, and the business would continue on a large scale well into the Twentieth Century. As the pine forests that fed logs to Minneapolis mills started to deplete, the industry shifted its operations farther north to the cities of Bemidji, Virginia, and Cloquet on the St. Louis River. Much of this product was shipped to Chicago and Buffalo via the Great Lakes.

Stagecoaches, Taverns and Roadhouses

Settlement of the Wisconsin Territory, in terms of any large numbers, began about 1835. Until that time, there had been only a paltry spattering of rugged pioneers, explorers, miners and fur traders inhabiting the frontier between the Great Lakes and the Mississippi River, but the next two decades saw a rapid growth in population, particularly in the southern portion of what would become the state of Wisconsin. Towns sprang up where only wildlife had previously occupied the land. Farms were cleared and cultivated, and the rich, fertile soil produced surprisingly abundant harvests. Manufacturing foundations were laid, churches were founded, and civilized society established a foothold, fashioned to meet the demands of pioneer conditions. The people progressed, and left to posterity a heritage more substantial than the customs of the time would indicate.

Public transportation facilities were reduced to simple terms – horse and wagon for freight; horse and stagecoach for passengers. The earliest roads amounted to no more than dirt trails etched through the countryside following the native Indian paths. They were poor, at best, and all but impassable during some seasons. Traveling was difficult and time consuming, and during the wet seasons – spring and fall – many journeys had to be postponed until the mud holes dried, or froze.

Over these crude trails were soon to be seen that vehicle of story and song – the stagecoach. Due to the constantly growing number of settlers coming into Wisconsin to make their homes, it was not long until regular stagecoach lines were operating definite schedules between settlements. Going over the roads in fair weather was a pleasant pastime, but the troubles and hardships that the drivers of the coaches and their passengers suffered trying to get through during the rainy seasons makes a sorrowful page in pioneer history. Nothing would stop them, however, and before long, there was a considerable network of stages in the territory.

The stagecoach provided an important factor in the development of the country when it was young. As the population pressed farther to the west from the Great Lakes, and east from the Mississippi River, so did the stage lines. By the mid 1840s, travel to and from any of the settlements – for business or pleasure – was usually done by stagecoach over routes that crisscrossed the territory. Until the railroads entered into the picture in the 1850s, the horse-drawn coaches remained the prime mode of travel, and were heavily relied upon for the movement of mail and light freight, as well as passengers.

People of the pioneer days traveled by stagecoach from Chicago to Racine, Milwaukee, Sheboygan and Green Bay. Routes were established westward to Janesville and Madison from Milwaukee, and to Fond du Lac from Sheboygan. These routes quickly extended into the fast growing regions farther west, and within a short time, an entire network of stage lines connected nearly every settlement. Madison based lines extended to Baraboo, Cross Plains, and Lone Rock. From Baraboo, connections were made to Sparta and La Crosse. Sparta was at the crossroads on a route between Black River Falls and Prairie du Chien. From Prairie du Chien, a stage line followed the old Military Road to Mineral Point, Cross Plains, Portage, and on to Green Bay. Countless numbers of local routes spiked off the main roads to reach new settlements.

In many regions of Wisconsin, the stagecoach lines remained active into the next century, when the railroads, and eventually the automobile finally took over. The stage was the accepted mode of travel, used regularly by doctors, preachers, lawyers, newspapermen, and lumbermen, as well as many of the newly arriving settlers seeking places of abode in this new country.

No one journey by stagecoach across the countryside was ever like another. So many unforeseen predicaments lurked along the route. A mechanical breakdown, a lamed horse, a blizzard or a downpour, a sudden confrontation by bandits or Indians – any number of reasons could turn a trip into an unpredictable nightmare. Or, the time might pass without incident and the travelers would arrive at their destination on schedule. A stagecoach journey was almost always an adventure, to be approached with either apprehension or calmness, but always with a tingle of anticipation.

The early Troy coaches were solid, offered little comfort, and overcrowded if more than eight or nine adult passengers boarded. By 1855 the traveling conditions improved with the arrival of the Concord coaches, built in Concord, New Hampshire. Pronounced as "the only perfect passenger vehicle for traveling ever built," the larger Concords weighed in at 1,800 pounds, boasted plush, comfortable seating for 15 to 18 people, and the passenger compartment was suspended on leather straps that absorbed most of the jolting experienced in the previous Troy models. The Concords' exteriors were elegantly painted and christened with eloquent names like Prairie Queen, Argosy, or Western Monarch.

Passengers aboard a stagecoach kept warm during the cold winter months under huge buffalo robes that trapped the warmth of a foot stove, a metal and wood apparatus that contained live coals, giving off heat for a considerable length of time. But little could be done to combat the sweltering conditions on a hot, dusty summer day.

Typically, a driver, perched high aloft on an open-air seat, unprotected from the elements, earned regal respect by virtue of his profession. Dressed in flannel shirt, corduroy breeches stuffed into high boots, a well-seasoned headpiece, and a fur or leather coat during inclement weather, he was the master of the four horses that drew his coach across the austere landscape at the amazing speed of four miles an hour.

When the Nineteenth century was young, during the period when the stagecoach attained its greatest vogue in this country, men commonly wore whiskers, and the important individual in the driver's seat of a stagecoach was certainly no exception. His position was one of so much exposure to drastic variations of weather that he usually endeavored in growing a more luxuriant crop than men in other occupations; his complexion, tanned by the sun and wind, showed a reddish tinge that was often heightened from frequent indulgence at the roadhouse bar.

And what magnificent use he made of his whip; in ordinary hands, it was nothing more than a braided buckskin lash attached to a hickory handle – but not so in a driver's hands.

The stage drivers seemed nothing short of showmen. Upon leaving for the next destination, he ascended to his high seat, gathered up the reins, and with an explosive crack of the whip, sent the horses and coach departing in a theatrical flourish amidst the common crowd of cheering spectators. When the stagecoach was well out of sight from the audience, he slowed the pace to a lazy crawl – most of the time, for good reason, as the trails presented grueling conditions for the equipment and the passengers. Few roads, then, had been improved and were tortuously laden with rocks, stumps, and unforgiving mud holes, crossing streams at the most favorable places, skirting elevations where there was the least resistance, and passing through woods along routes that were less demanding on the team.

It was a day when gentlemen wore towering top hats. The glossy silk "stove pipe" hats were particularly popular among doctors, lawyers, and others belonging to the professional classes, and they were recognized as an identifiable badge of the professions. Bouncing about as the coach wheels dropped into holes, and climbed over the stones and stumps, the passengers were sometimes suddenly tossed to the ceiling, crushing the gentlemen's hats down to their ears. Often, a gentleman found himself pitched into the lap of an unsuspecting lady, which was exceedingly embarrassing for both.

An eight-hour trip in a stagecoach could be exhausting – not only from the strenuous exercise in such confined quarters, but also from the possibility of ensuing arguments. This was a time when slavery practices were in paramount question. Whigs, Free-soilers, Democrats, and Republicans contended at the ballot box, and the fugitive slave law and other contentious political topics were discussed daily. With such live issues in the public mind, it may be well imagined that in more than one stagecoach there were plenty of sharply pointed debates; souls were set on fire by wordy friction, and in an atmosphere charged with these contending forces, it is not surprising that near brawls often erupted when passengers' political viewpoints clashed.

There were always enough exciting episodes packed into a stagecoach trip across the Wisconsin wilderness to last a lifetime. Nothing so colorful, perhaps, as the modern-day Wild West movie-depicted bandit holdup, although the possibility of such an occurrence was not a distant thought of the drivers. Quite often they were entrusted with large sums of cash – and, of course, the valuable mailbags – to be delivered at their next stop.

There were the talkative peddlers and shrewd speculators who cleverly began their sometimes-hypnotic presentations among a captive audience aboard the stage.

Frequently there would be suspicious characters – horse thieves, perhaps – who never had their eyes on the stage line property, but kept a sharp lookout for more spirited beasts to be had in an open pasture or unlocked barns. They would acquire a one-way ticket into the next town, never to be seen again upon arrival, and probably rode a pilfered horse back into Illinois to be sold to an unsuspecting buyer.

When the lumbering industry was beginning to flourish, it was not unusual to occupy a stage seat next to one of the many log rafters who relied on the coaches for transportation back to the north woods after floating a raft of logs or lumber downriver. They always had stories to tell of their harrowing experiences.

And during the Civil War, soldiers frequently rode the stages from a railway station to their homes on the frontier, supplying many a thrilling tale of the southland conflict, and often with an empty sleeve or pantaloon.

The arrival of the stagecoach was audibly advertised long before it could be seen. Approaching an upcoming stop, the driver blew loudly on a horn. That was the signal for the people to drop their routines; women tucked away stray locks and hurried from cabin doorways, children clustered about them; men rushed to the station or post office where they were all ears for the latest news, and invariably supplied the driver with their own local gossip to be carried on to the next town.

There was always excitement when the stagecoach rumbled into Madison from Milwaukee three times a week, deposited its passengers and baggage in front of the City Hotel at Main and Pinckney Streets, and then drew over to Webster Street where Postmaster David Holt received the mailbags.

Perhaps it would bring newcomers to add to Madison's population, a mere village of 600 in 1846. Or maybe it would bring news from the outside world, either by post, or by the voice of the well traveled, knowledgeable driver.

And so it was, the scene in any settlement that enjoyed the frequent arrival of the stagecoaches – almost like the arrival of a ship from a foreign land. Relatively speaking, they consumed about as much time in getting places. But that didn't really matter in a time when living hadn't yet shifted to breakneck speeds.

The trip from Milwaukee to Madison by stagecoach required all of two days' traveling time – about an hour jaunt in today's passenger car. There was no direct route between the two locations, and the road was nothing more that a rutted wagon path. Leaving Milwaukee in the early morning hours, the stage arrived in Janesville at about 11 o'clock that night. Passengers were offered sleeping accommodations for a few hours, and then were awakened for an early start on the journey's second day. If conditions were favorable, they reached Madison that evening in time for supper.

By the mid 1850s the Madison stagecoach stop had been moved to the United States Hotel. Eight coaches, most of them Concords, were regularly dispatched from there. Jim Cowles piloted one of the more popular lines that made its scheduled journey to Baraboo. Passengers could board any weekday at 7:00 a.m. for the eight-hour trip; the fare was two dollars.

The 35-mile route went by way of Lodi, and then continued northward to cross the Wisconsin River at Merrimac on a ferry. It was not unusual for the ferry to break loose from its cables and go wandering off downstream, stagecoach and all. That was an extra ride, without charge.

In winter, the stage crossed the river on the ice, but in seasons when the ice was not thick enough to support the weight, and the ferry not available, the route then diverted to Prairie du Sac and crossed over a toll bridge.

Stagecoach traveling in the pioneer days left much to be desired. The chief concern, however, was reaching a destination in one piece – and before old age set in. The stage was apt to be dragged from one mud hole to another, over the jarring corduroy roads, rocks and stumps, up hills and down, until the patience of not only the driver and passengers, but horses, as well, were near the breaking point.

Over the years, artists have usually rendered the horses powering a stagecoach as prancing, fire-breathing steeds, but in reality, most of that picturesque image is the product of imagination. It required highly practical teams to pull the heavily loaded coaches; the long monotonous journeys tended to produce conspicuous ribs, pronounced backbone, and other obvious indications of arduous toil. The animals were toughened by the hard hauls, conditioned to extreme heat and cold, and they were usually selected for this service by virtue of their subdued spirit and unusual patience necessary for the strenuous burden imposed upon them.

Occasionally, though, the horses possessed just enough spirit to create some unsuspected excitement and fright among the passengers. One night in Prairie du Sac, four horses hitched to a passenger-loaded coach were spooked by a sudden noise and ran away without the driver. After executing a number of fancy gyrations in the village, they were finally brought under control. Only a flowerbed or two were uprooted, a dozen roosting chickens scattered, and a rain barrel tipped, but no serious damage or injury resulted.

Not even the most farsighted citizen of those days ever dreamed that the stagecoach with plodding team would someday be relegated into oblivion. It seemed impossible to them that the bumping coach, the speed, and the extreme conditions of traveling comfort could advance to any greater degree, much the same as we look upon the improbable possibility of the automobile's extinction. The old stage routes were the main arteries of communication between all settlements, and they were the accepted mode of public travel. Older members of the population remembered back to the time when a traveler prodded his horse, mule, or oxen for miles along an Indian trail, fording unbridged streams, plunging through miring swamps, and penetrating dense forests beset with savages. It can be no wonder that they stood in admiration before a Concord coach with four sturdy steeds ready to carry them in a compartment sheltered from a blazing sun or torrential downpour of rain.

Although the iron horses gradually began stealing business away from the four-legged variety, the railroads could not completely eliminate the need for stagecoach service. Many settlements were bypassed on the rail routes, but were established well enough by populations that still held high anticipation of growth and prosperity for their communities. It was, perhaps, a smart move on the part of the railroad companies to advertise in their time schedules connections at various terminals to the outlying towns via stage. This could be observed as a means to appease the utter dissatisfaction and bitter attitudes stemming from the villages that had become isolated by the railroad building engineers' and surveyors' decisions. The Milwaukee & Mississippi Railway proudly announced connections at Durand with stage for Freeport; at Burlington for Rochester and Waterford; at Elkhorn for Whitewater; and at Springfield for Geneva. This meant more stringent schedules to be kept by the stage lines, but also proved that they had not yet outlived their usefulness.

In every settled community, and at many crossroads where there were no settlements, taverns were established and maintained. (The term "tavern," when referring to the pioneer era, should not be confused with the definition of modern-day drinking establishments – alcoholic beverages in pioneer days were consumed at a "saloon," however most taverns did sell whiskey.) The taverns, which were also important elements of the pioneer transportation system, provided a stopping place for the stage lines, and offered modest sleeping accommodations and simple meals for weary travelers. In time, many of these establishments evolved to grand hotels and eateries, and became the nerve centers of the communities for the people who lived there. These evolved taverns contained not only sleeping rooms, but often housed a great hall, generally on the second floor, that served well for dances, concerts, and entertainment functions of all sorts; it was the meeting place for secret societies, political campaigns, elections, religious ceremony, and most community gatherings.

These early houses, where the weary traveler might find needed shelter and refreshment as he journeyed through the country, were generally of the simplest design and construction. Their shadows fell on clearings amidst the lavish forests where the trees were cut and provided the logs to build them, or on the grassy plains dotted with wildflowers.

Construction of the log taverns was often an important event. Settlers came from miles to assist in the task, usually without compensation, except for the return favor when it came his turn to erect a structure.

Great care was taken to select the proper logs for size and straightness. A day or two before the cabin was to be erected, the foundation was laid and the first logs put in place, on which the puncheon floor – logs split and faced with a broadaxe – were laid. The puncheons were rarely fastened, but were merely held in place by their own weight. Logs forming the walls were then put into place, one layer at a time. Notches cut near the ends of the logs allowed the corners of adjacent walls to overlap and to fit together tightly. Shorter logs formed the wall where a door opening was placed, and the ends at the opening were fastened together with wooden pins.

If sawed lumber was not available, doors were fashioned by joining "splits" with cross pieces that extended beyond one side. Auger holes through the extensions provided the means to hang the door on wooden hinge pins.

Roofs involved labor-intense production of "shakes"—wooden shingles split from straight blocks of hardwood, red oak among the preferred choices. The shakes were supported by log beams spanning the length of the structure, and were held in place by long poles laid over them.

Early log house that survives at Prairie du Chien, Wisconsin. (Photo by aurthor)

Nails were rarely used to build the early log cabins, wooden pins being the primary fastening device. If nails were obtained, they were usually the product of a local blacksmith.

Every town had one or more livery barns, usually operated in conjunction with the taverns. Teams of horses were fed, cared for, and kept in ready at the liveries. When a long distance stage arrived, "fresh" horses were exchanged for tired ones, and the stage and its passengers continued on the journey without delay. Considering the distances traveled by some stage lines on a daily schedule – as was the case with the Beswick Line completing a 69-mile mail run between Racine and Janesville and return every day – several changes of horses were a must.

The taverns and livery stables served the public; anyone was welcome. A night's lodging cost the traveler ten cents, and he would part with twenty-five cents for a meal, usually cooked by the proprietor's wife. For the going rate of fifty cents, a traveler with a team of horses could sleep, eat breakfast, and have his team cared for at the livery.

Immigrants landing at Racine on Great Lakes steamers ventured inland by stagecoach to settle on the fertile farmland. Southeastern Wisconsin, the area that is now Racine County, saw some of the most rapid population growth during the 1830 – 1850 decades, and many of Wisconsin's first taverns were established there.

Perhaps, the first tavern established was that of Elisha Raymond, who brought with him a drove of livestock in 1835. He settled on a plot of land that would eventually become the town of Raymond, and his house provided lodging for the earliest travelers into the region.

In 1836, John Trowbridge built a two-story log tavern in the town of Dover, and the same year, Levi Godfrey opened the first tavern at Rochester, a double log house, where the first political convention in Wisconsin was held to nominate candidates for the territorial legislature.

The city of Racine became a transportation hub during that era; by the late 1840s, a plank road was constructed between Racine and Janesville, and a stage line ran from Chicago through Racine to Milwaukee and Green Bay. The Racine House, built in 1837 by Alfred Cary, and operated as a tavern by John Myers was the station for a change of horses, and where passengers were received, and was considered the best of the pioneer taverns in Wisconsin. The building burned to the ground in 1866.

A few families and friends known as the New England Emigrating Company first settled the site that would become the city of Beloit in southern Rock County, Wisconsin. They came from New Hampshire in 1837 and began building the first structure there that they called the boarding house. In time, this place would take on the name of the Beloit

House, serving as the settlement's first public tavern, and soon became a popular shelter for travelers passing through the area. The property, including considerable acreage, passed through the care of many owners over the years, but its popularity began with Capt. John W. Bicknell, who cultivated the adjoining land and raised a bountiful crop of vegetables to keep the tavern's table well stocked and the traveler well fed. Brothers Otis and Charles Bicknell assumed the duties of hotelkeepers in 1844, and about that same time, an agent for the Frink & Walker Stage Lines took up residency there and the Beloit House became a headquarters for the transportation company. They stabled their horses at the Beloit House livery barn, providing fresh teams for the coaches passing through on the north/south routes from Rockford and Belvidere, Illinois to Janesville, Wisconsin, and on the east/west routes from Delevan to Monroe. Unfortunately, this grand old hotel was demolished to make way for the first railroad entering the village in 1853.

At Janesville, a Frink & Walker stagecoach left the Stevens House every morning bound for Madison, forty miles to the north. Business increased with the growing population, and soon there were two daily stages running this route. The first stop for a change of mailbags was at the Leyden House, built by Ben McMellen in 1841 a few miles northwest from Janesville. (Later, the route was changed to a northerly course out of Janesville, the first stop being the Rock River House about four miles out of town.) From Leyden the stage traveled to Warren's Tavern, then on to the Ball Tavern near present-day Evansville, and then to the halfway point at Union, where passengers enjoyed a good meal at a tavern kept by Mr. Prentice, while a fresh team of horses was hitched to the stage. The tavern at Union was a lively place with four coaches loaded with passengers, all stopping there for dinner. After departing from Union, the next stop on the route to Madison was Rutland. The Rutland House, built by Albert Waterman, was one of the earliest taverns along this route, and offered whiskey in the barroom and a few groceries on the other side. From there, the stage went to a tavern built by C.P. Mosley at Rome Corners (now known as Oregon), then to Wm. Quivey's tavern and post office at Oakhall, and finally arriving at the City Hotel in Madison.

At the foot of a bluff in the narrow valley where the village of Cross Plains would soon emerge, Berry Haney established a post office in a log cabin in 1838. He was the second to settle there, but he didn't stay long. Haney spent a couple of years at Sauk City where he built and operated a ferryboat across the Wisconsin River. He sold the rights to that property and returned to Cross Plains in 1840, when he had builders construct a sturdy stone house that became known as "Haney's Stand," a tavern famed for its hospitality and lively reputation far up and down the roads that crossed there. It was here that the Military Road passed, and Haney also operated a stage line on that trail between Mineral Point and Fort Winnebago (now Portage), a popular route for emigrants heading to the lead mining region.

Many other taverns and roadhouses were established in the Southeast, and became well known to the early travelers. The Western Hotel, the City Hotel, the Exchange, and Congress Hall, all in Racine; at Ives Groves, ten miles west of Racine, Roland Ives conducted a tavern business for many years; Yorkville had the famous Searles House; and in Burlington, Hugh McLaughlin built the Burlington House in 1839.

From the early beginnings of settlement in the territory's southeast, the urge of discovery pushed settlers into the northern and western reaches. Solomon Juneau had been the first white man to settle on the site that is now Milwaukee in 1821 in his lone log cabin near the shores of Lake Michigan. Twenty years later, Milwaukee was a thriving village, and stagecoaches rumbled between it and the smaller outpost of Portage. Most of Wisconsin was practically unsettled; a few trading posts, tiny hamlets, and occasional cabins were scattered here and there about the region, and the trail between Portage and Milwaukee remained the only means of overland travel in the area. Verdant stands of timber alternated with prairie pastures. Deer stalked wild on the outskirts of the multiplying settlements and smoke from the exploring white men's fires frightened away the prowling wolves, still clinging tenaciously to their invaded territory.

Major Thomas Pratt followed a string of prairie schooners northward from Milwaukee, bound for the unknown. On that October day in 1841, he drove a team of oxen hitched to a clumsy, rumbling oxcart, winding his way through the quiet woodlands until he reached the site of present day Oak Grove, located in central Dodge County. There he stopped for the night and pitched camp beside the trail. Upon observation the next morning, the surroundings appealed to him; prairies dipped and rose in gentle swales between irregular patches of woods. This foresighted settler recognized promise in the land, and he decided to stay.

Pratt immediately set to work felling trees in preparation for the construction of a cabin. For several years, he conducted a tavern business in that log cabin where the early pioneers often found shelter. Two years after construction, 1843, the highway from Milwaukee was surveyed and established through Oak Grove, and stage drivers began pulling up their horses at the Major's tavern with regularity.

Ma's Place" in Oak Grove, Wisconsin. Building dates back to the 1800s, and still houses a modern-day tavern. (Photo by author)

Patronage of the little tavern proved quite profitable, and within five more years, Major Pratt erected a new, much larger and more pretentious hotel with "planed" lumber and shingles. It was furnished with the finest appointments available, and Pratt vowed to serve the best food, and the servants were to be the most accommodating to the traveler's needs.

Oak Grove was expanding, too. Due to Fox Lake's inability to furnish adequate office space for county officials, lawyers and businessmen relocated in Oak Grove, and it became the temporary county seat. It promised to become the largest settlement in Dodge County, and speculation of the permanent county seat to be located at Oak Grove drew great interest.

Even the Chicago & Northwestern Railroad contemplated altering its planned route from Janesville to Fond du Lac to include what was then one of the most promising communities in the county. The tavern keeper, Major Pratt, however, more strongly supported the plank roads, as he felt they would be more beneficial to the farmers. Ten miles of plank road could be constructed for the price of one railroad mile, and the farmers would have the freedom of using their own vehicles on the plank roads. He considered the railroads a monopoly.

But not everyone agreed with Pratt's way of thinking. Many people believed that the coming of the railroad was their only hope for a prosperous future. That attitude is probably what carried Oak Grove into a spiraling decline when the railroad company decided to route its tracks directly northward through Clyman and Juneau from Watertown, isolating the expectant village.

Major Thomas Pratt sold his hostelry in 1852, and it changed hands several times in the years to follow, still remaining as a service to the traveling public. But it didn't prosper again, quite as it had in the days of the stagecoach.

Another source of shelter extended to the early travelers was Rowan's Tavern near Madison. This much-celebrated inn consisted of two log buildings with an open space between, all under the same roof. The proprietor, Wallace Rowan, later maintained a hostelry at Poynette, and still later, built a cabin west of Baraboo.

Governor Doty once stayed at Rowan's Tavern, and after supper, as was the custom, he retired to sleeping quarters housed in the second building, rolled up in a blanket, and stretched out on the floor for a quiet night's sleep. In the night, the Governor felt something poking about him, and found it was a pet pig that the proprietor's children had running about the house. Annoyed with the disturbance of his needed rest, he probed the puncheon floor, finding one of the planks loose, which he carefully raised, grabbed the pig and thrust it under the floor. He was relieved of the unwanted company for the night, but the next morning there was a great search for the pig.

Under myriad stars twinkling in a darkened dome above, early travelers in the Baraboo valley were compelled to find their only available lodging in nature's vast out-of-doors. Their slumber was no doubt sweet, although an occasional prowling wolf or inquisitive bear may have interrupted it.

Then in 1843, James Webster erected a cabin at Lyons, west of Baraboo, and was the first to engage in the hotel business in the valley.

Webster was, in many respects, a remarkable man, being possessed of a superior mind, yet totally deaf. But such was his power of observation that he could get the substance of a conversation merely by watching the lips of the person speaking.

After spending some time at Webster's house, a traveler named Armstrong took pity on the proprietor, observing that he was deprived of hearing. Webster immediately exclaimed, "Neighbor Armstrong, you say it is a deprivation not to hear. Why, one-half that is told in the world is lies, and the other half had just as well not be heard."

Mrs. Webster was a woman toughened to the needs of pioneer life. One day an Indian came sneaking around and attempted to steal a pig. Mrs. Webster, always ready for almost any emergency, immediately gave chase, and for a brief period of time, three swiftly moving figures – the pig, the Indian, and Mrs. Webster – darted out across the prairie in rapid succession. The Indian finally vanished and the pioneer woman drove the pig home to root and ramble about the neighborhood.

Before the high bridge was constructed over the Baraboo River in the city of Baraboo, all the traffic passing over the stream crossed a lower bridge in a section of town known as "Under the Hill." J. W. Jackson built the American House in 1850 at the crossing, and soon became the typical community center, as well as an excellent source of lodging for travelers. The American House contained a great entertainment hall; travelers and area citizens alike frequently danced to the lively tunes played by Quiggle's Band.

Sometime after the name was changed to the Peck House in 1868 under the proprietorship of E. T. Peck, the frame structure burned to the ground, but was rebuilt and operated by Robinson & Sergeant, and was known as the Urban House.

James Burlin purchased land at Lyons (West Baraboo) and in 1848 erected one of the most noted taverns of the area, for here stopped many a familiar prairie schooner in the days when they moved at a snail's pace across the country, carrying the meager belongings of settlers in quest of Minnesota.

After ten years of proprietorship, Burlin sold the hostelry, and during the following twenty-five years, the name was changed to the Union House and saw nine different owners.

A fire reduced this grand old landmark to ashes in 1890; it was never rebuilt.

Michael Kornel who operated the little brick hotel and saloon for eight years built the Wisconsin House in 1850. It was at this establishment where the only war that Baraboo ever experienced – "The Baraboo Whisky War" – was initiated. In the spring of 1854 a great wave of the temperance movement engulfed the village. Led by several area ministers, it was decided by a band of temperance-supporting women to attack the evils of alcohol in its dens of iniquity, and sighted the popular Brick Tavern Bar as their first target. They invaded with fury in the early morning hours; in a short time, the fumes of liquor infected the air as bottles smashed and their contents rapidly absorbed by the parched earth in front of the tavern.

Needless to say, the momentum of their self-righteous destruction drew intense excitement as the army of women marched quietly to another nearby saloon. With cunning trickery they gained access through a back door, and once again, opened faucets and drained bottles, flooding the floor with Rum, Bourbon, and Rye.

By the time they reached "French Pete's" – their third destination – the news of the revolution had spread throughout the village, and a crowd had gathered. Deputy Sheriff Chapman advanced and began to disperse the onlookers, and then proceeded to take the intruders into custody.

A few days later, a number of the offending women appeared before Judge Wheeler in circuit court; damages were fixed at $150, which was immediately paid, thus ending the Baraboo Whisky War.

The Wisconsin House and the Brick Tavern received a frame addition in later years by its new owner, John Schlag. This historic old tavern remained in operation until it was torn down to make way for the Al Ringling Theater in 1915.

The distinguished widow of martyred President Abraham Lincoln visited Baraboo during the summer of 1872. She was a guest at the Cliff House at Devil's Lake, and the old Western Hotel in Baraboo.

Its builder, Colonel Edward Sumner in 1847, had originally christened the Western the Adams House, the name of the village at that time. By the time he departed for California in 1849 to seek gold, he had enlarged the house to an imposing three-story structure. Before leaving, Sumner rented the place to an innkeeper named Watson, and in 1855 sold it to the firm Dunn & Davis who subsequently renamed it the Western Hotel.

At this pioneer hostelry gathered all classes of people – court judges, lawyers, travelers seeking land, as well as townsfolk keeping attuned to the latest gossip. The Western even served as prisoner quarters, as there was no jail in Baraboo at that time. No doubt, prisoners of the law were not much inclined to break out from such elegant confinement.

Several owners presided over the Western Hotel over the years until it was consumed by fire in 1878.

While the stagecoaches rumbled in and out of Reedsburg during the early developmental years of that town, a great rivalry between hotels delivered much excitement. The first building of note in Reedsburg was a story and a half tall structure to which the citizens pointed with pride as the "tavern." J. C. Clark erected it in 1849-50, the materials coming from the principal industrial institution of the village, the Reed & Powell sawmill. A long list of proprietors followed Clark, and after its destruction by fire in 1877, it was rebuilt with brick.

J. S. Saxby constructed the second hotel in Reedsburg. It, too, saw many different owners, and was finally purchased and moved to a farm two miles west of the town.

But the real hotel business rivalry in Reedsburg involved the Mansion House and the Central House, built in 1855 and 1856, respectively.

An early proprietor of the Mansion House named Cooper carried a reputation that seemed less than desirable to the citizens of the village. For years the hostelry was credited with being the rendezvous for bad characters. On one occasion, when a law officer searched the place, portions of stolen harness were found and other evidence that indicated there was "something with an offensive odor in Denmark." Another incident is told of a wagon arriving one night, and when the injunction was given that no one should approach the vehicle, a resident bent with curiosity made a stealth investigation. He found a dead man in the wagon, but he said nothing about the matter until the wagon and the men accompanying it were long gone.

Feeling the pressure of scrutiny from the law, Cooper finally left the country. A number of proprietors greeted guests in this hotel during the years to follow. Nonetheless, the rivalry continued.

The rival was known as the Alba House for many years, Alba Smith its builder and proprietor, until the name was changed to the Central House.

Prior to and during the Civil War, the bitter rivalry between these two hotels stemmed from differences of political opinion. Democrats gathered at the Mansion House to hear news of important events, and Republicans congregated at the Alba House. Each place had an enormous dance hall, and in them the opposing factions assembled for the popular form of entertainment. During this time period, the minds of men not all cast in the same mold, sometimes led to physical combat. The political followings in the town were so strong that young ladies would ask to be escorted home if they learned their beaus were taking them dancing in the "wrong" house.

The Sheboygan-Fond du Lac trail became a popular route for the early settlers in that part of the territory, and had been in use as a wagon path since 1838, long before the plank road construction. Many immigrants had settled in the Fond du Lac area, and for them, Sheboygan was the nearest lake port, and the primary source for supplies. Because of the slow progress of the pioneers during their treks from the lake port to the interior, a number of taverns resulted along the trail. These hostelries and their stables provided feed and shelter for oxen or horses, and meals and lodging for the travelers.

One of the roadhouses, the Wade House at Greenbush, built in 1849 and opened to the public in 1850, remained in service as a public inn for nearly a century. Still preserved in its original state, the Wade House now serves as a museum and one of the many sites maintained by the Wisconsin State Historical Society.

Sylvanus Wade first built a substantial log cabin at Greenbush, the halfway point between Sheboygan and Fond du Lac, and brought his wife and nine children there in 1844. The cabin soon received two additions and served as an inn for the needs of the occasional traveler for several years. At that time, they were the only white settlers in the region that was nothing but dense forest populated with many friendly Indians, and not-so-friendly wolves. The Indian children proved to be good companions for the white youngsters, but the wolves proved to be a nearly constant menacing threat. When the wolves killed the Wade's watchdog, poison was distributed, and seven dead wolves were found, finally resolving the problem.

Then in 1849, business warranted the construction of the present building. The Wade House soon became quite popular; it is said that as many as 200 people might seek shelter there on a single night, but only a fraction of them could be accommodated.

Sylvanus and Betsey Wade built this classic inn that served as a stagecoach stop and hotel for travelers over the Plank Road between Sheboygan and Fond du Lac. (Photo by author.)

That would make it easy to understand why another tavern could be built within about four or five miles and still carry on a successful business. The Ehle House was better known for its excellent meals, although it is likely that many early travelers sought accommodations for an overnight stay there as well. Perhaps it would have been better remembered today had it survived through the years, as did the Wade House, however, a tragic ending that wiped out the entire family and the pioneer tavern in a matter of a few moments came in February 1886. By then the rush of emigrants into the interior from the lake port of Sheboygan had passed. Very few taverns were doing much of a hotel business, although some survived by maintaining a barroom and selling liquor, and by farming the adjacent land.

Abram Ehle was then eighty years old. His wife had died a year or two earlier, and his only son, James and his wife and their three small children lived there with Abram, maintaining the tavern and about 260 acres of farmland. The only guest at the Ehle House was an elderly woman, and occupying an upstairs room was a young hired hand, Fred Lambrecht.

Lambrecht was away the evening of February 16th, and when he returned about an hour before midnight, he noticed a light in the room occupied by the grandfather. He went right to bed and quickly fell asleep. Later in the night he was awakened by the smell of smoke and a whining dog. He jumped out of bed and opened the door to his room, only to see that the entire building seemed to be ablaze. He could hear James Ehle cry out, but by that time, Lambrecht's hair was singed and flames were eating into his room. It was utterly impossible to render any assistance to those downstairs, and he had barely jumped from the bedroom window when the roof collapsed. The house was old and the wood thoroughly dry, and within moments it was completely engulfed in flames.

Dressed only in his underclothes, Fred Lambrecht, the only one to escape the fiery catastrophe, made his way through the bitter cold to a neighbor's house a half-mile away. His conflicting statements placed him under great suspicion for a while, until later it was determined that he suffered, understandably, from shock and was a bit delirious after such an ordeal. Although Lambrecht was cleared of any blame, the feelings lingered for some time that the Ehle family may have been the victims of murder and robbery, but the bodies were burned beyond a condition for anyone at that time to make any such conclusions.

Years after the tragedy, it was still rumored that specters hovered in the little grove of trees where nothing remained but a crumbling stone foundation where the Ehle House once stood.

Robert Baxter owned a hotel at Prairie du Sac and operated stage lines out of that village, one of which went to Mazomanie, the nearest railroad depot at the time. But competition was as keen in the Nineteenth Century as it is today. Two brothers, Joshua and James Long, built a competitive hotel, and managed to secure the government contract for carrying the mail. (Probably with a lower bid.) This resulted, naturally, in a spirited rivalry. For a time, passengers were carried to the railroad depot, a distance of ten miles, for only fifty cents, and that included breakfast!

H.W. Kingsbury was awarded the contract to carry mail between Kilbourn (Wisconsin Dells) and Grand Rapids (Wisconsin Rapids) in 1857. He established a tri-weekly line of stagecoaches that ran between the two towns, and on the route made stops at Plainville, Point Fluff, Quincy, and Strong's Prairie. This was part of a route that connected the Mississippi River in western Illinois and the pineries of the Upper Wisconsin, and was scheduled to coincide with the arrivals and departures of trains at Kilbourn.

About the same time, Myers and Boham Stage Line operated between Portage and Stevens Point, with stops at Oxford, Necedah, Plainfield, and other settlements along the way.

The Charleston House, owned by Charles Nutting, seems to be the first establishment at the little village of Midway in 1861. Four years later, John Miller bought property nearby where he constructed a flourmill. Around these businesses a town sprouted, and by 1870 there were blacksmith, hotel, store, and a 10,000-bushel grain elevator. Charles M. Nichols platted the village first known as Charleston in 1871. Disaster struck in 1879 when fire practically wiped out the entire town.

But the doomed village sprang back to life the following year with the added businesses of a wagon maker and wheelwright. Paul Van Loon set up a store and acted as postmaster. And because the post office was located in a store, nearly all the postmasters were the storekeepers until the Midway post office was discontinued in 1934. The Onalaska office then handled mail delivery.

Morris Briggs drove the stagecoach that served Midway until 1904. He hauled the mail, passengers, produce, and freight on the route that took him to North Bend one day, and returned to Onalaska the next.

Now a private residence, this building in North Bend, Wisconsin was once a tavern that served as the stagecoach stop there. (Photo by Author)

This non-typical railroad depot structure still remains in Midway, Wisconsin, and is presently used as a warehouse by the Midway Lumber Company. The railroad that passed through this sleepy, little town was the Trempealeau & La Crosse line that became part of the Chicago & North Western Railway system. The grade is now a portion of the Wisconsin State Trails, great for bicycling and hiking. (Photo by Author)

The Madison-Monroe road was one of the 80 territorial mail routes laid out in 1838. This road passed through present-day Fitchburg, followed along the Sugar River to Belleville, and on to Monroe and Janesville. Branching off to the southwest was the Madison-Wiota road, so named because of an early mail route and popular trail to the lead region in the southwestern part of the state.

Now a private residence in Madison, the OLD SPRING HOTEL, also known as Gorham's Hotel, was a stagecoach stop on the Madison-Monroe road for travelers to and from the western part of the state. It was designated as a Madison Landmark in 1972. (Photo by author)

On this road just outside of Madison (at that time), the Old Spring Hotel, first built by Charles E. Morgan in 1854, entertained guests traveling to and from Madison on the busy highway. By 1856 when the railroad reached Madison, the city had attracted a lot of bright talent from the east, just as it had attracted Mr. Morgan, a merchant from New York. The Green Bay area and the mining region of the southwest were the important parts of the state then, as Milwaukee had not yet risen to a major city. The Madison Monroe-Wiota road was a very busy one, and the Old Spring Hotel became a popular stop for individual travelers as well as the stage drivers carrying the mail. Farmers bringing their large quantities of wheat and produce to the marketplace always tried to plan their trips as to arrive at the Spring Hotel for breakfast and a cup of coffee for which the place had become famous. The fifteen rooms usually filled with travelers arriving in the evening hours for an overnight stay before continuing on the next morning into the city or to the lead mines.

The old Spring Hotel hosted plenty of parties, too. During and after the Civil War, dances were held there for the soldiers, while Mike Hobbs, a famous fiddle player of the time reeled off the merry old-fashioned tunes that set many a light-footed patron twirling over the floor. University students found it the ideal place for dinners and parties at graduation time, and the parlor even heard wedding vows a time or two.

Just up the road from the Spring Hotel was another large brick house built at about the same time by Frederick and Amelia Paunack. It was operated by a Mr. Mayhew as a hotel, bar, and dancehall, and rivaled the Spring Hotel for popularity. It, too, served as a stagecoach stop. But this hostelry gained a rather rough reputation when a new owner, John Whare, a glass blower from England, took over its operation in 1857. He expanded the house with a brick addition, and it was known as the "Plough Inn" (named for the ploughs he sold) until 1865. Regular accommodations were for the gruff teamsters and reckless young fellows who were among the lead haulers. The place was witness to plenty of drinking, fighting, and fun-loving adventure.

The Plough Inn -- This historic structure served as a tavern and a stagecoach stop dating back to 1853. The Plough building is on the national register and is one of Madison's oldest existing homes. Travelers would hitch their horses outside on their way in or out of town for refreshments and dancing, and if necessary they could sleep in one of the bedrooms upstairs. It was a rowdy, loud tavern known for rough characters and some bar room fights, thus receiving the nickname "Plough Inn and Stagger Out." (Photo on left – ca. 1850s – obtained from the present owners, John and Cathie Imes. Photo on right by author – as it appears in 2006, the "Arbor House" Bed & Breakfast.)

Until the railroads pushed farther into the north, the stagecoaches were the only means of overland commercial transportation between cities in Wisconsin and St. Paul. As early as 1855 a stage line ran to St. Paul from Madison, Wisconsin by way of Eau Claire and Black River Falls. This stage ran three times weekly. Passengers from St. Paul arrived at Black River Falls on Monday, Wednesday, and Friday nights after a two-day journey. The next morning they could continue on the same line to arrive at New Lisbon that evening, and make a connection with an eastbound train that left the next morning for Milwaukee.

W.T. Price operated the line between Sparta and Eau Claire, passing through Cataract, Black River Falls, Augusta, and Fall Creek, known as the "Overland Route." He left Sparta daily (except Sunday) after the arrival of the trains from La Crosse and Milwaukee, and for a two-dollar fare, twenty hours later, his passengers were in Eau Claire in time to make connections on stages bound for Durand, Hudson, and Chippewa Falls. Milwaukee newspapers carried on this stage could be circulated in Eau Claire just thirty-three hours after they were printed! The return trip to Sparta arrived there in time for travelers to board the east- and westbound trains.

Richard Murphy and his son, William, came from Toronto, Canada in 1865 and settled at Augusta, near Eau Claire. They opened and operated a hotel, barroom, and store just south of Fall Creek. It became a popular stopping place along the Sparta-Eau Claire stage route where passengers were offered lodging and meals, and where the coach line stabled horses.

As the population increased, so did the demand for stage service, and this line eventually ran two daily stages each way between the towns. But as the West Wisconsin Railway progressed in steps northward from Sparta, the stage route shortened in corresponding increments. By 1871, when the rails reached Eau Claire, the iron horse had all but eliminated the need for the stage route.

Many early pioneers of the far northern settlements in the Lake Superior region had arrived via water routes. The waterways were always available as a means of transportation, and two canoe routes were most prominent. One was by way of the St. Croix and Brule Rivers, and the other followed the St. Louis River to Sandy Lake and the

Mississippi.

Dog teams were used as the first means of overland transportation on trails cut through the wilderness by explorers and woodsmen to Black River Falls, and to the United States land office at Hudson.

Congress appropriated the funds to build a military roadway opened for travel in 1856, and this route became the main artery of trade between Superior and St. Paul. At first, its main function was cattle drives and use by a few private vehicles. The mail was carried on foot or by mule, and canoe routes were still used from Kettle River to Taylors Falls.

Carlisle Doble started a wagon route in the late 1850s carrying mail, express, and passengers. His business was abandoned, though, when the Burbank Stage Company of St. Paul began operating a line of Concord coaches to Superior. Four- and six-horse teams pulled these grand coaches. Fourteen independently owned and operated relay stations between St. Paul and Superior were set up for exchanginteams, and where passengers could rest, refresh, and obtain meals while traveling.

The 160-mile route followed approximately the same line as present-day Interstate Highway 35 between the two cities, requiring six days to complete the trip. Later road improvements, however, reduced the travel time to three days. Although many of the stage stop settlements are long since gone, a few of the towns in Minnesota – Moose Lake, Willow River, Hinckley, Wyoming – can still be found on current maps, where the relay stations of this stage line were located. Horses were stabled and fed, and hospitable inns offered passengers a welcomed meal and a comfortable bed.

Railroads brought an end to the St. Paul to Superior stage route in 1870. But it wasn't the end of usefulness for these coaches. The company continued to operate in the Minnesota Red River Valley, and when the Black Hills area opened, new owners, Carpenter and Blakely, established the Northwestern Stage, Express and Transportation Company and ran these coaches on a line between Bismarck, North Dakota and Deadwood, South Dakota.

Moving the Mail

When the surveyors' reports came in, Congress had a problem on its hands that insistently demanded a solution. The biggest concern was the mail, and the means by which it should go overland. Delivery of mail had been the government's obligation since the republic's infancy, but in practice much of it was contracted to private carriers using any suitable form of transportation. By the mid-1800s, that was not a problem in the East where roads, rails, and waterways were well established. But on the frontier wilderness it was a different story.

Mail did not simply mean letters from home for the lonely emigrant settlers in the backwoods. It also encompassed newspapers, printed government matter, business documents, bank drafts and currency. Telegraph lines were still a novelty, limited to only a few Eastern areas; print remained the sole medium of communication that could inform the spreading population of happenings around the world, of Congress debates, and of decisions and laws that could affect their lives. Mail service – or more accurately, the lack of it – was becoming a crucial concern.

The usual procedure in establishing a new postal route was for Congress to designate the route, set a delivery schedule, and to decide on the maximum allowable compensation to a contract carrier. The Postmaster General then advertised for bids on the contract, and awarded it to the lowest bidder who could commit to its stipulations. If the contractor failed to perform properly, his contract could be annulled. In the event that his costs exceeded expectations due to increased volume or, perhaps, natural conditions, his only recourse was to appeal to Congress to raise the level of pay. Legislators were not always able to honor such a favor. That arrangement meant obvious risks for the contractor, but also a promise of handsome returns.

The earliest mention of mail arriving at Milwaukee via stage was in 1836, when that town was barely more than a trading post. The stage, conducted by Lathrop Johnson who kept the New York House at Chicago, was no more than an open lumber wagon. Some preliminary work had been done to the road, but it was still merely an Indian trail crossing four streams where a wagon would get mired most of the time.

Three years later, Milwaukee boasted a population of 1,000 inhabitants; increased traffic to and from Chicago wore a more permanent path, and a stage leaving Chicago could reach Milwaukee in 48 hours, with an overnight stop midway in the village of Racine. By 1845, two stage lines advertised daily express and passenger service between the cities.

As the regions within the Wisconsin Territory populated, villages and towns sprouted and grew. The people who courageously penetrated the frontier had left behind family and friends in their homelands of the East and South, and many had braved the treacherous journey from across the oceans. Communication was nonexistent, except for the personal messages brought by others arriving after them.

One important event took place in every community – the arrival of the first mail. It occurred in Janesville, just a tiny village in 1837. Virginia native, Henry Janes, like any other land speculator, was attracted to the availability of waterpower, settled on a bend in the Rock River, 1836, and platted the town on the east bank of the river that was first known as Black Hawk, but was soon changed to Janesville. He established the first ferry across the Rock River, enabling the town to become the focal point for the movement to the southwestern Wisconsin mining region and the Mississippi River Valley. With his little town established, he petitioned the government for a post office.

A lone horseman, Joseph Payne, appeared on the west bank of the Rock River carrying a mail pouch. It contained a single letter addressed to Henry F. Janes. The pouch had been locked at Racine, and when it arrived, there was no one to open it, as there was no post office or postmaster.

Doctor B. B. Carey, the Racine postmaster was on his way to the young settlement to inaugurate Mr. Janes as postmaster. Until he arrived, there was nothing to do but wait. Luckily, he brought a key with him; the pouch was opened and the mail delivered. There was much excitement in the settlement on this important occasion and Mr. Janes and his letter were the center of attraction for many days. In those days, the receiver of a letter was looked upon with much reverence.

Henry Janes was duly appointed the settlement's first postmaster, and letters could now be addressed to residents at "Janesville, Rock County, Wisconsin."

The establishment of a post office did not mean the immediate erecting of a large, well-equipped building. For months the Janesville post office resided in a cigar box nailed to a stump in front of Mr. Janes' tavern. Nor was it a common occurrence to send or receive a letter. Only the most urgent matters were transmitted by post, as sending a letter or a package meant the investment of twenty-five cents. During the first year of Janesville's post office operation, $90 in postage revenue was collected. As the population in southern Wisconsin grew, mail carrier contracts were awarded to the stagecoach lines, and Janesville emerged a central hub for several additional postal routes. Four years later, the volume had increased to $3,000 in annual revenue.

During the summer months by the mid-1800s, steamers carried much of the mail and express on the rivers. But come November, the waterways closed for navigation until the ice left in the spring. In November 1851, J.C. Burbank of Minnesota created an Express Agency and began carrying the mail on foot between St. Paul, Minnesota and Galena, Illinois. At that time, Galena was the western terminus of the American Express Agency, and also the primary depot for the steamboat trade on the Upper Mississippi. Burbank traveled a route through Wisconsin by way of Hudson, Black River Falls, Prairie du Chien, and then into Illinois to Galena.

Within two years, the business had expanded tremendously and Burbank partnered with a Mr. Whitney to organize the Northwestern Express Company, and by then could rely on the services of a fleet of stagecoaches known as the Walker Line, established a few years earlier. But by 1856, Burbank and Whitney became quite dissatisfied with Walker's service; they acquired their own line of coaches and established an Express route from St. Paul to Dubuque, Iowa by way of Decorah.

Burbank & Co. soon added more Concord coaches, included the passenger business to their enterprise, and in a short time had edged out their former competition with the speedier service. In 1858 they were awarded the contract for down river mail, which until that time had been monopolized by the Walker Line. Later that same year, Burbank & Co. joined forces with Allen & Chase to establish stagecoach service into

La Crosse, Wisconsin – an important step, as the railroad had then reached La Crosse. There was no wagon bridge at La Crosse until 1891, but there were ferryboats operating. One of the first things the promoters of the new town of La Crescent on the opposite shore from La Crosse had accomplished was to build a road to the ferry landing, thus making stagecoach communication between Minnesota and Wisconsin a practical means of moving passengers and mail across the river. The following spring, the two companies merged to form the Minnesota Stage Company, and within a year had established such efficiency, they were given a contract for all outlying mail delivery in Minnesota. By 1867 their immense mail and passenger operation network employed 200 men, 700 horses, and covered more than 3,000 miles of roads and trails, even though they had sold off their express territory south of St. Paul in 1863 to American Express Company. Rushford remained the western end of the line of the Southern Minnesota Railroad for nearly two years, but the Burbank stagecoaches were there to carry passengers and express from the Rushford depot to points as far west as Winnebago City.

The people settled in Franklin Township, Sauk County, Wisconsin desired mail service. An impending crisis – that would eventually evolve into Civil War – lurked among all citizens everywhere, and the political tension produced curiosities that could only be satisfied by communication with the outside world. Settlements located within Wisconsin during the 1850s were, in fact, still rather remote; mail routes seemed their only hope to connect with the rest of the country.

A petition for a post office at White Mound, a tiny settlement just north of present-day Plain, Wisconsin, was introduced to the US government, but before it could be granted, the citizens were required to prove their need by carrying the mail from Spring Green weekly for a year at their own expense, as a test of their sincerity. Taking turns, the settlers diligently fulfilled the agreement every Saturday for a year, and in 1860 they were granted the establishment of a post office with William Hudson as the first postmaster. Congress awarded a contract to John R. Lewis and the Spring Green Stagecoach Line to convey the mail to Franklin Township on a route that soon extended all the way to Reedsburg.

Bernard Strong, who, in later years was elected to the State Senate, was one of the earlier drivers, making one round trip per week between Spring Green and Reedsburg. In 1888 the stage service expanded to two round trips each week, and in 1893 the route was split, with drivers leaving Reedsburg and Spring Green daily, meeting in White Mound to exchange mail bags and passengers, and then returning to their respective home terminals.

By the 1870s, a number of settlements had appeared in south central Wisconsin along the Military Road. Although the very first letter to be carried any distance across the state traveled on this route, it wasn't until 1874 that the Post Office Department in Washington let a contract to the lowest bidder to carry the mail from Madison to Dodgeville. Timan Knutson and Ole Olson of Blue Mounds won the contract for four years with a bid of $517 per year. Knutson, a Norwegian emigrant who had served with the 23rd Wisconsin Infantry during the Civil War, drove the mail and passenger stagecoach.

Mail service in those days was a slow process, as the times presented difficult conditions. Poor dirt roads lined with tall weeds and brush sometimes made it necessary to take to the adjacent fields in order to avoid miring mud holes, and in winter it often became blocked with snow. Only during the dry summer months could the road be considered fair. But the mail must go through, according to contract, and Knutson spent three days to complete the appointed round-trip that he accomplished twice each week.

His route began at 7 a.m. Monday from his home village of West Blue Mounds and his stage would arrive in Madison at 4 p.m. Mail was exchanged and passengers boarded at 7 a.m. Tuesday, and with the crack of a whip, the stage rumbled off toward Blue Mounds again, making the first stop at the East Middleton post office. The post office at West Middleton was located in a farmhouse at the halfway point to the next stop in Pine Bluff, a modest little community that consisted of one blacksmith shop, two saloons, and a veterinarian.

Then it was a long, grueling uphill pull for the team to Postmaster Andrew Levorson's little store at Mount Horeb. One more stop at the East Blue Mounds general store kept by Postmaster Frank Brackenwagen, Sr., and the stage was bound for Knutson's headquarters at West Blue Mounds, arriving at 4:30 in the afternoon. (It might be noted here that the post office of West Blue Mounds was located in Pokerville, just west of the present village of Blue Mounds. Blue Mounds was not located until after the railroad was built. Pokerville had two general stores, two hotels, three saloons, a harness maker, two blacksmith shops, a wagon maker, and a doctor. The town no longer exists.)

Bright and early on Wednesday, Knutson rolled his stage westward toward Dodgeville, making two stops on the way – at Jennieton, a tiny hamlet two miles west from the present village of Barneveld where a blacksmith shop, an inn, and a small store run by Ben Evans housed the post office; and at Dan Jarvis' grocery store in Ridgeway.

Dodgeville, the first established town in Iowa County, and one of the oldest places of business in Wisconsin, got its start in 1827 as the center of the lead mining district. By the time Timan Knutson's stagecoach rumbled through its streets, Dodgeville was already a thriving, busy place with several large hotels, many stores of wide variety, farm implement manufacturers, furniture makers, doctors, lawyers, a newspaper, a brewery, and, of course, a post office where Knutson arrived at 11:00 a.m. By 1:00 p.m., mailbags were exchanged, and stage, passengers and eastbound mail rambled off, returning once again to Blue Mounds at 4:30 in the afternoon. Thursday morning, the same routine began again.

Numerous stagecoach lines were established between Minnesota, Iowa and Wisconsin towns, most of them for the purpose of carrying the mail. Even after the railroad brought about a diminishing effect on the passenger service provided by the stage lines, many continued successfully long after the iron rails were in place, transporting mail, light freight, and some passengers to outlying towns not situated along the railroads. Stagecoaches remained an important part in the way of life until after the turn of the Twentieth Century, when the motorcar evolved into trucks and buses.

Stagecoach Stop
Lorette House

c.1871

In its day, the Lorette House (also Loretta) was a well-known landmark on the ridge about eight miles west of La Crescent, Minnesota, along the territorial road traveling west from La Crosse.

(Present-day Houston County Highway 25) Seth Lore built the original log cabin sometime before 1856, the exact date unknown. As the first stagecoach stop west of La Crosse, he operated the establishment until 1861 when his daughter, Mrs. C.B. Carpenter became the hostess.

The original two-story log structure was 18 by 20 feet. It offered for the stagecoach travelers three sleeping rooms on the ground floor and one chamber upstairs. It was a very popular stop, and by 1859 a 20 by 30 foot two-story frame addition was constructed to accommodate patrons of three different stage lines. As many as 70 people were fed at a single meal.

The climb up the long, steep hills from La Crescent was grueling work for the four- and six-horse stagecoach teams, so the Lorette House complex also included a blacksmith shop and livery stables where the horses were exchanged and cared for. The next stop was another eight miles to the west at Cooper's Tavern in the present-day village of Ridgeway.

A post office established in 1856 at the Lorette House, E.S. Lore its first postmaster, operated until it was discontinued in 1869 when another office was established at near-by Mound Prairie.

Farm buildings now occupy the spot where this grand little inn once stood. Nothing remains of the Lorette House except for its sign, kept at the Houston County Historical Society Museum in Caledonia, Minnesota. (Picture and information courtesy of the La Crescent Area Historical Society)

Mail for the Northwest Frontier

Although mail service had an early start in the St. Croix River Valley, there was very little postal activity during the early years of settlement. A post office had been designated at Ft. Snelling in 1834, but it was only occasionally that a letter might arrive with soldiers or a chance traveler

87

coming from Ft. Crawford at Prairie du Chien. Mail service was expensive, and few people could afford the twenty-five cent charge for transporting a single sheet, folded and sealed with hot wax. As the rates were reduced – five or ten cents, depending on the distance in 1845, and then in 1851 to three or six cents – the use of the postal service increased, and so did the demand for more post offices. These new offices, though, still had little to do at first, as mail was generally received only semimonthly along the Upper Mississippi, and irregularly, as the steamboats that brought it ran only when they could obtain enough cargo.

Despite the irregular service, post offices usually were quick to follow a new settlement, even though a town had not yet been officially founded. The first post office to be established in Minnesota (outside Ft. Snelling) in 1840 at Point Douglas was first known as "Lake St. Croix." The mail was carried by canoe or on foot up the St. Croix River. The men who made these trips, usually twice per month, received six dollars per trip to the northern terminal, also established in 1840 at St. Croix Falls.

The federal government established another post office at Stillwater in January 1846, and a few months later one at St. Paul. As early as 1847 the mail traveled over a road connecting the two villages, but deliveries to Stillwater were still only occasional, as the mail from Prairie du Chien continually suffered delays – sometimes for weeks – at some point along the Mississippi River.

During the late 1840s, an overland postal route was established from Prairie du Chien via Black River Falls, Wisconsin into the St. Croix Valley and followed the eastern bank of the river northward. Minnesota residents had to cross the river to pick up their mail. The inconvenience provoked complaints from the citizens of Marine Mills and Stillwater claiming their need for better service. As a result, a direct postal route from Point Douglas at the mouth of the St. Croix and Marine Mills was established on a newly opened road via Stillwater. This road was eventually continued on to Taylors Falls, where another post office was authorized in February 1851. The first mail didn't arrive there, however, until the following April, and that only amounted to one letter sent from St. Paul.

With no money to spend on roads, the state of Wisconsin could do little for the far west settlers or the young Minnesota Territory, and relied strictly on the federal government for any improvements. The mail service continued to suffer because of the poor road conditions. Then in 1853 a military road up the west side of the St. Croix that eventually connected Point Douglas with Lake Superior was completed past Taylors Falls. It was a great day, indeed, when, in addition to the occasional steamboat delivery, four-horse coaches began delivering the mail to Stillwater tri-weekly from St. Paul. Carlisle Bromley, a liveryman at Stillwater was the carrier on the route, and he also ran a mail carriage once a week to Taylors Falls. And about that same time, the sister city across the river, St. Croix Falls, started receiving some of its mail via Hudson, but, even with these few improvements, the service was far from being adequate.

Most of the complaints were aimed at the carriers. George Nettleton contracted to carry the mail from Taylors Falls northward along the eastern bank of the river to Superior, Wisconsin. After the route was expanded, he found himself obliged "to pass the mail over a road some 60 miles of which is not worked at all and impossible to pass with a horse," so he wrote to Washington. Such difficulties must have been discouraging, for in the following year, Superior was without mail service. Citizens' complaints were accompanied by the concessions that the route was rather difficult, and by 1860 the road was reported to be in good condition. Superior wanted its mail.

More post offices were added on the route along the St. Croix: on the west bank at Lakeland, Milton Mills (later changed to Afton) and a speculator's village, Vasa, that was later dropped because of the lack of development. On the east bank, offices were authorized at Prescott, Osceola, and Kinnick Kinnick, the village that is now River Falls, Wisconsin. Yet, the problem of poor mail service persisted. In the entire Northwest, there was no official postal supervision. Riverboats traveling north from Galena did not make proper connections with trains from the East, and on the overland routes, mail was left behind to make room for the paying passengers. Schedules were often altered to meet the carriers' convenience.

By 1858, the year Minnesota was admitted to the Union, the mail situation had seen little improvement. But with statehood came the appointment of a special agent to travel up and down the route along the

Mississippi to ensure that carriers fulfilled their contracts and to better organize the system.

Although this supervision was not the total immediate solution, some benefits were noticed. Mail reached St. Paul on a regular schedule; there was daily mail and stage service from there to Stillwater; and mail deliveries reached the towns to the north three times weekly.

But the system was still not at its best potential. Instead of steamboats bringing the St. Croix Valley mail directly to Stillwater, it was first routed to St. Paul, causing unnecessary time delays. An attempt to remedy that problem came early in 1859 when the steamer *Equator* started carrying the mail on the St. Croix, but a disastrous storm completely wrecked that boat. Then in 1860, Captain Isaac Gray put his little stern-wheeler, the *H.S. Allen*, on the postal river route and became the "Regular St. Croix River U.S. Mail Packet," establishing service between Prescott and Taylors Falls.

One boat could not completely satisfy the demands, and in 1862 another steamer, Captain Oscar Knapp's Enterprise joined the Allen. On alternate days, they managed to provide daily mail service to the villages of the upper river. Schedules were still sometimes difficult to meet due to low water, log jams, and occasional equipment breakdowns.

During the winter months when the boats couldn't run, delivery schedules were reduced to three times per week. The frozen river provided a better, smoother route for the stages, although thin ice resulted in an occasional accident.

Cold weather and deep snow often caused backlogs of letters and papers bound for Bayfield and La Pointe on Madeline Island, and during some summers like 1863 and 1864, extremely low water made steamboat navigation difficult on both the St. Croix and the Mississippi. Captain Knapp complained that a good-sized pickerel lying crosswise in the channel interrupted navigation, and that his boat could no longer jump over the sandbars. It was suggested that the government should ban all catfish from using what little channel was left.

And, of course, the greatest competition for use of the St. Croix River that steamboat pilots faced was that of the lumber industry and their log drives. Frequent logjams blockaded the river, causing long delays for the packets. Needless to say, the people of the St. Croix River Valley were continually plagued with the lack of dependable postal service.

Not all the problems incurred were the fault of the river, and sometimes the river became the temporary cure. In 1871 another steamer, the *Wyman X* functioned as a mail boat for a short period after a stage line was forced to discontinue service because the road along the river was in such poor condition. As the stage driver put it: "This road is not passable, not even jackass-able."

By 1875, there was only one mail packet remaining on the St. Croix – the *G.B. Knapp*. The Taylors Falls run had ended in 1873 when that town began receiving its mail communication via the village of Wyoming that was now served by a railroad. George McNeal, a liveryman at Marine Mills who held the mail contract found it more profitable to carry mail sacks and passengers by boat rather than team. That era ended, though, when he disposed of his contract in late 1875. The *G.B. Knapp*, for so long a familiar sight on the St. Croix, was the last of the river's mail boats.

Major changes came in 1876 with the development of improved roads. Until the mid-1880s, four stage lines handled the mail carrying business with the aid of ferryboats to take them across the river to reach the Wisconsin villages. And when the Stillwater branch of the Lake Superior & Mississippi Railroad started transporting mail in 1871, the stage route between St. Paul and Stillwater was discontinued. But not until December 1887 did rail service reach Marine Mills when the Minneapolis, St. Paul & Sault Ste. Marie Railroad – better known as the Soo Line – was completed and replaced the horse-drawn stages once and for all.

No other event during the pioneer days seemed to draw as much attention with such excitement as the arrival of the first railroad train into a town. In a carnival-like atmosphere, there was always a band playing, speeches delivered by prominent citizens, fun and games for the youngsters, and the women of the town went to great lengths in preparing a fabulous meal to serve the attending crowd, including the many visitors arriving aboard the train. The opening of the Hudson & River Falls Railway in 1878 was no exception.

To anyone who had made the trip between Hudson and River Falls in dark nights or stormy weather, they could appreciate the advantages of the thirty-minute trip in the comfort of a railroad car. It can be assumed with little doubt that there were plenty of hats in the air when the guests from St. Paul, Stillwater, and Hudson arrived on that first train, welcomed with great frivolity by the citizens of River Falls. Over 600 people partook of a fine dinner, and then listened to the many speeches by notables such as the railroad company president, a Minnesota ex-governor, the man who had run the first stagecoach line between Hudson and River Falls twenty-three years earlier, judges, and others. Their messages conveyed appreciation of the warm welcome, as well as praise to the development of this great advancement of civilization.

Upon adjournment, the band and a throng of citizens escorted the visitors back to the depot, and sent them on their way home with hearty cheers that were cordially returned.

At last, the people of the St. Croix Valley were freed of the mail hindrance by low water, log jams, and muddy roads.

Iowa Stagecoaches

Stagecoaching began in Iowa about 1838 and remained the prime source of overland transportation until the 1870s when the railroads had become well established. From the 1850s through the 1870s the stagecoach lines conducted business in conjunction with the railroads. By 1854, the Western Stage Company was the largest line in Iowa, conducting nearly all the stage traffic over 14 routes, most of which originated in Iowa City.

Stagecoach trails were a significant factor in Iowa history, although they were short-lived. By 1855 the popular "Diamond Trail" was a system of roads that helped close the gaps between the Mississippi River towns, the new state capitol at De Moines, and many other western cities. During the pioneer times, public travel was exclusively by stage. The various stage lines were created, initially, to serve the function of federal, state and county governments, as well as for mail delivery and public passenger service.

But by 1870, the competition from the railroads became too strong, and the stagecoach lines quickly disappeared. Many of the routes they traveled, though, continued to be used for local and regional travel by wagon and teams, and some of the modern-day highways follow those original stage routes.

Wagon Builders

Small companies that were often one-man operations produced most wagons built in the United States during the early 19th Century. Production was slow and in varying degrees of quality. America's surge to move westward changed all that. Scores of companies sprang up to supply vehicles for the transport of people and goods, with long distance hauling in focus. Some firms boasted of specialties such as Schuttler Wagons of Chicago making wagons that could be coupled together in tandem. However, Schuttler's output never matched that of the industry's two giants: the J. Murphy Company of St. Louis and the Studebaker Brothers Manufacturing Company of South Bend, Indiana.

Studebaker featured an extensive line of vehicles ranging from military ambulances to elegant carriages. But both companies concentrated on freight wagons as the staple product, built as meticulously as their finest surrey. Joseph Murphy would not allow his workmen to bore holes with an auger for bolting planks together; instead they burned the holes through with red-hot irons to keep the surrounding wood from cracking. The Studebaker Brothers insisted on equally high standards. The hardwood lumber used in their wagons was aged three to five years to prevent shrinkage in the dry western climate, and their black hickory axles were boiled in oil to drive out moisture.

The cost of most freight wagons was held to less than $200 by virtue of quantity production. By 1874, the 550 Studebaker plant employees were turning out more than 30 wagons a day.

Many early professions relied on the wagons just as modern-day businessmen rely on motor vehicles of all sizes. But perhaps none were quite as picturesque as the peddlers, or "drummers" as they were often called. "Peddler" and "drummer" are typically American terms. The Old World "peder" or foot salesman (of Scotch origin) became the "peddler" in America, and although in England they traveled only on foot (a "hawker" traveled by wagon) anyone in America selling wares door-to-door was commonly known as a peddler. The term "drummer" originates from a time when drums were used to attract public attention: the first American peddlers "drummed up" business in such a manner, but by the time men of that profession began plying the streets and trails of Wisconsin Territory frontier, that practice had probably been all but abandoned, and only the name "drummer" arrived with them.

Itinerant peddlers traveled from settlement to settlement, stopping at every farmhouse along the way. They traveled great distances and were away from their homes for long periods of time. The sides of the specially designed wagons, usually drawn by one or two horses or mules, opened to expose compartments stocked with all sorts of houseware items from pots and pans to stationery and sewing supplies. Many peddlers carried patent medicines, perfumes, clothing, spices, hardware, boots and shoes – virtually a compact department store on wheels. These sales entrepreneurs made possible for the average rural family to obtain needed items that were otherwise unavailable to them at the limited "shopping" facilities in nearby towns.

Edmund Evans and Sons planted orchards of apples, plums, blackberries, raspberries, and currants on a farm they purchased near La Crescent, Minnesota in 1860. They relied on their own wagon transportation to deliver the abundant produce to markets in La Crosse, Wisconsin. (Photo courtesy of Evans family descendants.)

Wagon Builders
Of Early Wisconsin

Henry Mitchell, a dark-haired, hunched little man drew up his horses in front of a grocery store at Racine in 1854. He climbed down from the driver's seat, and as his boots clattered across the wooden sidewalk to the front door, a crowd with envious admiration was gathering about his brightly painted green wagon.

Mitchell had come to Racine from Chicago, where a few years earlier he had established the first wagon factory there. He arrived with little money, but with an attitude that disguised his financial condition. A short time later, he turned out Racine's first manufactured wagon in a small workshop, and from that meager beginning, an impressive business known as *Mitchell, Lewis & Company* grew to a proud and respected enterprise. Hard work and dedication resulted in constant growth, until fire completely destroyed the plant in 1880.

But determined to continue, Mitchell rebuilt it all, and eventually the operation was housed in a five-story brick structure capable of producing a finished wagon every twenty minutes.

The company prospered for a time, and then came financial reversals and the automobile; Mitchell abandoned wagon making, the enterprise fell into other hands, and the old Mitchell glory faded.

The Stoughton Wagon Works began operation in much the same manner in 1865. T. G. Mandt was only nineteen years old when he moved from his father's farm in the town of Pleasant Springs to the village of Stoughton, just five miles away. As a youngster, he had thoroughly learned the art of making a wagon at his father's country shop, and unlike most mechanics, he had mastered both the wood and iron work.

With only forty dollars capital, but plenty of energy and determination, young Mr. Mandt used half of his available cash for the down payment on a plot of land, and the other half he paid toward the purchase price of eighty dollars for an old warehouse that he tore down, using the lumber to build his shop.

In the summer of 1865 his shop was running at full blast with five employees, operating on capital obtained in advance by selling a wagon before it was manufactured. During that year, one buggy and five wagons were produced.

The following year, business boomed; another lot was purchased and additions to the blacksmith shop were built. Production increased that year to ten wagons, four buggies, and five sleighs.

Late in that same year, 1866, George Getz came in as a partner, and remained for only three years. Although production increased to forty wagons per year, very little improvement was made to the facility other than adding a larger labor force. A cautious businessman, Getz thought Mandt was pushing the growth factor a little too quickly, and sold his interest in the business back to Mandt.

Subsequent years brought even more growth; more lots and more buildings were added, and the business expanded to include a sawmill and foundry. Then in 1869, the young entrepreneur took on another partner, an uncle, G. T. Mandt. Previous to that time, there had only been local trade for the wagons, but the new partnership afforded the business to extend westward, and the first carload of wagons was delivered to Mr. P. K. Everson, an Iowa dealer. By 1881, Everson had sold more than 850 Stoughton wagons.

Seventeen months after the partnership formed, it was dissolved. The uncle thought, too, that his nephew was over-reaching, and left the firm. But young Mandt pressed on. His trade now extended into a considerable portion of Iowa, Minnesota and Dakota.

Then came the hard and crushing times of 1873, '74, and '75 for all kinds of businesses. Widespread crop failures in the west rendered agents who had been selling Mandt's equipment unable to collect from farmers and could not meet their obligations to him. Consequently, Mandt could not meet his obligations to Eastern wholesalers, and after a difficult struggle, had to give up, making assignments of all his property for the benefit of his creditors. Liquidating the assets, though, meant sacrificing great loses, as values had drastically shrunk. After careful consideration at a meeting of the creditors, they determined that the causes of the slump were beyond Mandt's control and agreed to allow Mandt to regain command, accepting a small percentage of the due debts as payment in full.

After only four weeks of shutdown, Mandt re-opened his shops, and work resumed at full capacity. Abundant crops of 1877 throughout the West, and brilliant business practices rewarded Mandt for his persistence; old debts owed to him were repaid, and in turn, Mandt paid his creditors in full – even though he was not obligated to do so – recognizing the value of the business relationships he had established with them, and appreciating the help they had extended to him during hard times.

Over the years, Mr. Mandt spared neither time nor money to produce the easiest running, best finished, and best-proportioned wagons, buggies, sleighs, and other farm equipment in the country. Continuous development of improvements always remained top priority, and his efforts were well recognized; wherever the products were introduced, they were generally used exclusively.

Long gone are the days of wagons and buggies, however, the business still remains into the 21st century in Stoughton, Wisconsin. It is known now as *Stoughton Trailers*, manufacturing semi-trailers for use by modern-day freight transportation companies across the nation.

Another interesting account of a wagon builder in the history of Wisconsin is that of Herman "Long John" Barkow, that begins in 1879. Barkow was 26 years old when he first came to Wisconsin from Germany, where he had learned the wagon making trade. He founded the business in Milwaukee, and was soon dubbed "Long John" for his towering height.

"Long John" and his five sons quickly became a familiar institution. They began their workday in the early hours of dawn, calling on the various freight haulers, taking orders, and by 7 a.m. had a full day's work ahead.

Eventually, one son left to join the ministry, and another went to work in a motor factory. But Herman Jr., Fred, and William stayed, learned the wagon building art, and carried on the family business.

"Long John" Barkow knew the art of business, too. Frequently, he took the squeaks out of a new wagon by sipping beer in a tavern. If a customer complained of squeaks, "Long John" would say: "Let's have a beer and talk it over." Invariably the beer was the oil that quieted the squeaks, and the customer soon forgot them.

Barkow's office was a plank resting across two wooden sawhorses, and his bookkeeping system consisted of a chalkboard hanging behind the forge. Because the smoke from the forge would smudge the chalk marks, he made certain that bills owed to him were paid promptly before the records were destroyed.

In 1893, fire ravaged Milwaukee's third ward where Barkow's shop was located. He lost everything and had to start over. But soon lumber, milk, coal and beer wagons built with the finest white oak were rolling out of the new shop, and business as usual continued until 1910 when motor trucks came into the picture. "Long John" quickly adapted to the new era, and was the first in Milwaukee building truck bodies for the *Sternberg Motor Company*, which later became the *Sterling Motor Truck Company.*

Wagon building stopped about 1923, but "Long John" did not live to see that end; he died in 1918. His son, Fred, took over management and ran the company until he died in 1934, and the business was passed on to the third Barkow generation, Alvin and August.

Revival of the wagon days came in 1942 when the H. Barkow Co. rejuvenated two old milk wagons for a local dairy trying to meet the problem of truck and tire shortages. The sight of the sturdy wagons – built 45 years earlier – rolling along the streets of Milwaukee was reminiscent of a time when stomping Belgians pulled huge, creaking beer wagons, and a horse was still a man's handiest means of transportation.

Bicycles and Motorcars

The 1890s saw the arrival of bicycles in Wisconsin at an alarming pace; by 1894 the numbers had increased to over 15,000. This popular new mode of transportation faced a suppressing obstacle: no good roads on which to ride. Bicycle owners united to form the League of Wheelmen, and in turn achieved the support of commercialists; together they formed the League for Good Roads, but the struggle was far from over.

These advocates of road improvement engaged in some head butting with the taxpayers. Even with an improving agricultural economy, the farm community was not necessarily in favor of their tax dollars being shoveled into the roadbeds. Perhaps they didn't realize then that it meant a better means for them to market their produce and decrease their rural isolation, but nonetheless, they resisted the higher tax burden. They were satisfied with what they had and very much in agreement with the constitutional ban on spending tax money for internal improvement, including roads.

Enter – the motorcar – 1899. Gasoline-powered automobiles started appearing in Wisconsin, and by 1908 nearly 6,000 of them splashed through the muddy trails we would hardly call roads today. Their speed, economy and usefulness – not to mention man's growing obsession with the mechanical contraptions – conceived an even greater need for improved roads.

Wisconsin was the first state to number its roads and to place signs along the routes to aid the motoring public. This occurred as a result of James Drought, chairman of the newly formed Wisconsin State Automobile Association, when in 1907 he marked the trail from Milwaukee to Madison with bright yellow signs and arrows, tacking them to fence posts and trees. The struggle to attain the state's aid in improving roads with tax dollars, however, had already been as rutted as the roads, and it would be several more years before legislators approved the state spending.

By then, the Wisconsin Automobile Association had successfully lobbied for the motorists, and state residents voted the approval to change the constitutional spending rules. In 1911, the State of Wisconsin finally began providing financial assistance for the creation of good roads.

Despite the efforts, the development of dependable roadways throughout the state proved a long-lasting endeavor, as evidenced in an article appearing in the *Westby Times*, November 1926:

> *The big busses that have been going through here*
> *from La Crosse to Madison have discontinued coming to*
> *Cashton on account of bad roads and are going by way of*

Coon Valley. The last trip around was made Sunday and the bus that was due here from Madison at eight o'clock in the evening did not reach here until two o'clock Monday morning. It got stuck several times and when between Cashton and Newry ran out of gasoline.

And perhaps at least one discouraged car owner placed this advertisement in the same newspaper in March 1927:

For Sale, cheap if taken soon, Ford touring car, with starter and demountable rims.

It is not known whether the seller was discouraged by the bad road conditions, or maybe by the notice that all automobile drivers would be required to attain a driver's license the following year.

The Great River Road

Our pioneers' efforts to create roads was marked with deserved distinction in 1938 when the Department of the Interior first proposed the idea for the Great River Road. Initially conceived as part of a grand system to link North and South Americas from Canada to Chile, the Great River Road concept was put on the back burner for Congress-approved funding to study the project until 1949. At that time it was determined that such a road system would greatly benefit the entire nation, and the designated route should concur with established scenic federal, state and local roads along the Mississippi River. In the late 1950's, the route was marked with the distinctive green and white ship's wheel logo signs. Some fifteen years later, the first funds specifically for improvements of the Great River Road were authorized by the Federal Highway Act of 1973, providing $250 million to enhance existing roadways, build links to complete a continuous route and develop roadside amenities for travelers.

In its earliest development, the Great River Road nearly bypassed the southern-most portion of Wisconsin, the route crossing over to the Iowa side of the river and excluding the village of Cassville. R.J. Eckstein, one of the early advocates of the Great River Road idea, and who served on the Cassville village board for 50 years, much of that time as its president, was instrumental in urging a second route following the highways on the Wisconsin side as well, extending his community continued representation on the Mississippi Parkway Commission. Thanks to his persistence, Wisconsin now enjoys its entire Mississippi River shoreline caressed by the Great River Road.

And an honorable monument it is, to those pioneers who first blazed the primitive ox-and-wagon trail from Prairie du Chien to La Crosse, and later extending south from Prescott. As part of the prestigious 3,000-mile route between Canada and the Gulf of Mexico, that which threads its way through Wisconsin is embraced by some of the most breathtaking scenery found anywhere in the country.

The Mighty Mississippi River main channel at Alma, Wisconsin. (Photo by author)

The Rivers

Most people today are left with the impression that the American frontier was pushed Westward almost solely by wagon trains and the railroads, but the prairie schooner carried little cargo, and the iron horse, for all its final dominance, did not reach the Mississippi River until 1854 and the northern Continental Divide until the late 1880s. In conjunction with a vast network of far-reaching tributaries, the rivers remained the most important single means of entry into the wild and empty country that lay beyond the settled east.

The rivers served as roads for explorers and for all who followed them. They were the channels of commerce for fur traders and miners. The Army used them to establish and supply outposts. Rivermen penetrated the unknown and opened the way for settlers seeking virgin soil. And their usefulness would not soon be outlived.

The Mississippi River is, with little doubt, an overwhelming element of American geography, and no less important is its strategic place in American history. With its source in northern Minnesota and the numerous tributaries, its watershed encompasses all or part of twenty-two states – where lies some of the richest agricultural land the world has ever known – and discharges an average of 611,000 cubic feet of water per second into the Gulf of Mexico. Before Thomas Jefferson concluded the Louisiana Purchase in 1803, control of the Mississippi River was the focal point of several foreign powers, as this main artery proved to be the key to a future economic splendor. It was the doorway to the interior of the new continent. But with the Louisiana Purchase came the proclamation that the Mississippi was truly an American possession. Americans had been gradually pushing westward from the Appalachians and filtering into the Mississippi valley. Settlements along the river grew to villages, towns, and cities where only wilderness had once been, and by 1830 the great pilgrimage to settle the West was clearly underway. Thousands of European emigrants bypassed New York and entered at New Orleans, traveling up the Mississippi in pursuit of opportunity in this new land.

Prior to the age of steam, navigation on the river was accomplished with a variety of craft; Indians rode the currents in "bullboats" – circular, clumsy little vessels made by stretching the hide of a buffalo bull over a framework of willow branches. But these small boats could only float minimal loads across streams or down short distances of the big river, and they were far less useful than the sharp-prowed Mackinaws constructed by white settlers. The Mackinaws were flatboats up to 70 feet long, which could be quickly slapped together from whipsawed lumber, and with oars and a rudder were quite maneuverable. They could float tons of cargo downstream; however, Mackinaws could not be worked against the current, and usually, upon arrival at a destination, were dismantled and sold for lumber. The long upriver voyages were usually negotiated in dugout canoes or the graceful keelboats.

Keelboats were built up to 70 feet long and 15 to 18 feet wide with a roofed midship cabin. Cleated narrow walkways flanked both sides on which crewmen labored in poling the vessel upstream. A small brass cannon was usually mounted on the keelboat's bow, and its captain stood atop the cabin to shout commands and handle a steering oar fixed at the stern. The keelboat also had a mast to support a sail when favorable winds could aid propulsion.

The first steamboat on the Mississippi came in 1811, when Robert Fulton's *SS New Orleans* successfully steamed down the Ohio River from Pittsburgh, entered the Mississippi at the southern tip of Illinois, and continued on to New Orleans. Although it was underpowered for the strong currents and not well suited for upstream navigation, other steamboats soon followed with more powerful engines, multiple decks to accommodate passengers in comfort, and cargo in large quantities. The steamboat era was well on its way to become a major transportation media that would last into the twentieth century. By 1860 over 800 steam-powered vessels plied the western waterways.

As homesteaders streamed into the vast regions between the Great Lakes and Louisiana, settlement tended to follow the navigable rivers. The inland waterways provided cheap and easy passage to frontier zones as well as lines of communication linking western producers to markets in New Orleans and points on the eastern seaboard. Rivers became crowded with houseboats (that often served as floating general stores, saloons, and other dens of varying entertainment) as well as log rafts, barges, flatboats, keelboats, and eventually steamboats.

The early boatmen had to have stamina, nerve, and a fair measure of skill, as navigation was a ticklish business. Most early crews were the rugged backwoodsmen type who had signed on because – in addition to money – the job promised fun, adventure, and freedom from responsibility. Their lifestyle lacked in refinement and they were usually in a sad state of poverty – probably due to squandering their wages ashore on wenching, drinking, gambling, and fighting. These early boatmen – along with river pirates, cardsharps, and ladies of easy virtue – provided an extravagantly colorful and wild phase in the development of America.

The advent of the steamboats brought about little change at first, as the crewmen aboard these vessels were mostly carryovers from the keelboat days. Roustabouts (or roosters, as they were called in river slang) led an exhausting and thankless life. Firemen stood four-hour watches, but the deck hands remained on call day and night, slept when they could amid the freight, and were expected to carry cordwood, bales and crates over narrow, flimsy gangplanks that were often slippery with rain or ice. Their food was frequently appalling – pans filled with scraps and leavings from the passengers' tables – however, some of the packets sent hunters ashore for game, which was shared by everyone aboard.

Black roosters were considered the most compliant to toil; German immigrants rated next in dependability; Missouri farm boys, many of whom joined steamers to escape the plow, were thought to be a shade too independent, but were forgiven for it since they were Americans. Irishmen were considered to be the most rebellious and unreliable of all. At this time when steamboats were advancing America's trend toward engine power and speed, they were magnifying other American attitudes. Steamer officers were certainly not alone in a kind of cheerful contempt for ethnic minorities, but they were in a position to display their bias more dramatically than most. Slaves were used as roustabouts – their owners charged wages for them, and they were treated with some care since the owner always billed the boat if they were crippled or lost. But the European immigrant was another matter. "Oh, hell!" blurted one pilot, steaming on after being informed that a deck hand had fallen overboard. "It's only an Irishman!"

Steamboat mates – bullyboys who had little or no part in the actual operation of the vessel – were in charge of administering orders to the roosters. Some managed their crew with fists and a continuous volley of profanity. But some used clubs and carried pistols, since the roosters carried knives, and it was not above a few of the brutal ones to shoot a disobedient deck hand and heave the corpse overboard.

Deck hands of the era were not as discontented as the conditions might suggest. They still held certain leverage: they could desert a boat when she needed them most, especially during harvest seasons when alternative employment was abundant. They could win higher wages and better working conditions – for one voyage, at least. Since they were paid in cash (though poorly) most of them skipped every third or fourth trip to heal their bruises and foolishly splurge their earnings in the river town bars and gambling houses.

For decades, steamboat engineers had no way of gauging steam pressure or the limits imposed by crude safety valves, or of measuring how much horsepower their engines could produce. All they could rely on was that a hotter fire under the boilers produced more steam pressure, so in times of stress they simply ordered the firemen to dispense more fuel into the fireboxes, tuned their senses to the resulting vibrations, and by virtue of experience and good judgment estimated the strain on the boilers. The single cylinder, high-pressure engines used in those earliest steamboats exhausted steam every few seconds with a sound resembling that of cannon fire – a racket that could be heard for miles, even under normal operating conditions. The noise amplified as the pressure increased, and sometimes culminated in the hideous roar of boiler explosions when the safety limits were exceeded in radical proportions, often claiming lives, the boat and its cargo, and sending crew and passengers in a survival frenzy. But the traveling public had grown accustomed to the normal exhaust sound, and passengers seemed as exhilarated as the pilot and engineer when a boat labored noisily against a rushing current with the safety valve tied down.

A riverboat pilot's view of the Mississippi River just south of La Crosse, Wisconsin. (Photo by author taken from the pilothouse of the Steamboat Julia Belle Swain, 9/24/05.)

If life on a steamer in those days was crude, and if the vessels were dangerous contraptions engaged in an unpredictable confrontation with nature, they were also a mirrored image of the frontiers they served, and were admirably received without criticism by the pioneers for whom risk and hardship was the way of existence. Captains and pilots were men of dignity as well as adventure, navigating their massive craft through all the river's treacheries with encyclopedic knowledge, natural skill and instinct, and their boats were serious instruments of a serious trade; they penetrated the river wilderness a little farther upstream on each trip, landing every few miles to deliver or pick up goods and passengers. Their appearance to the pioneers was reassurance that they had not been forgotten, and that hope for a future in this untamed country seemed a little brighter.

In time, particularly after the Civil War that had interrupted river travel for four years, tremendous improvements in steamboats and their crews offered the traveler a more appealing experience with greater comfort and speed. Most steamboat lines boasted luxurious staterooms, entertainment of all sorts, and dining as fine as could be found in any big city restaurant. The working and living conditions for the crewmen improved, as well, with sleeping and eating facilities added for them on the Texas (top) deck. Seeming as almost a contradictory statement compared to the description of earlier boatmen, famed author Samuel Clemens (Mark Twain) wrote: "[Rivermen] were in the main honest, trustworthy, faithful to promises and duty, and often picturesquely magnanimous."

What better tribute could be given to one of the grandest professions on this earth?

Prior to the Civil War, Daniel Smith Harris was the most well-known and highly respected riverboat captain on the waterways. He had arrived at Galena, Illinois in 1823 at the age of fifteen with his father, James Harris, whom, because of financial difficulties, sought promising security in the lead mining region along the Fever River. But instead of mining, James Harris took up farming, and soon enjoyed great success in supplying the miners with the much-needed agricultural products.

The trip to Galena from Cincinnati aboard a keelboat fascinated oldest son Daniel. When they reached the mouth of the Ohio River at the Mississippi and began the slow journey against the current northward, the *Virginia*, bound for the Minnesota frontier, quickly overtook them.

The sight of the steamer chugging swiftly by their sluggish keelboat made an indelible impression.

A year later, Daniel and his younger brother, Robert Scribe Harris, had pursued lead prospecting with little success. Daniel's determination to earn enough money to build his own steamboat kept his ambition high, and so it is not surprising that his persistence finally led him and his brother to discover one of the richest lead deposits in the area. Some 4,000,000 pounds of ore would eventually come out of the mine that had previously been abandoned by its original claimants. Needless to say, Daniel Harris was well on his way to becoming a riverboat captain, although he or his brother would not ever discontinue their activities in mining.

Captain David Bates, one of the best steamboat captains on the Upper Mississippi, recognized Daniel's success and enthusiastic character. When a vacancy occurred in the pilothouse on his busy lead transporting steamer *Galena*, Bates offered Daniel Smith Harris an appointment as a cub pilot, which he accepted without hesitation. A little later, an assistant engineer was needed, and Daniel's brother, Robert filled the position. They could not have received better training in the steamboat business than they did under the direction of Captain Bates.

Then the Black Hawk War brought panic throughout the Mississippi Valley and Galena became an armed camp. River transportation interrupted, Daniel Harris enlisted in Captain James Stephenson's regiment and actively served throughout the entire war.

At the close of the war, Harris returned to Galena, Illinois and a substantial income from his mines. He still had the desire to own and operate a steamboat, and now he and his brother had gained ample training and experience from Captain Bates. There was a definite shortage of transport boats for the lead trade; there was no better time to answer a dream. While Daniel rejuvenated the hull of the old keelboat and constructed a cabin on its deck, Robert Scribe Harris left for Cincinnati to obtain an engine. He soon returned with the prize.

Christened the *Jo Daviess*, in honor of the county, it was a relatively small craft in comparison to the other Mississippi packets – only 90 feet by 15 feet and measuring 26 tons – but it would serve a bold purpose with Harris in command.

In July 1834, eleven years after the *Virginia* probed into the north on the upper Mississippi, tributary navigation added to the riverboat transportation network; the *Jo Daviess*, loaded to capacity with troops and military supplies, commanded by Captain Daniel S. Harris, ventured up the Wisconsin River to Fort Winnebago at present-day Portage, and made two more similar trips during that same season. Steamers continued that route from the Mississippi for many years to follow.

The Wisconsin, though, had peculiarities that eventually attributed to its shorter life span for supporting riverboat navigation. A river of great volume and swift current, it was subject to flooding from melting snow and heavy rains, but unlike many other streams, the Wisconsin is rarely flanked on both sides by high, steep banks, with the exception of the Dells area. This characteristic afforded adequate room for the extra volume during periods of flooding to spread out over the adjacent lowlands, rather than containing it in a narrow channel, resulting in less damage due to a less forceful flow. But the trade-off for that was a continuously changing main channel. Fast-moving currents constantly washed large amounts of sand downstream, and wherever an obstruction disrupted the smooth flow, the sand settled to the bottom, eventually forming a permanent bar or island. Where there was a good, deep channel, the following year might be shallows or even dry land. This led to extensive government expenditures in attempts to improve navigational conditions by building wing dams to collect the sand and to direct the water flow into a deeper main channel. It seemed, however, a losing battle; eventually, many stretches of the Wisconsin became too shallow for riverboat navigation.

But in its heyday, the Wisconsin saw plenty of steamboat traffic. Travel on the Wisconsin had been extended by the *Enterprise* as it penetrated through and beyond the Dells, and by 1854 two steamers made regular weekly runs from the Mississippi to Portage, and the *Ellen Hardy* offered regular service between Prairie du Sac and Portage.

Before the railroad, several attempts were made to navigate the Wisconsin River between Stevens Point, Mosinee, and Wausau. William Fellows and a Mr. Walton were the first to engage in the venture. Their boat made several trips from Stevens Point to Little Bull, but it was soon abandoned and dismantled, as the project proved to be a losing proposition. The Mosinee Fire Station bell was the only remaining memory of the failed steamboat. A few years later another futile attempt was made, but again, after just two or three unsuccessful trips, the boat was beached at a place called Bean's Eddy and was converted into a sawmill. W. W. Mitchell of Stevens Point challenged the navigational problem. But the river would not cooperate, and no more successful than his predecessors, Mitchell gave up the endeavor that only rendered unfavorable results.

The *Ellen Hardy* on the Wisconsin River. (From a newspaper photo made in 1876)

Old post card view of steamboat navigating through the Dells of the Wisconsin River.
(From private collection.)

The Portage Canal

The Fox and Wolf Rivers were also navigable, and in 1837 it was deemed advantageous to make a connection from the Fox to the Wisconsin River at Portage; a canal would open a continuous water route across the territory. The Portage Canal Company with $10,000 of private capital was chartered to build the waterway between the two rivers, and digging commenced the following year at a point on the Fox. Funds were soon depleted, work was abandoned, and the project lay idle for eight years.

As a route for military transportation, the canal concept drew government attention; land grants were made to the new state of Wisconsin to aid in the construction of the canal, and in June 1849, work began on a new and longer route a little farther to the north from the original site. But because of misunderstandings between the contractor and the state, progress crawled. Wages were withheld for months at a time, forcing the labor crews to abandon the operation, once again leaving the project unfinished. By March 1851, its condition was in a sad, neglected state; the canal banks were caving in and shoring timbers floated in the water.

However, the situation was resolved, as repairs were made a short time later. In May of that year, the steamer *John Mitchell* attempted to pass through the canal from the Fox River, and the steamer *Enterprise* entered the canal from the Wisconsin River. They both eventually retreated to their respective rivers, and neither could make a successful first passage through the too shallow Portage canal.

After that ceremonious failure, the water was drawn off and the work of shoring up the banks and bottom continued throughout the summer. What a devastating sight it must have been the morning after the water was let back into the canal to witness most of the shoring timbers and planks floating, nearly covering the entire surface. Unfortunately, that was not the end of the trouble. Less than a month later, floodwaters from the Wisconsin ravaged the southern banks of the canal, undermining several warehouse buildings, and even floating away a few other houses. Most of the shoring planks disappeared into the Fox River.

This destruction proved to be more than an easy fix, and the canal would exist as nothing more than a water-filled ditch severing the town for more than 20 years. When the Wisconsin-Fox River Improvement Company failed to meet its three-year obligation in a contract with the state to rejuvenate and restore the canal, the government stepped in and turned the project over to the Army Engineer Corps in 1874. Steam excavators were brought in, and this time, pilings were driven to secure the planking for bank reinforcement. Now the 2½-mile canal was 75 feet wide and 7 feet deep. And because the water level of the Fox River was eight feet lower than that of the Wisconsin, it was necessary to install locks to accommodate boat entrance and exit, and to control the water level during flood stages. As constructed, these locks were 45 feet wide and 160 feet long, with a lift of 9 feet at the Wisconsin River end, and 6 feet at the Fox River.

Two years after the beginning of this construction attempt, the government steamer *Boscobel* made the first successful trial run through the canal starting at the Wisconsin River. We can easily imagine the distinguished group of passengers aboard couldn't help but wonder how "Louis Jolliet regarded it, if his spirit was floating about in the vicinity." A little over two hundred years before, he had carried his canoe across this same portage on his famous voyage of discovery.

With the locks operating just as they were intended, and the canal of adequate depth and stability, it was immediately opened for navigation. Barges loaded with farm produce, lead ore from the Southwestern mining district, lumber from the northern reaches, and a steady flow of passenger traffic along with privately owned pleasure craft made regular use of the waterway.

The *Boscobel* was the first steamer to pass through the Portage canal in 1876.
(State Journal photo)

At the Wisconsin River end of the Portage Canal, the locks remain intact and can be viewed from the city park adjacent to downtown Portage. (Photo by author)

Although the canal would remain in service to the public for 75 years, it is ironic that upon its completion, after so many failed attempts, at enormous expense, steamboating had been on the decline for a decade. Railroads and other overland transportation means would eventually bring to an end this wonderfully romantic era. Navigation dwindled to a mere trickle and in July 1951, the locks were closed for the last time.

The locks at the Fox River end of the canal were removed and replaced by an earthen dam, however, the locks at the edge of the Wisconsin River in Portage remain and are accessible for viewing. Culverts and fill have replaced all the swing bridges at street crossings, but segments of the original canal with its planked shoring can still be seen.

Segments of the navigation canal still remain in downtown Portage, Wisconsin. Notice the planked shoring at each side. All the swing bridges have been replaced with culverts and fill to accommodate through streets. (Photo by author)

The Fox and the Wolf

The Fox River and Lake Winnebago waterway had long been considered the key route to Wisconsin's interior. A cavalcade of explorers, traders, and missionaries had traveled this route in canoes between Lake Michigan and the Mississippi River. The canoes gave way to the bateaux, and eventually the flat-bottomed, square-sailed Durham boats were the common vessel.

But then the lusty era of steamboats came to the Fox River Valley. It was an exciting time when the brawny steamers brought settlers and goods into the heart of Wisconsin, and they played a glorious and colorful role in the growth of the new state. As early as 1821, the steamboat *Walk-in-the-Water* came across the Great Lakes to Green Bay, but the venture up the Fox River was not attempted. The heavy steamers were unable to navigate past the rapids at Grand Kakalin, now known as Kaukauna.

As the population in the Fox River Valley expanded, making the river a more useful, navigable route became an important issue. Improvements to the waterway could make it possible for a vessel to travel from Green Bay to the Wisconsin River via the Fox, then down the Wisconsin to the Mississippi, and then to anywhere in the world. But the improvements would not come right away, and until statehood in 1848, steamboat traffic was limited to Lake Winnebago, the Wolf River, and the Fox River only as far as Princeton.

Getting the first steamboat to Lake Winnebago proved a difficult task. That boat was the *Black Hawk*, an odd-looking craft that was nothing more than an Erie Canal boat propelled by a small but powerful engine and a stern paddle wheel. Captain Peter Hotaling of Buffalo, New York, and pilot Joe St. Pierre, with a surly crew of Frenchmen, half-breeds, and Indians started up the Fox River with the Black Hawk in late summer, 1843. They made it over several rapids, but at Grand Kakalin, they could go no farther. It was decided to dismantle the boat, and with rollers and levers cut from the surrounding forest, they attempted to portage the craft. But discouraged by the extremely difficult task, they abandoned the *Black Hawk* at the edge of the river and continued their journey to Lake Winnebago on foot.

At the village of Manchester on the shore of Lake Winnebago, Captain Hotaling was determined to build a new steamboat. The keel was laid that fall, and the next spring, he and his crew returned to the dismantled *Black Hawk*, stripped out all the machinery and other valuable equipment and materials, loaded it onto Durham boats and hauled it to Manchester. They installed the machinery into the new side-wheel boat they christened the *Manchester*. Unlike their first boat, this one was built with a cabin on the lower deck that provided quarters for the crew.

It had taken Hotaling nearly a year since he had left Green Bay with the *Black Hawk*, to navigate onto Lake Winnebago with the first steamer in the Fox River Valley. Although the *Manchester* was not known for speed or maintaining a reliable schedule, she steamed around the lake between the settlements of Oshkosh, Fond du Lac, Taycheedah, Manchester, Pique Village, and Neenah, landing any time or place a passenger wanted to board or disembark. Sometimes it took weeks to make the trip around the lake. When asked by a passenger when the boat would arrive at Neenah just as it was leaving Oshkosh, the captain replied, "How should I know? I'm no prophet."

The *Manchester* set out with a load of supplies bound for the far northern lumber camps, making it the first steamboat to ascend the Wolf River from Oshkosh. The voyage was plagued with problems. At numerous bends in the winding Wolf River, the crewmen were obliged to cut away jammed lumber rafts and driftwood in order to proceed. Then at Shawano, the engine crankshaft broke. Two crewmen carried the broken piece weighing hundreds of pounds on their backs through dense forest and over unbridged streams for nearly forty miles back to Green Bay to secure a new casting, which they carried back to the crippled boat several days later.

The *Manchester* was rebuilt in 1850, and three years later sank in the Wolf River. The machinery was once again salvaged and installed in the *W.A. Knapp.*

By then, work had begun on the Fox/Wisconsin improvement plans. In addition to the canal project between the Fox and Wisconsin Rivers at Portage, the improvement plan called for dredging the upper Fox and constructing locks at the worst rapids on the lower Fox. It wasn't until 1876, however, that the project was finally completed, as financial burdens hampered progress of the difficult task, especially on the lower Fox where the river drops 170 feet between Lake Winnebago and Green Bay.

The opening of this water route from the Mississippi to the Atlantic was as important to the settlers of the Fox River Valley as the transcontinental railroad would later be to the people in the western territories. A grand celebration was planned. Charles Green of Green Bay went to Pittsburgh to bring a steamboat down the Ohio, up the Mississippi and Wisconsin, and into the Fox. Stephen Hotaling, the son of Lake Winnebago's first steamboat captain, Peter Hotaling, captained his boat, the *Aquila.* When the *Aquila* reached Lake Winnebago in mid-

June, great excitement swept through the valley, and there were dances and parties and speeches all up and down the river as she steamed toward Green Bay. Another steamer, the *Pioneer*, started from Green Bay to greet the *Aquila*, and when the two vessels met, the editor of the *Appleton Crescent* grandly proclaimed "the marriage of the waters of the Mississippi and Lake Michigan."

When the grand era of steamboating had officially arrived, Oshkosh became the important center of activity. Numerous steamers from that port established reliable river transportation down the lower Fox to Neenah, Menasha, Appleton, De Pere, and Green Bay, and on the upper Fox to Omro, Eureka, Berlin, Montello, and Portage. These boats carried every commodity from coal, produce, and cattle to lumberjacks and Sunday excursionists. Unlike the majestic riverboats of the East and the Mississippi, the Fox River vessels were not necessarily plush or particularly handsome. Because of the shallow waters of the Fox, these boats had to be much smaller than their counterparts on the Mississippi – most of them not more than 100 feet long, drawing only three to six feet of water, and traveled at a top speed barely over ten miles per hour. Although they were not noted for speed or luxury, they were sturdy little craft, built to withstand the choppy waters of Lake Winnebago.

The Oshkosh Steamboat Company built and operated several vessels on the Fox and Wolf Rivers. The first of this series were the *Northwestern*, a side-wheeler 100 feet in length, and a sister ship, the *Tigress*. These two boats ran daily between Oshkosh and New London, leaving simultaneously at 7 a.m. from each city and arrived at their destinations about 3:30 in the afternoon.

This was a period of rapid growth in the Fox River Valley. Until 1850, freight had largely been moved on Durham boats (flat-bottom barges powered by men with poles) along the Fox River from Green Bay. Nathan Godell was heavily engaged in the business, and he began to realize the urgency for improvement, as the Durham transportation method quickly became inadequate to meet the needs of the ever-increasing population. He acquired the *Indiana*, a side-wheel steamer from a company in Grand Rapids that was well adapted for the trade route. Upon the completion of the locks around the rapids near Kaukauna, the *Indiana* began a regular schedule from Green Bay to Appleton. The business so rapidly developed that another boat, the

Pioneer, built at Fort Howard, was added the following spring with a daily run.

The *Indiana* sank the following September at the mouth of Apple Creek near Wrightstown. Her machinery was salvaged and installed in a replacement boat, the *Morgan L. Martin.*

Numerous steamers worked the Fox River, among them, the *Montello*, the *Chittenden*, the *Fox*, a small government steamer, and the *Northport Belle* operated by Kelsey & Lewis of Montello. The *Northport Belle* was nearly new in 1865 when it was put into service making regular runs between Montello and Berlin.

Another of the earliest steamers to appear above the rapids of the lower Fox River was the *Peytonia* in 1850. The 85-feet-long side-wheel vessel was brought to Green Bay, and then up the Fox River to DePere. There it was hauled ashore, the upper structure and machinery dismantled, and the hull cut in half. The parts were then transported overland to Menasha where it was lengthened by twenty feet and reassembled, and began its service on the Fox River with Captain Estes in command. A few years later, Enos Drummond took over as Captain, and the *Peytonia* went into service on the Wolf River. Early in spring, 1859, before the ice was completely gone, Drummond attempted to take the vessel to New London. Prospects appeared good with a wide expanse of open water as the boat entered Lake Poygan. But farther upstream, the open channel narrowed, and finally the ice closed in and sliced the hull in half. The crew reached safety on the banks, and later began salvage efforts. Only the engines and boilers were saved.

Oddities occurred with boats built during this era, often due to poor design. Perhaps the strangest vessel on the Fox and Wolf Rivers was the *K.M. Hutchinson.* Originally built as a two-masted schooner for use on Lake Winnebago, Captain Thomas Bangs bought it, installed a steam engine to drive a propeller, and ran it in the wood hauling trade. Because of its unsuitable hull design, it would roll violently when caught in the wash of other boats. Captain Bangs finally cut her in two, added in 20 feet, and converted her into a stern-wheeler. After change of ownership sometime later, the *Hutchinson* burned and sank between Lake Poygan and Winneconne.

Another poorly planned steamboat was the *O.B. Reed*, eighty feet long and only twelve feet wide. It was designed with an engine having only one crank for both side paddlewheels, and developed the nasty habit of lying over to one side after getting up to speed. The traveling public refused to trust its safety, even though stabilizing projections called "bustles" were added to both sides. The boat was soon replaced with a larger, better design.

The *Abel Neff* was named for the man who owned it, and who, in Oshkosh ran a store with a dance hall on the second floor. Somehow, Mr. Neff came into possession of a cabin door, and to make some use of it, he built a steamboat to put it in. The boat was designed with a rather tall superstructure and tended to list easily because it was so top-heavy. On the very first excursion, crewmen kept busy by rolling casks filled with water from side to side, attempting to compensate for the lack of stability. Mr. Neff sold the craft immediately after its first and only cruise.

Just as unusual, the most notable feat for a riverboat and its captain on the rivers above Oshkosh is credited to the *Ajax* and Captain Tom Bangs. This was the first propeller driven steamer on the Fox and Wolf, used for hauling hemlock from far above New London back to the tannery at Fond du Lac. But on one occasion, the *Ajax* powered an extraordinary load. A Mr. Mase had purchased a four-story gristmill at Winneconne, and wanted it moved to Oshkosh. Because there were no adequate roads, transporting a building that large, that far overland was impossible. Dismantling and reconstruction would take too long. Although the risk was quite high, the *Ajax* towed the mill supported on two barges down the Wolf River and delivered it safely to Oshkosh.

During the week, the Fox River Valley steamers were working boats, hauling farm produce to the markets, logs to the mills, and marsh grass to the rug factory at Oshkosh, as well as all the manufactured goods such as butter, flour, sugar, hardware, stoneware, all sorts of dry goods, and barrels of whiskey.

But on the weekends, these rugged vessels were scrubbed down for the Sunday excursion trade. Fare for a leisurely trip from Berlin to Oshkosh was only ten cents, and beer was served as soon as the boat left the dock. Occasionally, some of the boats offered a "shopping special" for the ladies, with the same low fares.

Steamboats served the Fox Valley well, transporting people and freight, and provided a special charm to everyday life. But those halcyon days were numbered. The river channel was expensive and difficult to maintain, and the introduction of the railroads offered a reasonable alternative to river travel. Most of the steam vessels of the Fox were relegated to hauling freight on the lower Mississippi, some being converted to barges. Some met their end at a wrecking yard near Omro, where they were broken up for firewood, while others were simply dragged up on shore and abandoned. Gradually, the steamboats on the Fox River sadly disappeared.

The *Valley Queen* was the last of these majestic boats to ply the waters of the Fox. She could carry 550 passengers and a crew of thirteen, and was serving as a floating dance hall when she burned in 1922. Although the lower Fox River still sees limited commercial use, the river above Lake Winnebago now only supports pleasure craft to explore its memorable course through time.

Chippewa River Steamboats

The Chippewa River has a drainage area of nearly 10,000 square miles in northwestern Wisconsin, making it one of the Upper Mississippi's largest tributaries. With the vast logging operations in and adjacent to the Chippewa Valley, the deforestation resulted in tremendous sediment flowing down the river, and eventually, lumberjacks found great difficulty in floating their log and lumber rafts over the sandbar that formed at the mouth of the Chippewa as it entered the Mississippi.

In 1877 the Corp of Engineers built constricting dams to direct a current such that it would scour out the sandbar, and within three years the mouth of the Chippewa was once again clear, making the waterway a busy avenue for log rafts and navigation, and by then, improvements were under way on the fifty-seven miles of channel to Eau Claire. Steamboats carrying freight upstream used this route extensively, but use of the main channel of the Chippewa turned almost exclusively to log rafting, and most steamboat traffic had ceased by 1884.

Read's Landing, the town on the Minnesota bank opposite the mouth of the Chippewa River at the lower end of Lake Pepin (which the

Mississippi flows through) had become a popular place for the early lumberjacks to lodge and acquire their provisions before continuing the journey to the pine forests of the upper Chippewa Valley. Many of them, as well as the pioneers who established the early settlements, traveled up the Chippewa by canoes or keelboats. Because the keelboats loaded with freight required twelve to twenty men with poles pushing the craft against the current, it was an ideal opportunity for many to work for their passage to Eau Claire. Since all the lumber produced by the mills was rafted down the Chippewa to the Mississippi, involving a pilot and eight or nine oarsmen for each raft, there were always more than enough able bodies to power the supply boats back up the river.

A stagecoach line was established to Eau Claire, too, and in the mid-1850s a few small steamboats started making trips up the Chippewa. They would load whatever freight had been left at Read's Landing by the northbound Mississippi packets, and their decks were usually crowded with passengers, as well. The trip from Read's Landing to Eau Claire took an entire day.

Some of the boats to navigate the Chippewa River were the *Monitor*, the *Johnny Schmocker*, built at La Crosse, the *Chippewa*, the *Minnietta*, the *Minnie Herman*, the *T.P. Benton*, built at Onalaska, the *Silas Wright*, and the *Ida Campbell*, one of the last steamers to maintain a regular schedule on the Chippewa River.

The *Johnny Schmocker* and the *Silas Wright* would occasionally run through to Chippewa Falls in high water, and the Union Lumbering Company's Mississippi raft boats, the *Union* and the *Saint Croix* would also occasionally go all the way to "The Falls." The steamer *Saint Croix* was the last to land at the Chippewa Falls levee in 1873.

In the earlier days when the thick saw blades were making lumber and sawdust in about equal quantities, much of the goods shipped to Eau Claire and Chippewa Falls were hauled with horses and wagons from various stations along the railroad as it progressed across the state to La Crosse. Ingram and Kennedy were manufacturing lumber at that time, and they also maintained a store to supply their workers, and sold to others to some extent. In 1857 their merchandise was hauled by team from Portage; a little later, from New Lisbon, and then from Sparta. When the railroad reached La Crosse, they had their goods sent to Read's Landing by Mississippi packet, and when there was "good water" in the

Chippewa, a little steamer brought it the rest of the way to Eau Claire.

A degree of uncertainty in schedules at that time prompted Ingram and Kennedy to build their own steamboat, and to maintain a regular schedule between Eau Claire and Read's Landing. They contracted with an experienced boat builder to construct the *Silas Wright* at Eau Claire.

The name was given the craft in honor of a recent and popular New York state governor at the request of a representative from the wholesale house where Ingram and Kennedy bought much of their product, in exchange for flags, life preservers, and a very nice damask spread for the table in the dining cabin.

The Eau Claire lumbermen ran the *Silas Wright* for three years on the Chippewa River with Captain William Lee commanding, making daily round-trips hauling freight and passengers between Read's Landing and Eau Claire. Passengers then were mostly raftsmen.

During those years, the area farmers raised a large quantity of wheat. Ingram and Kennedy built a warehouse on the west bank of the river, and engaged in the grain trade, shipping the wheat in sacks to the Mississippi. Their steamer, the *Silas Wright*, was a busy little boat.

Steamboats on the St. Croix River

Throughout the long winter months after the river had frozen, very few visitors made their way into the St. Croix valley, and business slumped. But each spring, as soon as the paddle wheelers could churn ice-free waters, nearly everyone rejoiced and started making plans for trips on the river.

The shrill whistle of the season's first steamboat arrival was most welcomed, and was generally greeted at the levee by nearly everyone of the village with cheering and hat waving. It officially announced the opening of navigation, and that meant renewed contact with the outside world and an improved quality of life along the St. Croix River.

Residents of the valley liked the informality of river travel where a man could stick his feet up somewhere, light a cigar, and become acquainted with all his fellow travelers. Sunday excursions, moonlight rides, and a journey to a picnic aboard a steamboat did not lose popularity until after the turn of the Twentieth Century. These outings were always an important part of St. Croix River life, as entertainment in this remote area was limited. Packet boats like the *Kate Cassel* provided occasional pleasure cruises, and even the 162-foot *Falls City* navigated the unpredictable St. Croix channel to bring tourists from St. Anthony and St. Paul to visit the Minnesota and Wisconsin towns along the river.

More than twenty-five steamers navigated the St. Croix above Stillwater during the 1850s. Many of these maintained regular passenger schedules, while some ran less frequently according to freight volumes. The boats varied in size from the large 226-ton *Minnesota Belle* to the little 21-ton *Queen of the Yellow Banks*, perhaps the smallest of all the steamboats to ply the St. Croix.

One of the more popular steamers was the little stern-wheeler *H.S. Allen*. Rated at just 41 tons, she was only one third the size of the larger, more elegant rivals, but because of her size, more dependable in the shallow river. The captain, former innkeeper Isaac Grey boasted – as did most steamer captain who navigated American rivers – that if the St. Croix dried up completely, he would still get through on a heavy dew.

With an early spring in 1858, Captain Green in command of the steamer *Equator* planned a gala grand excursion in March to compete with the *H.S. Allen* for the patronage of valley residents. Two hundred guests accepted his invitation to take part in the trip with music and refreshments provided.

Spirits were high as the crowd boarded the *Equator* anticipating a festive journey. But this would be a day when everything went wrong for Captain Green. First, a careless deckhand fell overboard and a fruitless search for him caused an hour's delay. Then early in the afternoon, just above Marine Mills, the engine ceased to operate, stranding the *Equator* in midstream. The excursionists had little choice but to wait for help to arrive, or to swim to shore and walk home. Many just kept dancing to pass the hours, while some worried about the food supply.

The climax of the day must have been humiliating, indeed, for Captain Green, when the rival *H.S. Allen* approached on her return trip from the Dalles and rescued the marooned passengers, returning them safely to Stillwater. Upon making some temporary repairs, the *Equator* limped back to port the next day.

Steamboats did deliver other forms of entertainment: on a bright June morning in 1858, a steam calliope announced the arrival of two St. Louis showboats at the Stillwater levee – the James Raymond and the Banjo. Although the circus they carried didn't feature performing elephants, dancing bears, lion tamers, tigers jumping through hoops of fire, or even prancing white horses, it was, nevertheless, a circus. The Spaulding and Rogers' "Great Monkey Circus and Burlesque Dramatic Troupe" presented performances with monkeys, trained dogs, and a variety of other amazing curiosities never before seen in the Upper Mississippi Valley.

Generally, Stillwater, Hudson and the other larger settlements were fortunate enough to be visited by the traveling theatrical troupes, although the Medicine Shows requiring much less accommodations on the regularly scheduled packet boats frequently entertained the people of the smaller villages, and their barkers made good money hawking the "patented cure-alls."

During the halcyon days of steamboat navigation on the St. Croix, which lasted into the 1890s, the riverbed had not yet filled in with silt and sand from eroding hillsides stripped of their earth and water retaining forests. In those earlier years there were few natural obstructions for boats of relatively shallow draft, as this river, even then, was not extremely deep. In dry seasons, low water brought the sandbars nearer to the surface, creating natural deterrents to trouble-free river travel. At times, pilots were forced to patiently wait days for rain to raise the water level enough to float a stuck vessel from a sandbar, and often it was necessary to unload freight in order to sufficiently lighten the craft.

The lower St. Croix log boom just above Stillwater especially irritated riverboat pilots. This area of the river was often so filled with floating timber that the navigable channel was completely blocked. The boom companies paid heavy damages when the packets could not pass through, however, the lumbering was deemed more essential to the economy, and despite boat owner complaints, the problem was never solved. Yet, an incredible number of steamboats arrived at Taylors Falls – 230 recorded in 1869 – to unload passengers and freight.

In 1851 the *Excelsior*, a 182-foot side-wheeler with carrying capacity of 272 tons, reached the Falls without problem, and a few years later, the *Metropolitan*, an even larger vessel from St. Louis navigated up the St. Croix to Marine Mills. Upon witnessing the *Minnesota Belle*, another large packet, discharging its heavy load of cargo for local merchants, a reporter for the *Stillwater Messenger*, evidently attempting to encourage and promote more business on the river, wrote, "The largest class of boats do not encounter the least difficulty in reaching Marine."

People of the St. Croix Valley depended almost entirely on the river for transportation. It was their only route of communication with the rest of the country, and they desperately needed the steamboats to help settle the region, to bring in supplies, and to stay in touch with the outside world. This was especially true for the people at "the end of the line" in the somewhat isolated settlements of Taylors Falls and St. Croix Falls.

Stillwater had developed a good riverboat landing by 1849, and thirty-four steamers were recorded as users of that levee, but not all of those were run exclusively, or even on regular schedules on the St. Croix. Many of them were Mississippi packets on their way to or from St. Paul making the trip to Stillwater to land passengers and freight. The service beyond Stillwater was rather haphazard – anything but scheduled.

Boats came and went at irregular intervals until 1852 when the little steamer *Queen of the Yellow Banks* began making tri-weekly trips from Stillwater to the head of navigation. Captain Albert Eames charged one dollar per round trip ticket, and was the first to offer regular service on the upper river. This boat could carry twenty tons and burned one cord of weed every twelve hours.

Another diminutive craft – the *Humboldt* – also appeared later that year making tri-weekly runs between Stillwater and Taylors Falls. Unattractive and lacking any luxury, this boxy little boat was slow, underpowered by an engine with the power of a teakettle. But it provided a good service, stopping anywhere along the river to pick up or discharge passengers or freight. The accommodating little *Humboldt* served the valley well, upriver to the Falls one day, and back to Stillwater the next. Larger boats like the *Asia*, the *Montello*, and the thirty-stateroom *Blackhawk* made only occasional voyages above Stillwater. Then in 1857 the *H.S. Allen* and the *New St. Croix* advertised regular packet service to Taylors Falls.

There was a lack of regular service from Stillwater south to Prescott and Point Douglas, where Mississippi steamers bound for St. Paul often left freight. To answer this need, the 106-ton stern-wheeler *Eolian* came in to carry mail and serve the trade on the lower river.

Merchants were soon displeased with the Eolian – freight charges from Prescott to Stillwater were exorbitant (as much as from St. Louis to Prescott) and it wasn't long until the same businessmen who had begged for the service were ready to boycott the boat providing it. Their threats were successful; freight rates were lowered and the *Eolian* continued to operate.

William F. Davidson had been operating two boats on the Minnesota River, and in 1860 expanded his fleet to begin a La Crosse to St. Paul trade on the Mississippi. Davidson's often ruthless methods of bullying the competition in order to gain control of the packet business soon led to a lengthy rate war. His attempts to monopolize were felt on the St. Croix River as well.

The St. Croix and Mississippi Steamboat Company entered the La Crosse to Stillwater trade with Captain Oscar Knapp's side-wheel steamer *Viola* in 1865. Davidson forced them out of business within two years.

Davidson ran the packet boat *Enterprise* doing business on the St. Croix. But there was general surprise the vessel was withdrawn shortly after the *G.B. Knapp* launched at Osceola in June 1866. Davidson and Knapp had come to agreeable terms regarding river transportation above Stillwater. By doing so, it was felt that Davidson had made many friends on the St. Croix. The feeling of good will, though, didn't last long. He came back with the stern-wheeler *Nellie Kent* two seasons later. With this boat, expressly built for the St. Croix trade, the rate war began. The following year, more boats were fighting for supremacy; in addition to the *Nellie Kent* and the *G.B. Knapp*, the *James Means* represented the Northern Line, and another local steamer, the *Wyman X* of Taylors Falls joined in the competition. They were the first of numerous craft to take part in this battle that would last for many years.

The bitter rivalry grew to include the entire Upper Mississippi from St. Louis to St. Paul, with freight rates and passenger fares dropping so low that a pleasure cruise was cheaper than living at home. Twenty-five cents was considered the top price for passenger service from Prescott to Taylors Falls, and that generally included meals!

It was believed that such a conflict as the one between the riverboat companies could not last, and that compromise would soon come. But the *Nellie Kent* held out until it needed rebuilding at Davidson's La Crosse boatyard facility in 1878. Other boats came and went to keep the competition hot and strong until 1880.

Steamboat racing provided plenty of excitement and became a common, popular event. At first, the passengers took pleasure in the sport and overlooked the risk of boiler explosions and fire, but soon realized that the prestige gained for the winning captain did little to promote good service. In seeking this form of river supremacy, boats would depart from the Stillwater port at unpredictable times, neck and neck with a competitor and making irritatingly brief stops at village landings along the way. The afternoon return trip was conducted in the same manner. Steamboating on the St. Croix was fast becoming a poor source of reliable travel. Complaints from merchants and the public did little good.

It wasn't competition, price-cutting, logs, or low water that eventually saw the end of packet business on the St. Croix. Steamboating everywhere on the inland waterways declined with the introduction of railroads. That decline first began in the St. Croix Valley in 1870 when rails reached Stillwater and Taylors Falls.

For a while the tourist trade boomed when the boats started meeting the trains. But in time, the popularity of summer resorts developed at White Bear, Forest Lake, and Lake Elmo caused the magical river attraction to fade. The primary reason for boats running on the St. Croix – to provide reliable transportation to the people of the valley – was slowly becoming a thing of the past. Railroads were taking over.

Several attempts were made after 1880 to keep steamboating alive on the St. Croix, but with little success. By 1886 the commercial fleet consisted of only two regular packets hauling freight and passengers to Taylors Falls.

Excursions, though, for social groups – Sunday schools, library associations, singing societies, and other chartered assemblies – remained popular to the very end. In 1901, two thousand railroad conductors in route to a convention in St. Paul arrived at St. Croix Falls, boarded the *Columbia* and the *Lora*, and cruised downriver to Stillwater.

A group of 1,100 retail grocers enjoyed a July 1905 trip upriver from Stillwater aboard the steamer *Purchase* and its excursion barge the *Twin Cities*. That boat carried only one more excursion of some 800 sightseers to Taylors Falls in 1914.

Unceremoniously – but not without regret – the magic of steamboating on the St. Croix River was gone.

Logging and the Rivers

A certain halo of romance can be connected to the important industry through which Wisconsin earned a large portion of its earliest wealth from natural resources. Researching the history of the lumber business also reveals its direct correlation with the waterways that contributed tremendously to its development and success, and such bold advancements.

The land must have appeared as a paradise to Jean Nicolet as he and his exploration party skimmed their canoes between the verdant banks of the Wisconsin River in 1634. It would be difficult to speculate whether or not he gave the slightest notion to the potential of a future empire standing there before him, in terms of commercialism. For it was nearly two hundred years before the harvest began.

Pinpointing an exact time when logging and lumbering began in Wisconsin is difficult. Undoubtedly, the fur trappers and traders cut logs to build their cabins in the wilderness long before the arrival of any substantial settlement; we can hardly consider this as commercial lumbering. But as the lightly timbered country along the Mississippi developed, settlers seeking home sites and fortunes began exploring the Mississippi's tributaries, and soon entered into the work that would become, for a time, Wisconsin's leading industry. A glance at the map will show that the Wisconsin, the Black, the Chippewa, and the St. Croix Rivers, with their smaller tributaries, drain nearly half of the state into the Mississippi, and provide access to an equal proportion of great timber tracts.

This was a great industry, but greater than the forests that the strong, resolute, fearless men conquered, and better than the wealth they earned, is the good they contributed to national life. We may censure the ravages of the woodman's axe, but we must admire the enthusiasm and dedication of those early pioneers. Seeking to carve out of the wilderness homes and fortunes for themselves, they brought together the important elements, and through their efforts, opened the way for enrichment of the future.

When the very first steam-powered vessel, the *Virginia*, chugged its way to Fort St. Anthony (now Fort Snelling) in 1823, there were few people to witness one of the most remarkable accomplishments that ushered in a century of economic growth for the Wisconsin Territory. By the early 1850s, as more courageous riverboat captains ventured northward into the new frontier, other industries began to flourish, as well, and the territory started to enjoy an alarming wealth in its natural resources. Thousands of immigrants poured into the North Country with the opening of navigation on the upper river. New opportunities seemed more plentiful there than anywhere else in the nation: land was available for homesteading; the water was abundant and pure; the soil was rich; the immense empires of timber in northern Minnesota and Wisconsin promised unlimited work and gave birth to the industry that grew to colossal proportions. Logging camps sprang to life, some maturing to the status of villages and towns.

The logging and lumber industry was assured of a strong foothold, as pioneers found an overwhelming abundance of virgin timber covering most of the territory. It provided more than adequate building materials for their homes and other needs, and it seemed quite clear that a profit could be earned from it by supplying other parts of the growing country. But transport of their product presented a particular obstacle – the problem of getting it to the people who would pay them for their efforts.

The lack of overland roads greatly restricted conveyance of any notable quantities of the forest products. Railroads were merely a speculative dream, and remained far in the future. The Mississippi River and its tributaries, though, offered the perfect solution, forming the only connecting link between the pioneers and the world they had left behind. Passenger steamers crowded with immigrants, freight steamers piled with supplies, towboats and barges began filling the river. In a short time, the number of log rafts floating downstream continuously increased, and the logging industry had boomed into full swing. Over the years, thousands of acres of land would be cleared by the lumbermen, opening the way for farming, essentially making the territory more self-sufficient. In time, Wisconsin, as well as the entire Upper Mississippi River region, would become even more appealing for its fertile soil, earning the attention of those seeking agricultural opportunities.

Seasonal changes contributed to the success of the lumber industry in this lucrative new land. The freezing temperatures during the long winter months kept the landscape icy and slick, ideal for skidding the cut logs to nearby streams and rivers. When the warming springtime swelled the rivers with floodwater as the ice and snow thawed away, the logs were rolled into the rushing streams and sent on their journey, destined for the mills.

In late fall, the cutting crews migrated, usually on foot, to the remote camps located in the dense northern woods. The camps were established and operated by the lumber companies owning or leasing the timberland tracts – usually thousands of acres in size. Disconnected from their families and friends for the entire duration of winter, these men endured the blinding blizzards and numbing sub-zero temperatures, living by the simplest means with only the gear they could carry in a single pack. They slept in a common bunkhouse, heated by a centrally located wood stove that sometimes barely kept the chill off. They ate their meals in a common dining hall, and perhaps as a trade-off for all the other inconveniences, they were fed well. The company owners knew these men needed ample nourishment, above all else, to perform the duties that were expected of them, much of the time in adverse conditions.

From the first light of day until darkness fell upon them, they toiled in the woods, felling the tall pines, cutting and skidding the logs to be piled parallel to the river at its banks in huge stacks called rollways, 20 – 30 feet high. These rollways lined the streams for miles waiting for the spring thaw.

A distinct breed of men – the river drivers – came into action in the springtime. Their work was demanding and dangerous, riding the tangled masses of logs on the raging floods, ensuring arrival at prescribed mill destinations or the sorting booms on the Mississippi. Often, the logs would jam in the river bends and rapids, calling on the skillful talents of the jammers to break up the mess. Occasionally, the more serious jams required the use of dynamite to free the stuck log mass. It is not surprising that there were frequent injuries and occasional loss of life among these men.

They were a rugged lot, toughened by the work they performed, and bound together in a strong fraternity to help and protect one another. They knew the dangers they faced daily, yet at every emergence of trouble they rose to the call, dedicated to their purpose, undaunted by the unavoidable threats to their safety. All ages were represented, but the younger, more agile dominated the number. There was no distinct uniform in dress other than all wore woolen trousers stuffed into leather boots reaching to the knee, the soles of which were clad with rows of one-half to three-quarter-inch-long spikes or caulks to provide sure-footed navigation over the slippery, floating logs. These boots were the only outward symbol of the river man's unique profession.

"Breaking out" the rollways once the ice had left an open channel and the spring freshets sufficiently raised the water level provided the most excitement, and perhaps the most spectacular of all activities of the entire operation. Only the most experienced and skilled members of a river drive crew were permitted to engage in breaking the rollways. Teasing and prying at the lowermost log of the stack facing the river would invariably bring the upper layers of logs cascading down with a roar, a crash, and a splash. The man who had done the prying had to be quick-eyed, of cool temperament, and very agile to avoid being buried under the tons of timber rushing down. Often the men standing near lost sight of him entirely in the spray and confusing blur of the breaking rollway, until it seemed certain that he must have perished. But he always appeared at the right or left, and sometimes nonchalantly balanced on a log adrift on the water. To him it seemed an easy escape from the destructive power he had turned loose! Afterwards the rest of the crew rolled into the river the logs that remained on the bank.

Once in the stream the logs ran their appointed course, watched by the men who herded them on their way. The formation grew with each rollway breakout until for miles and miles the river was nearly a solid mass of logs. A man could surely walk down the middle of the river as down a highway.

The crews then had their hands full to keep the logs running. The slightest obstruction at any one point, sometimes, meant a jam, for there was no way of stopping the procession. The logs behind floated gently against the obstruction and came to rest. The mass thickened and the water's surface was concealed completely. Then, as the slow pressure developed from the three or four miles of logs forced against each other by the current's push, the head of the jam began to rise. Timbers up-ended, crossed, interlocked, slid one over the other, and mounted higher and higher.

Immediately and with feverish activity, the men nearest at hand attacked the situation. Logs on top were rolled and tumbled into the current below. Men beneath tugged and pried in search of the key logs causing all the trouble. Some worked at the outer edges, opening a channel for the current to flow around the ends, hopeful to create a "draw" on the tangled mess. As the stoppage of the drive indicated to the men up and down stream that a jam had formed, they converged on the scene – those from above over the logs, those from below up the riverbank trail.

Rarely, unless in case of unusual complications, did it take more than a few hours to break the jam. Once the culprit key log was discovered and dislodged, the jam went out with a rush. Slowly and reluctantly the miles-long mass upstream stirred and silently began moving forward, but it was still necessary to watch carefully until the onward flow steadied itself, and the congestion was spaced and orderly again. Then the men moved back to their posts as the drive resumed.

Jams on the river were a very common occurrence. Throughout the length of the drive, there would be at least three or four hang-ups a day. Each had to be broken, and in that was danger. The smallest misstep or slowness in reading the signs of the break, the slightest lack in alertness or the agility to leap from one moving log to another, still maintaining perfect balance, or the faintest deviation from rigid attention to the changing monster underfoot could mean instant death. Thus, each of these men was called upon almost daily to wager his skill against his destruction.

At night the river was left to its own devices. Rivermen were touched with a bit of superstition; they believed that "logs run free at night." Though it might be expected that each morning would reveal a big jam to break, such was rarely the case. The logs had usually stopped, but generally in so peaceful a situation that a few minutes work would easily get them started downstream. This was usually because they had come to rest in the slow, still portions of the river where the current had little effect on their movement without some prodding and urging from the crew.

The log driving crews on the river didn't enjoy the luxury of a bunkhouse or dining hall. Protection from the elements at night was merely a tent, and during rainy spells, that tent did not necessarily mean a dry place to sleep. Their meals were generally eaten around a large campfire, fitted with makeshift racks made of saplings for the purpose of drying out wet clothes. The cook and an assistant who traveled with the crew prepared the meals over a second fire with the supplies carried in the "wanigan," a shack constructed on a crude but sturdy barge or raft that also served as the conveyance of all the bedrolls, tents, clothes, and the crew's personal belongings, along with the provisions and cooking utensils. Each day after breakfast, the cook and his helper broke camp, loaded the gear in the wanigan, and slid the barge from its high and dry spot on the riverbank into the water. With poles and oars they guided and maneuvered the rather clumsy craft among the flow of logs until evening, when it could be towed up onto another suitable campsite.

At the rear of the drive followed the "sacking" crew. In addition to assisting the cook to launch the wanigan, their job was to retrieve logs that had strayed from the mass, stranded in shallow water or caught up in weeds, snags or rocks. Although not a spectacular position, theirs was equally important, as every retrieved log meant fewer penalties for losses at the end of the drive.

Upon reaching towns at the end of a drive, the boys were usually ready to celebrate, and celebrate they did with plenty of drink and song, and many a fight. Every sidewalk and every saloon and store floor showed the marks from their spiked boots, and their adventurous spirits gave ample color to the pioneer towns. And when the party was over, they were always ready to return to the north woods for more of the heroic work that tested muscles, skill, and courage.

On the Wisconsin – "The Nation's Hardest-Working River"

is a phrase coined to describe the Wisconsin. It descends 1,071 feet over 430 miles, and 26 dams harness its flow to annually produce one billion kilowatt hours of electrical energy. A unique system of 21 reservoirs in the upper valley store water during high flow periods to release for use during periods of low flow. In addition to enhancing power production, the system reduces flood damage, greatly improves the recreation qualities of the river valley, and since its creation in 1907 has enabled the Wisconsin River to earn the title "The Nation's Hardest-Working River."

But long before the installation of power plant dams, the Wisconsin River was hard at work in another capacity, as it played a vital role in transportation for the logging and lumber industry.

Although there is only mention of a sawmill owned and operated by Pierre Grignon somewhere on the upper Wisconsin sometime prior to 1820, Jefferson Davis was, perhaps, the first to perform what could be called lumbering that involved a large quantity of cut timber in the Wisconsin River Valley. He arrived at the site that would become Fort Winnebago at Portage, Wisconsin in the fall of 1828 as a messenger from General Henry Atkinson at St. Louis Headquarters. Second Lieutenant Davis delivered the plans for the proposed fort to Major Twiggs, and was assigned to the company commanded by Captain William Harney, where he remained for two years.

Determined to use the very best building materials available, Major Twiggs dispatched Davis and part of the company fifty miles upriver to cut pine logs and float them down the river to the portage, where they were carted the rest of the way to the building site. There, the logs were cut into lumber with hand tools. Within two years, enough timber was cut to construct seven barracks buildings, two blockhouses, and outside of the fort proper, wash houses, commissary store, icehouse, blacksmith shop, carpenter shop, bakeshop, and stables.

Then in 1835, George Whitney erected a mill at a place called Point Bauss at the head of navigation, but during all this time and for the next decade, little was done in the line of commercial logging.

About 1845, however, the business began to expand, and soon a strong demand for the excellent quality of lumber came from the growing settlements downriver. This demand caused the occupation of nearly every point along the river offering good waterpower, and the erecting of more than twenty mills. Consequently, settlements sprang up around the mills, and several prospered and grew into cities – Wisconsin Rapids, Stevens Point, Wausau, and Merrill, to name but a few.

A notable feature of the industry's work along the Wisconsin River is that the majority of logs cut were sawed into lumber at the riverbank. The nature of the upper river made rafting of finished lumber more manageable than logs.

As the lumber interests of the territory grew in importance, the

Old post card view of lumber rafts negotiating the Dells of the Wisconsin River.
(From private collection.)

Wisconsin River became a great highway for rafts from the upper river and its tributaries, on their way to markets on the Mississippi. Henry Merrill is given credit for piloting a lumber raft from Portage to St. Louis in 1839, perhaps the first enterprise of this sort attempted in that region, although smaller rafts were frequently run between local points.

For a lumber raft, the trip through the Dells was hazardous and could only be made under the guidance of an experienced pilot. Even then the rafts were sometimes broken up and occasionally a man was drowned. (Riverfront landowners downstream often managed to retrieve quantities of lumber from disintegrated rafts, free of charge.) During extreme high water of the springtime floods, many acres of rafts were tied up at the head of the Dells, waiting for a safe water stage and their turn at passing through. Rivalry was great; each pilot was anxious to make his name and fame as "first through the Dells." Sometimes the current was so strong that the rafters were obliged to help each other; all the men boarded one raft, two or more at each oar, until the quieter water below the Dells was reached. This meant several trips down the river and walking back each time to take the next raft through.

With a good stage of water, the trip from Wausau, Wisconsin to St.

Louis, Missouri was made in about twenty-four days. But occasionally, prevailing weather conditions could more than double the traveling time.

On the Black River

On the Black River – When lumbering first began in earnest in the regions of the Black River, dozens of sawmills sprang up along its banks, and like the practices along the Wisconsin, much of the timber was processed into lumber near the place of cutting. But the plentiful stands of tall, straight pine attracted more lumbermen, many whose interests did not necessarily focus on the local mills. Log drives soon dominated the stream by the men who were more interested in the quick revenue raw logs could generate at La Crosse or farther down the Mississippi, and rafted them to points in Iowa, Illinois, and Missouri, where many of the largest and most flourishing mills in the Mississippi valley were located. The milling industry had been lively along the Black River until log-driving operations literally monopolized the stream; attempts to run rafts of sawed lumber became quite impractical, and in time, many of the mills died. Only a few remained in the manufacture of lumber to meet local demands.

The earliest record of lumbering activity on the Black is of the Rollette expedition, originating in Prairie du Chien and arriving at the site that is now Black River Falls in 1818. A good source of waterpower was discovered and a sawmill built, however, its usefulness was short-lived as the native Indians burned the mill before it could produce enough lumber to build even one house. The project was abandoned until 1839 when Jacob Spaulding led another expedition, also originating in Prairie du Chien, to the same location. His efforts were better planned and more adequately equipped; his successful mill helped build the settlement known as Black River Falls.

It was in this area, too, that a company of Mormons, between 1830 and 1840, conducted some lumbering activity to obtain materials for the building of their temple at Nauvoo, Illinois.

Averill E. Sawyer had come to the West from New York in 1858 and first established a general store and lumberyard in Brownsville, Minnesota. He settled at Black River Falls in 1860, where in conjunction with a general store he pursued the logging business, in addition to maintaining a stagecoach line between Sparta, Wisconsin and St. Paul, Minnesota.

Joining forces with W. T. Price, they took a contract to furnish the ties for the Southern Minnesota Railroad. Sawyer began directing more of his interest to the logging, and in 1872 entered into partnership with David Austin. They purchased large tracts of land, and with a constantly growing enterprise, continued the logging operation until 1882. Most of their product was sold on the riverbank, but much of it was floated down the Black River to a mill in La Crosse that Sawyer and Austin purchased in 1882 from R. M. Moore.

Sawyer died three years later, but the mill continued to operate under the original business name, and in 1887 Sawyer-Austin incorporated with Sawyer's son, William E., as secretary and treasurer of the firm.

The lumber industry that sprang to life along the Mississippi River tributaries during the last half of the Nineteenth Century was the primary reason for the successful growth of many upper Midwest cities. Although many of the lumber mills at La Crosse obtained logs that were rafted down the Mississippi from the Chippewa, the Black River played a more important role in the prosperity of early La Crosse than any other single factor. The prime Black River timberland had been surveyed and put on sale in 1848-49. It attracted lumbermen and speculators, and at the mouth of the Black River, La Crosse was considered by lumbermen to be one of the best sites to establish milling businesses. Dozens of enterprising businessmen invested their entire personal capital, and many made liberal use of bank credit to enter into the lumber trade, speculating on adequate profits the following season. In many cases, large tracts of timberland were purchased long before their mills were constructed.

Early mill owners built booms to contain their logs for removal from the river. These booms were constructed by connecting timbers end-to-end with chain. The ends were secured on each side of the channel to hold the logs coming down the river until they could be taken out of the water. This held up the log drives and resulted in bitter feuds between loggers and mill owners. After several unsuccessful attempts to establish some order, the Black River Improvement Company was formed in 1864 for the purpose of regulation and control, as well as maintaining the channel by removing snags and building booms and storage dams for handling the logs. A drive master was appointed each year to oversee its operation, and police committees to guard against theft and unfairness. The main booms were constructed such that the logs could be sorted according to the owners' marks (put on the logs at the time of cutting) and directed into specified holding areas for that owner.

Generally, the timber cutting and log driving was let out to contractors that maintained sorting booms, such as the MacDonald Brothers. However, some mill owners, such as the Island Mill Company, maintained its own logging crew. The labor force in the pineries was largely from the Norwegian and Swedish settlers, supplemented by French Canadians. These crews gravitated to the larger metropolitan areas after the cutting season, and the mills employed many during the summer months. By the 1870s, La Crosse became the most prominent of these cities on the Black River. No less than a dozen sawmills operated there at one time, making it truly a lumber town.

One of the largest of these was the Coleman mill, started in 1854 when C.L. Coleman, who had been operating a small shingle mill at Fond du Lac, decided to locate in La Crosse. He loaded his horse-powered shingle outfit on wagons and hauled it across the state to the banks of the Mississippi. The mill was set up in a small building erected by Peter Cameron next to the river, and soon Coleman purchased another small shingle mill operated by Goldthwart and Brown. His combined facilities could produce about 14,000 shingles per day that were sold at that time for five dollars per thousand. A steam engine was added, and in 1862 Mr. Coleman acquired the machinery from the Denton and Hurd mill. Production increased to 350,000 shingles daily. Operations continued in this mill until 1868 when it was completely destroyed by fire.

Coleman immediately built another mill, this time designed to manufacture lumber as well as shingles. The large plant was equipped with the most modern machinery of the time.

Then in 1875 another fire destroyed the mill, and again, Coleman rebuilt with an even larger facility, and was back in business the following year.

Yet another fire ten years later, this time starting in the neighboring

John Paul Lumber Company, spread so quickly into the Coleman storage yards and factory that firemen were unable to contain the blaze that destroyed much of the southern extremities of the town, despite aid from Winona and other adjoining town fire departments.

Coleman was still not willing to give up. Plans were once again immediately under way for rebuilding a larger saw and planing mill. Offices were located at Second and Cameron Streets, where the business was conducted until 1903.

As the log supplies from the north exhausted, and the lumber business started to dwindle in the early 1890s, the many sawmills in La Crosse, one by one, ceased operations, and the owners disposed of their property. The Coleman Mill at the foot of Cameron Street next to the Mississippi River was the last to operate, as they still had a limited supply of pine timber in the north and continued as long as there were enough logs to keep the mill running. In 1893 the mill finally closed.

The Colemans continued in the lumber business until 1926, however, operating a string of retail lumberyards located along the Southern Minnesota Railroad, as well as many locations throughout Wisconsin and Iowa.

On the Chippewa – Logging on the Chippewa River began in 1836 but the volume of trade didn't start to escalate until around 1850. From then until the turn of the Twentieth Century, the output of product transported on that river ranged between 30 million and 1 billion feet of lumber annually. Many mills were built and operated at various points on this river and its tributaries in Buffalo, Pepin, Dunn, Eau Claire, and Chippewa Counties; Eau Claire, Chippewa Falls and Menominee are among the many flourishing towns and cities whose beginnings can be attributed directly to the lumber interest.

Eau Claire's first sawmill, started in 1846 on the Eau Claire River by McCann, Randall & Thomas was short lived, as it was swept away by the great flood of 1847. Simon and G.W. Randall rebuilt the mill over the next winter, and in 1856 it became the property of Chapman and Thorp, who operated it and another mill they purchased that had been built by Gage, Reed, and Dix. This firm evolved into the Eau Claire Lumber Company.

One of the most impressive mills along the Chippewa River began operation as Pound, Halbert & Company. Men with little investment capital purchased the mill from the United States Marshall in 1860, but they possessed good business tact and strong perseverance. Within a few short years, this mill was recognized as one of the most successful lumbering companies in the United States, and can be credited with rising Chippewa Falls from a tiny village to a flourishing, bustling city.

The business incorporated in 1868 as the Union Lumbering Company. Three hundred employees kept the machinery running, including ninety saws, a blacksmith and machine shop, and a wood turning shop, producing massive amounts of lumber, shingles, and lath. The company held ownership of eighty thousand acres of pine forestland.

Another one of the largest early Wisconsin lumber concerns was that of Knapp, Stout & Company. From its beginnings on the Red Cedar River, a tributary of the Chippewa, sprang the city of Menomonie, still a busy municipality today.

In 1846, William Wilson ventured from his Ft. Madison, Iowa home into the northern pine forests of Wisconsin. Quite impressed with the vast woodlands, he returned to Iowa and persuaded his friend, John Knapp, to invest with him in a sawmill in the Chippewa River Valley. Like Wilson, Knapp recognized his life's best opportunity and joined in on this adventure amidst the wilds of the Chippewa.

The two men came to what is now the city of Menomonie and purchased a half interest in a little single sash sawmill from a Mr. Black for $2,000. They began their lumbering operation in June 1846. In the fall of that same year, Mr. Black died; Wilson and Knapp bought his interest and formed the new partnership.

That mill was primitive and its output exceedingly small, but it was the seed from which grew a great enterprise. Over the next few years, Wilson and Knapp took on more partners; among them were Andrew Tainter in 1850, and Henry Stout in 1853, and the firm then became known as Knapp, Stout & Company.

By 1873, the firm owned 115,000 acres of forestland, and operated mills in Menomonie, Cedar Falls, Downsville, and Rice Lake in Wisconsin, and at Ft. Madison, Iowa. At Menomonie, 800 men were employed at the

500-acre complex that consisted of three mills, warehouses, foundry, machine shop, flourmill, stores, a large boarding house, and a number of dwelling houses. The company operated its own electric light plant and water works; the mills and shops were powered by water and steam. Lumber output from the Knapp, Stout & Company mills reached 90 million feet annually.

A mammoth quantity of lumber was manufactured at other mills, too, and if we were to float down the Chippewa River, starting at Jim Falls in the hardy 1870s or '80s, the voyage would reveal the strenuous days when a vast number of busy and prosperous mills lined its banks. The voyager would hear the steam whistles blowing and men on the river shouting, and the constant loud drone and whine of the great saws. It is easy to understand why Eau Claire earned the nickname "Sawdust City," but it seems the title could very easily apply to the entire Chippewa Valley.

At Jim Falls were two big mills, one owned by the French Lumbering Company, and nearby the Chippewa Log and Boom Company. That mill was destroyed by fire, and was replaced with one of the largest mills in the state.

Five miles above Chippewa Falls, there was a place called Sap Town, where H.H. Rumsey and Seth Webb built a steam mill. On July 4,1870, most of the crew was in town celebrating when the mill caught fire and was totally destroyed. It was never rebuilt.

A little farther down the river, at Chippewa Falls and Eau Claire, were many mills: we first come to the Wheaton Mill, and the Gravel Island Mill built by James Taylor and John Hall in 1863. And just a little farther down was the Badger State mills operated by John Barron, who used Lake Hallie as his reservoir.

H.S. Allen built the first flourmill of the county on Duncan Creek in 1852. Five years later, he added a very successful sawmill.

Alexander and Henry O'Neil built a sawmill at Chippewa City on O'Neil Creek. It was sold to B.F. Manahan and A.C. Fair, who operated it until 1880, and then sold it to L.C. and F.G. Stanley. They closed the mill when their timber was gone. Chippewa City became a ghost town.

The next mill downstream was that of Burdick and Prescott. This mill was later moved to Eau Claire and was then known as "The New Dells." It remained in operation until 1929.

Directly across the river was the Farwell Mill, and then the Eddy Mill owned by Ingram and Kennedy. This mill was eventually taken down and moved to Winona, Minnesota.

Next on the journey downriver was the mill of Chapman and Thorp located on the Eau Claire River near the Dewey Street Bridge. This was a fine water mill and steam mill, producing lumber and shingles.

Just below that was the Rose Mill. It was, however, doomed before it even began operations. Just as it was being made ready for business, the Rose Mill blew up and burned from some mysterious cause. It was never rebuilt.

Next were the Marston, the Smith and Buffington, and the Dick Wilson mills, the Pinkham, Easterbrook, and the Boyd. Then there were the mills of Porter and Moon. These mills flourished until the Wisconsin pine forests were exhausted, and then were moved to Calgary, Canada.

Across the river stood the Gordon Mill, and a little farther down, the Meridian Mill. Then was the Noah Shaw Foundry and Machine Shop where nearly all the repair work for the lumber mills was being done. Nearby was the Daniel Shaw Lumbering Company. This mill used the Half Moon Lake as its reservoir and log storage.

At Half Moon Lake was the shingle mill of Charles Parker, and also the McVickers Sawmill. This area hosted many lumber facilities in succession: the Kaiser Mill, the Sherman (also known as the "Snag"), and the Evans and Lee Lumber Company.

These mills (not nearly a complete list of all the mills operated on the Chippewa) rafted their lumber down the Chippewa to Read's Landing, and from there they were towed down the Mississippi to the mill-owned lumberyards and other southern markets.

A tremendous number of logs were run down the Chippewa River. But the economic panic of 1857 caused serious depression in the lumber trade, as it did in so many of the important business interests of the entire country. Revival soon came, however, and in 1867 the Beef Slough Manufacturing, Booming, Log Driving and Transportation Company organized; its efforts in improvement to the estuaries at the mouth of the Chippewa greatly aided running logs and lumber into the Mississippi, a valuable contribution to the business traffic there. Volume and expediency became an issue, and mill operators farther down the

Mississippi developed an intense interest in the Chippewa valley timber. The area soon became the principal source for logs and one of the notably prosperous regions of the state; the volume of logs from Beef Slough at the Chippewa mouth kept seventy-five towboats busy for entire seasons.

On the St. Croix – One hundred twenty-five miles of Wisconsin's northwest boundary is designated by the St. Croix River. The region drained by this stream and its tributaries rivaled the southern counterparts in the richness of its timber resource. On the St. Croix was located the first commercial sawmill in Minnesota, and eventually this area produced tremendous amounts of lumber and continued to do so long after the regions to the south had depleted their stock. But the beginnings, though, were small.

When all of Minnesota (except Ft. Snelling) and a large portion of Wisconsin still belonged to the Indians, three fur merchants trading in the wilderness territory of the Upper Mississippi and St. Croix Rivers made an agreement in March 1837 with the Chippewa chiefs, and were the first white men to obtain permission to cut timber from a large area flanking either side of the St. Croix River, and to build sawmills along its banks. In exchange, annual payments of goods were to be made to the St. Croix and Snake River bands of Chippewa over a ten-year period.

To the three traders – Warren, Aitken, and Sibley – it was a good deal, because the designated area encompassed a vast stand of valuable pine, easily accessible from the St. Croix River, and it spelled out their exclusive rights.

As it turned out, their negotiations were in vain, for in July the Chippewa signed a treaty with the government that ceded this land and much more, opening the region to land purchase and settlement. Warren, Aitken, and Sibley vanished from the St. Croix lumbering scene.

The ink was barely dry when missionaries reported seeing other pioneer lumbermen busy in the pineries. Joseph Brown was ambitiously felling trees and trading with the natives at a place on the west bank that is now Taylors Falls. John Boyce, who had traveled from St. Louis in a Mackinaw boat, began operations with eleven men and six oxen at the Snake River, and was perhaps the first on record to take a logging crew into this area.

But neither of these operations was of any consequential size, and they, too, disappeared within a short time.

Another early lumber speculator executed more permanent plans. Immediately after the treaty of 1837 had been signed, Franklin Steele and a companion hurried off from Ft. Snelling to stake a claim. Following their canoe to the falls of the St. Croix was a scow loaded with tools, supplies and laborers. These men quickly constructed a warehouse and two log cabins at the foot of the rapids. A year later, soon after the treaties with the Sioux and Chippewa were ratified at Washington, the steamer *Palmyra* left St. Louis loaded with tools and machinery for building a sawmill and shops, four months' provisions, and about fifty men. Among them were millwrights, carpenters, masons, lumbermen, teamsters, and laborers. The *Palmyra* was, perhaps, the first steamboat to navigate the St. Croix.

But as well furnished and manned as it was, this was not the first mill to produce lumber on the banks of the St. Croix. Steele returned to St. Anthony to accept an appointment at Ft. Snelling, and work on the mill, dam, and millrace was not completed until 1842.

Meanwhile, another group of men in the town of Marine Settlement near Alton, Illinois learned of the treaty ratification, and by northern travelers they were told of the magnificent pine forests and the great lumbering opportunities of the St. Croix region. Their particular interest was to become of great importance to the future of the valley. Twelve men assembled at the tavern of the three Judd brothers – Albert, George, and Lewis – and plans were laid to organize and locate a lumber company. Two of these men, David Hone and Lewis Judd, the youngest of the brothers, were chosen to explore the St. Croix to choose the most ideal site for a sawmill.

Hone and Judd left Illinois aboard the northbound steamer *Ariel* in September 1838. At the head of Lake St. Croix, they left the steamer and poled a flatboat upriver to the falls where they found the millwright and other members of the Steele organization constructing a sawmill. The two continued their search, and on the return trip downriver, they selected a spot for their mill about halfway between the falls and the head of Lake St. Croix. There they found a stream cascading into the St. Croix where they staked a claim. This site would later become the

Minnesota village of Marine.

The two land lookers returned to Illinois for the winter, joined their fellow partners, and completed preparations for the future logging and sawmill firm they would call the Marine Lumber Company.

The following April, eight of the men chartered the side-wheel steamer *Fayette* and loaded it with complete machinery for the mill, farming equipment and cows, household goods, three yoke of oxen, and all the other supplies needed to set up their new business and homes in the unknown country. When they departed northward, traveling with them were a millwright, a blacksmith, and Mrs. Hone, who would handle the cooking responsibilities. About two weeks later, the steamer arrived at the St. Croix. Heavy rain had raised the water level, covering dangerous sandbars, so the *Fayette*, the second steamboat to ascend the river beyond Lake St. Croix, had no trouble in reaching the proposed Marine Lumber Company mill site.

Much to their dismay, the colonists found their construction site occupied by claim jumpers, who were actually two of Frank Steele's employees at the Falls, Jeremiah Russell, a blacksmith, and millwright Levi Stratton. They had learned of the newcomers' plans the previous fall and decided to take advantage of the opportunity for some extra money. They had one of their laborers clear some land, build a cabin on the claim, and keep possession through the winter. Then in the spring, Russell and Stratton returned to the cabin, paid the carpenter $100, moved into the cabin, and waited for the men from Illinois to return.

Since both parties were squatters on public land, the new arrivals had no choice but to agree to the jumpers' terms, and paid Russell and Stratton $300 to vacate the claim.

The Marine Lumber Company, under the direction of Orange Walker, immediately commenced construction, and only three months later, August 24, 1839, the first commercial sawmill on the St. Croix cut its first lumber, and one of Minnesota's greatest industries was off on its meager beginning.

Mrs. Hone, the first woman in the area, tended to the cooking while the men tended to business. During that first winter, 2,000 pine logs were cut upriver and floated down to the mill in the spring. With the slow up-and-down saw driven by an overshot water wheel, the company managed to cut 800,000 feet of lumber.

The first few years proved difficult, but tireless work and dedicated interest soon brought prospering results. One of their biggest boosts came in the mid-1840s when the company established a yard at St. Louis, under the direction of George Judd, to handle the sale of Marine-cut lumber.

The 1840s saw the beginnings of other lumber operations, as well. The St. Croix Falls company finally cut its first timber in 1842, and mills at Osceola, Arcola, and Hudson became operational. And at Stillwater, the beginning is another interesting story.

Early in the 1840s, four young men from the New England states – John McKusick, Elam Greeley, Elias McKean, and Calvin Leach – arrived in the pineries of the St. Croix Valley. They found employment at the newly established St. Croix Falls lumber mill, building dams and cutting timber for the fledgling company. Then in 1843, an extraordinary spring flood decided their future. Unusually heavy rains enraged the river, and the log-holding boom above the mill could not withstand the pressure, giving way to 400,000 feet of timber sent crashing thirty miles downriver into the quieter water of Lake St. Croix. This event had all the potential makings of a financial disaster if it hadn't been for the quickly responding actions of a discerning riverman, Captain Stephen Hanks. He collected much of the scattered timber, assembled a raft, and floated it to the southern markets at Clinton, Iowa. This was the first commercial log raft ever to go down the Mississippi.

Until that time, shipments from this northern region had comprised solely of sawed lumber, lath and shingles. This stroke of bad luck, actually, might take credit for the beginning of a new, prosperous market for the St. Croix Valley lumbermen. A seeming disaster turned to enormous benefit, for thousands of rafts were to follow, supplying logs to the treeless areas of the South.

When payday rolled around for the four Easterners (McKusick, Greeley, McKean, and Leach), as part of their wages from the lumber company at the Falls, they were awarded the rights to the renegade logs still hung up along the St. Croix River. They pooled their resources, and that fall they contractually united in the sawmill business. With the gathered logs stranded by the earlier flood comprising their initial raw material, the four entrepreneurs bought a building site on the river from Jacob Fisher, a carpenter at the Falls Lumber Company. The narrow plateau facing Lake St. Croix was part of his claim along the west bank, and seemed the ideal location for a mill, as waterpower could easily be supplied by another upland lake (later named for McKusick) just to the west of the site. By 1845, a sawmill, a tavern, a general store, and a half-dozen wooden houses occupied the plateau backed by steep bluffs. Jon McKusick named the place Stillwater after his home village near Bangor, Maine.

Newspapers soon predicted that Stillwater would become another Milwaukee or Chicago, for within just a few years its population grew to more than 200; stores, shops, and hotels lined the main street, a school flourished, and the striking wooden viaduct that carried water from the lake to power the sawmill stretched high above the rooftops of many fine houses. Although McKusick's mill (he came into complete control when his partners sold him their interests in 1844) had not been the first, and it certainly wasn't the largest lumber operation on the St. Croix, Stillwater rapidly became the industry's headquarters and principal supply depot for all the St. Croix Valley lumbering operations. More new mills sprang up in the Stillwater area, and there was a notable increase in the milling business.

Another near catastrophic event struck in May 1852. Torrential rains along the St. Croix caused the river to rise dangerously, and after several days of constant downpour, everything was thoroughly saturated, and the ground could absorb no more. High on the bluff behind Stillwater, McKusick's storage lake was overflowing. The villagers were suddenly startled by the roar of water as the dam ripped open. Not only water, but also a tremendous mudslide rolled down the ravine carrying trees, topsoil, sand and gravel across Stillwater's Main Street in what has sometimes been referred to as the greatest movement of real estate in the history of the valley. Many buildings – stables, several houses, and McKusick's mill were almost completely buried by mud and gravel. But when the townspeople inspected the results, they discovered that the landslide had deposited about ten acres of new real estate at the waterfront, adding substantial land area, plus an excellent steamboat landing, both of which would permanently benefit the town. The ordeal put McKusick out of business for just a short time. He rebuilt his mill, and Stillwater continued to thrive. But several new, much larger sawdust-burning steam-powered mills had been established, backed by wealthy eastern and southern firms. John McKusick found it difficult for his small operation to compete with Schulenburg and Boeckeler from Missouri, and Hersey, Staples and Company from Maine, who had created the best mills in the Minnesota Territory. By 1856 he abandoned the milling operation and turned his efforts to the real estate business.

Nearly all the lumber manufactured by Schulenburg and Boeckeler, the biggest producer in Stillwater for many years, was rafted down the St. Croix/Mississippi to the company's lumberyard in St. Louis. Although this mill was of economic importance, its owner never became a civic or social factor in Stillwater.

Rival lumberman, Isaac Staples, on the other hand, built a small empire in Stillwater, and remained a prominent figure for half a century. By 1854, he and his partner had established a general store handling dry goods, groceries, clothing, and miscellaneous merchandise. Early that fall, they began construction on a mill, and by June 1855, Hersey, Staples & Co. was sawing lumber.

Isaac Staples was instrumental in forming the boom company at Stillwater. The St. Croix Boom Company had been chartered in 1851 and a boom constructed six miles below Taylors Falls in an attempt to control the unorganized log drives. There the logs would be corralled, sorted according to ownership, and rafted to the owners' mills. But the company proved not entirely effective. Staples acquired control of the failing operation in the mid-1850s, and persuaded other mill owners' co-operation for incorporating a new boom company, with the boom site located about two miles above Stillwater. Long, narrow islands that divided the river into several channels at this point provided the ideal set up to corral, sort, scale, and raft the millions of logs coming down the St. Croix during the spring drives. It was an essential addition to the prosperous industry, even though its massive collection of logs frequently blocked the channel, creating navigational nightmares for the riverboat pilots and passengers.

Lumbering and a growing nation's appetite for its products decided the success for many St. Croix settlements. Logs were, for over half a century, the foundation of their prosperity. Most St. Croix lumbermen were convinced that the vast northern pineries were inexhaustible, and as long as there was timber to cut, the St. Croix Valley remained a great factor in the lumber trade of the West. It furnished a constant supply of quality building products to the people from Minnesota to Missouri, as well as provided profitable employment for thousands of men.

Lumbermen of the St. Croix Valley enjoyed their most profitable years during the 1890s, but as the turn of the Twentieth Century approached, so did the end of the glorious lumbering era. By the early 1900s, most of the magnificent primeval white pine forests of Wisconsin and Minnesota were gone from the St. Croix Valley, and the lumber industry was moving on to the Pacific Northwest.

So, the lumbering era is all but forgotten along the St. Croix, but other manufacturing and agricultural interests continue to keep it alive. Excursion vessels remain popular, and pleasure boat marinas have become big business. With its numerous parks and breathtaking scenery, the St. Croix Valley is now a recreational paradise.

Pirates at Two Rivers

Two Rivers was just a small village in 1849. Located on the shores of Lake Michigan in the northern portion of the state, it was distinctively a sawmill settlement, lumber manufacturing its chief industry. Not far away stood the primeval forest of majestic pine, hemlock, oak, maple, and birch, yet untouched by the woodman's axe. The nearest choice pine had been cut to build the town, but the other trees remained unmolested in all their original grandeur, just as they had when only the red men wandered beneath them, and wildlife sought shelter and sustenance in their shadows. Although lumbering employed the largest number of men of the village, fishing, coopering, and shingle making were carried on, as well.

The fishermen were mainly French Canadians, although other nationalities were among them. During the long winters when it was unsafe and generally impossible to go out onto the lake in their small, open mackinaw boats, they engaged in making shingles and fish barrels to enhance the income derived from their nets.

In those days, shingles were all hand-made, each one split from a block of pine, called a bolt, and was shaved and trimmed into shape by the skillful use of hatchet and draw knife. Staves for fish barrels were made in the same manner. The bolts, or blocks, from which the shingles and staves were made, had to be of the very choicest of timber with sound, straight grain and without knots or blemishes. Consequently the most perfect pine trees were selected by woodsmen for bolts, as they brought better returns than they would if cut into lumber.

Because the shingle and stave bolts were more valuable than logs for lumber, there came to be a class of men who paid little attention to honesty, and soon gained the label of "river pirates." They usually operated in gangs, going up the rivers in canoes, ravaged the forests of these choice trees, and sometimes helped themselves to unattended logs already cut. Once the logs were sectioned into bolts, there was no means to prove ownership. The bolts were then rafted down the rivers and sold to the men in the little shanties scattered along the banks where the shingles and barrel staves were made.

As long as their money lasted, these river pirates were a rowdy lot, and they terrorized the town with their unruly ways, frequently making it unsafe for anyone to appear on the streets of Two Rivers in 1849.

A man named Fox was recognized as the leader of one of these riotous bands, numbering about twelve. From the time they disposed of one bolt raft until they started upriver after another, this dangerous set of ruffians held the village in siege, frightening and assaulting innocent townspeople, and maliciously damaging property. When their money ran out, they disappeared, only to return a few weeks later with another raft of pillaged bolts.

In the spring election of 1849 it was decided to rid the town of the gang; a man named McCullom was elected constable. It was believed that he had the courage to hold the gang in check, or to drive them out. One afternoon, while Fox and his followers were on one of their rampages and were making themselves generally despised, they passed by the little brewery owned by Edward Mueller. At the front of the brewery stood a flagstaff flying a small flag, planted there by Mueller's twelve-year-old son, Richard. Being the rowdy bunch they were, the gang members challenged Fox, betting a keg of beer that he could not climb the pole and bring down the flag. Immediately, Fox accepted the challenge and began the ascent. But as he reached a height of about ten feet, the staff toppled over, landing Fox in a mire of mud. Unrestrained, noisy laughter emerged from the gang, and that, in turn, set a nearby flock of geese owned by Mueller into frantic squawking. Furious with the mishap, Fox was just crazy enough to think that the geese were laughing at him. In anger he seized a large stick, rushed toward the flock and began clubbing and killing the defenseless creatures.

Mueller suddenly appeared and ran to defend his geese from the fatal attack. Fox clubbed him, too, and knocked him senseless. Knowing that there was apt to be more trouble of insurmountable proportions, Fox and his gang retreated.

Mueller soon recovered, and did not hesitate to go immediately before the justice of the peace to swear out a warrant for the arrest of Fox. The gang had scattered, but about nine o'clock that night, McCullom discovered Fox hunkered down in one of the shingle shanties along the river. McCullom was well aware of Fox's temperament, and saw fit to recruit the assistance of several men from the lumber mill, one of whom was a young German named Linstedt, almost a giant, and a powerhouse of strength capable of dwarfing Fox's meanness.

McCullom entered the shanty alone and found Fox sitting on a stool, stupefied by liquor. Taking him by the arm, the constable told Fox that he was under arrest and ordered him to come peaceably. Court was about to be in session.

But Fox was not willing to give up so easily. As he arose from the stool, he lunged at McCullom with a knife that he jerked from his belt. McCullom had expected some resistance from the desperado, but his reaction was not quick enough to escape a severe wound. Fox darted for the door, only to find Linstedt blocking the exit. "Drop that knife, Fox, or I'll kill you," growled Linstedt. Fox sobered quickly, and saw at a glance that the big German meant what he said. He cowered to the command, released the knife, and allowed Linstedt to lead him to the waiting justice of the peace.

Court was called to order in another little shanty. Fox remained quiet and submissive, but during the trial, he asked to use a nearby privy. Permission was granted. Under the watchful eye of a guard, he was marched out into intense darkness. Once outside, Fox managed to slip away and disappeared, never to be seen in Two Rivers again.

The rest of the Fox gang vanished, too, and the river-pirating era soon ended.

Log Rafting on the Upper Mississippi

Once the logs reached the Mississippi, they were corralled into large holding areas, sorted, and then lashed together to form huge rafts, making them manageable for navigation downriver to lumber mills in Iowa, Illinois, and Missouri. Some rafts contained up to 10 million board feet of lumber – enough to build 500 houses. One such raft, recorded in 1869, covered 3 acres.

Assembling the rafts was hard, dangerous work. Crews began by fastening the logs or lumber into a wood frame called a crib. A typical crib measured about 16 by 32 feet. A dozen or more cribs were linked end to end to form a string. Several strings were then lashed together to form the raft.

Until the 1860s, the rafts relied solely on manpower and the river's current. Each string required two oarsmen – one at the bow, and one at the stern; thus, a raft of ten strings employed a crew of twenty or more, all under the direction of a pilot.

The massive log rafts presented a picturesque sight to behold as they drifted silently downriver in the shadows of the hills. As for the hardy men who guided them – the "rafters" – their profession seemed peculiar in itself, and yet, their presence painted alluring, indelible impressions. Danger was extreme, but they knew no fear and bravely faced the occasional disaster. Generous wages, though, compensated for all the hardships.

These floats with their long sweep of oars at bow and stern and little shanties perched in the center where the men ate and bunked, was home for weeks on end to the red shirted oarsmen as they leaned into the oars in obedience to the orders of the pilot. Boisterous dancing, singing and gambling with which they whiled away the hours not spent at the oars was their way of life on the long journeys down the Mississippi. Only during fog and storms were the rafts tied up at shore.

To safely navigate these great unyielding masses through and around reefs, sand bars, and the thousand turns and windings of the river required courage, a cool head, instinctive resources, and marvelous exact knowledge of the river. During the early days of raft navigation, searchlights were unknown; the white "diamond boards" marking the channel were not yet in place, and the river was full of snags. At night the pilot had to grope his way in inky darkness with only the shadowy outlines of the bluffs or such marks as an isolated tree, projecting rock, woodpile or cape of land to guide him.

The U.S. Lighthouse Service began marking the channel with the white diamond boards on the shoreline in 1874. Lights were kept burning on them at night. These lights were placed in the care of local people, and many of the little riverside trading stores appeared as a result of the new marking system. Periodically, a government steamer tied up at the landing and delivered oil and lamp repairs to the light keeper. It was the job of the "keeper" to maintain his assigned light, fill the oil reservoir every day, and to ensure it was burning brightly at every sunset. Many of the added landings became well known and popular among the steamboat men and rafters, as they could easily obtain milk, eggs, butter, ice, and other store supplies.

With the advent of towboats to propel the rafts with greater speed and efficiency, searchlights to make nighttime navigation more advantageous were introduced – but not until 1881. Prior to this, accurately steering the long rafts down the winding Mississippi at night demanded the pilot's expert, detailed knowledge of the channel and the landmarks along its banks. Even without lights to guide them, these pilots would hardly scrape a sandbar on the darkest night. Competition among the pilots was keen during this period; contests were waged to bring down the largest raft, run the darkest night, make the quickest trip, and incidentally, make the most money for the boat owners.

The pilot who could get his raft through the bridges using the most efficient method made quickest times. Because the piers supporting the railroad bridges at Winona, La Crosse, and Dubuque created a narrow passage, rafts would have to be split into two sections to get through. "Double heading" was the term given to the method of placing one raft section ahead of the other, and then lashing them side-by-side again after passing through the bridge. Another way was called "double tripping," which involved one section to be tied above the bridge while the towboat pushed the other through the bridge. This section was separated from the boat and allowed to "make a fly" or float on the current. The towboat then retrieved the first section and caught up to the other below the bridge.

The fastest recorded trip was made in 1884 with a lumber raft twelve strings wide (192 feet) and sixteen cribs long (that's nearly the length of two football fields end to end) by the steamer, *Menomonie,* Captain S. B. Withrow commanding. The boat and raft departed from Reads Landing one Monday at sunup and the raft was delivered 622 miles downriver at Alton, Illinois the following Sunday morning.

Captain C. A. Bradley is credited with the first successful attempt to drive a log raft with a steamboat, the *Union*, in 1864, from the mouth of the St. Croix River to Clinton, Iowa, although a similar attempt had been made the prior summer with the same boat, Captain George Winans at the helm. A mechanical failure curtailed that first attempt from Reads Landing at the mouth of the Chippewa River, and the *Union* was laid up at Winona, Minnesota for repairs. This venture was promptly followed, and a decade later, the towboat had all but replaced the slower floating method; nearly 100 boats were employed in this work. For a time, the crew of oarsmen at the bow of the raft were retained to aid in directing its course, but in 1890, the hand powered sweeps gave way to the bow boat – a small steam powered vessel placed across the front of the raft at a right angle with the current, which readily directed the raft to starboard or port as the towing boat might require. Captain George Winans devised this innovation with the *Satellite*, a little steamer constructed for that purpose. The plan was an immediate success.

A similar boat, the *Lotus*, had previously been used by the A. B. Youmans Lumber Company for the purpose of helping the rafts through the Winona bridge, but it never made entire trips down the Mississippi.

The introduction of the bow boat marked the beginning of the end for Mississippi rafting since it permitted much larger rafts; pilots could now safely take downriver the entire amount of logs and lumber accumulated during the winter in a much shorter time, virtually working themselves out of jobs.

The steamer *Saturn*, Captain Winans commanding, towed the largest lumber raft ever taken down the river in July 1901 with the *Pathfinder* at the bow. This raft left Reads Landing 256 feet wide and 1,408 feet long.

From 1830 to 1915, lumber companies in western Wisconsin floated millions of pine and hardwood logs and bundles of cut lumber down the Mississippi River, originating from areas along the many tributary streams. During the peak of this era – the 1860s – the scene along the banks at any given river town boasted the same sight of logs and wood products piled high, while countless rafts lie at water's edge, waiting for a crew of oarsmen and pilot.

Old Post card view c.1890s of a Mississippi lumber rafter.

But that scene gradually changed as the northern pine stands began to deplete. The thousands of saws that once buzzed and screamed near the river towns were silenced; many of the mills were abandoned and their armies of workers scattered. What lumber was being cut, then, was too costly to risk in the river. The river was changing, too: an added dam at Keokuk, Iowa prevented the log rafts passage beyond that point.

Log rafting ended on the Upper Mississippi in 1915. At the helm of the *Ottumwa Belle*, Captain Walter Hunter of Winona, Minnesota, and with the *Pathfinder* at the bow, piloted the last raft of lumber – a fitting climax to a period of feverish activity on the Mississippi River and its tributaries in the North. A hundred or more majestic steamboats and their pilots, and thousands of hard-boiled, courageous crewmen had delivered to America's marketplace the finest timber from Minnesota and Wisconsin. Never again would there be a similar generation.

The beginning of a new commercial shipping era on the Mississippi came in 1916 with the installation of a fleet of steel freight barges, capable of transporting huge amounts of products, and put the raft men and pilots adrift without a business. As for the scores of boats that had pushed the rafts downriver, they lay idle on the shores, or were sold to the excursion companies.

Ferryboats and Bridges

Although the rivers and streams provided an important means of transportation to the earliest explorers and settlers for many years, they presented obstacles and restrictions as overland travel developed. Bridge construction was challenging and costly. Some crude log bridges were constructed over many of the smaller streams in makeshift fashion, or the route was simply diverted to a shallow crossing where men, horses and oxen splashed their way across. But on the wider, deeper rivers like the Wisconsin, ferry boats and rafts remained the more practical choice.

In June 1825, John P. Arndt was granted license to establish the first ferry service across the Fox River some distance south of Fort Howard. Controversy soon became the issue. Military law had governed the region surrounding the fort for the first ten years of its existence; Major Whistler, the commanding officer, refused to recognize a license given by civilian authority, and immediately issued an order forbidding any passenger to land on the west bank of the Fox River without first obtaining a permit from the commanding officer. Guards were posted to enforce the decree, and several persons attempting to cross were apprehended and "put to much inconvenience."

Ferryboat owner Arndt, justifiably displeased with the military action, decided to put an end to the tyranny. He crossed the river, was seized by a military guard as anticipated, and was taken to the fort. Upon release, he filed suit against Major Whistler for false imprisonment. Judge James Doty ruled the Fox River as a public highway on which a ferry could be operated without military interference, and awarded Arndt a judgment of fifty dollars plus costs.

Soon after the Military Road between Green Bay and Prairie du Chien was first used in the 1830s by troops conveying supplies to Fort

Crawford, it became the highway for fur traders, and later the great wave of emigrants into western Wisconsin and northern Iowa flowed over it. A pole ferry was established at the Bridgeport crossing, and eventually was owned by Peter Barrette who had the contract for carrying the mail between Prairie du Chien and Platteville. Barrette operated the ferry for nearly twenty years until a covered wooden toll bridge took its place in 1854.

Wherever possible, an ingenious method of propulsion was utilized. It required a strong current present the entire width of the river, and few such places could be found. A heavy manila cable was suspended squarely across the channel from shore to shore, and to it, lines attached the boat at each end from a windlass. The lines were connected to grooved wheels that rode on the heavy cable. By winding up the line at the leading end of the boat, the operator adjusted the craft to a diagonal with the current. He usually had to start the momentum by pushing the boat away from the bank with a pole, but once started, the current pressing against the angle propelled the boat across the channel.

One such ferry, first chartered in 1848, is still in operation today as part of the State highway system on Route 113 where it crosses the Wisconsin River at Merrimac, about 25 miles northwest from Madison. The huge diesel-powered craft that now transports vehicles and passengers is a far cry from the first wooden boat that ferried wagons, teams, and a daily stagecoach across the river.

That first boat used was a flat-bottomed scow, only forty feet long and sixteen feet wide. Wooden platforms at each end could be lowered to the shore to enable teams and wagons to drive onto the boat deck. Two double teams were about the limit of its capacity.

Chester Mattson first came to that place on the banks of the Wisconsin River in 1847. That winter, he succeeded in getting a state road chartered from Madison to Baraboo, and a ferry service crossing the Wisconsin River to complete the route. The road was soon laid out, and by the time stagecoaches began making regular runs between Madison and Baraboo, Mattson's ferry was in operation to take them across. The meager beginnings of the place was known as Matt's Ferry, and hence, the road was known as Matt's Ferry Road. It meandered about the rolling hills northwesterly from Madison to the settlement of Lodi and then to Matt's Ferry. Across the river, it took a northerly course, passing the eastern edge of Devil's Lake on its approach into Baraboo.

Mattson began construction of the town's second structure for use as a tavern, but he did not complete it. In 1849, W. P. Flanders entered into the business as a partner, and within a short time purchased Mattson's share of the unfinished tavern and ferry for a sum of $700. Flanders completed the tavern – or more accurately, a hotel – in 1853, and by 1856 it was doing a thriving business, as delays in crossing the river on the small ferry boat made it necessary to stop there for meals, and quite often, lodging.

The Merrimac Ferry is the lone survivor of about 500 ferries chartered by territorial and state legislatures before 1900. The State of Wisconsin assumed responsibility for its maintenance and operation in 1933, after which the service has been provided without charge. (Photo by author)

The Chicago, Milwaukee & St. Paul Railroad engaged in extending its line to La Crosse about this time, and Flanders recognized a soon approaching decline for the ferry enterprise. He decided to sell out. The opportunity came when H. M. Jones, a livery operator in Madison, became quite impressed with the operation, and displayed an enthusiastic interest in taking advantage of its ownership. He had made frequent trips over the Matt's Ferry Road with passengers, stopped often at the hotel, and saw the prospect for a money making venture. However, the threat of railroad competition escaped Jones' observation, and he bought the hotel and ferry for $3000.

Jones soon discovered that he had purchased a dying horse. With

Construction began in 1847 on the Ferry House located near the north bank of the Wisconsin River at Matt's Ferry, now known as Merrimac. (Photo from *Stagecoach and Tavern Tales by Harry E. Cole*)

the railroad completed to La Crosse in 1858, through traffic by way of Matt's Ferry all but ceased, and both the hotel and ferry became unprofitable to their owner, although operation did continue.

The name of the hamlet was changed from Matt's Ferry to Merrimack in 1855 by settlers who came from a county in New Hampshire with the same name. But the old original name did not die easily. Guide boards pointing the way to Matt's Ferry remained for many years.

The first means of crossing the Wisconsin River at Sauk City was a flat boat built by Berry Haney in 1839. He was one of the first dozen pioneers to settle there. A short time later, 1840, a Hungarian emigrant, Agoston Haraszthy, backed by his father Charles, and another Milwaukee man with plenty of money to finance the undertaking, purchased Haney's west bank riverfront property (or more accurately, his squatter's rights to it) and entered a claim on the land that would become Sauk City, although the town would carry the Haraszthy name for a number of years until the Indian name, Sauk City, would finally become official. Haraszthy also was granted the right to operate the only ferryboat service. Until the bridges were constructed – one in 1852 at Prairie du Sac, a sister city just upriver, and one at Sauk City in 1860 –

the ferryboat monopoly proved a lucrative business. The service consisted of simply a skiff to handle the pedestrian traffic, and a barge big enough to accommodate three teams of horses with loaded wagons. But the crossings were slow, sometimes quite inconvenient if the craft happened to be landed on the opposite shore, and always expensive. The citizens of the village, as well as area farmers on the east bank anxiously anticipated bridge construction.

When first settled, the site that is now Wisconsin Rapids on the upper Wisconsin River was actually two towns – Grand Rapids and Centralia – one on either side of the stream. In those early days, travel was light, and the settlers who had chosen to make their homes among the pine forest were content to stay – for the most part – on the side where they had located. There seemed to be little need for ferry or bridge, as almost everyone had his own flatboat, dugout, or canoe to facilitate crossing, should the need arise. But as time would prove, adequate transportation would become essential. Under a charter from the state, Eusebe LaVigne put into regular service the first commercial ferryboat between the two settlements in 1858. The thirty feet long by sixteen wide flatboat ran on an overhead cable and used the river current as motive power.

This method of transportation served adequately for about ten years, and then an enterprising businessman, George Neeves, was granted a charter by the Wisconsin legislature to construct and operate a toll bridge for public use. A charge of five cents per pedestrian and twenty-five cents per team and vehicle was authorized. The bridge put an end to the ferry business, and although the tolls were reduced when the traffic increased, there were still those thrifty citizens who crossed with their own boats to avoid the charge.

The charter had been written with provisions for the county to purchase the bridge and make it free for public use. The bridge had been instrumental in the growth and prosperity of the entire county, not to mention the two communities it connected, and it seemed advisable for the county to take it over. Naturally, Mr. Neeves did not favor the transaction, as the bridge was proving to be a profitable endeavor, and he fought the purchase plan, but with no success. The transfer was completed; the bridge rebuilt and strengthened, was reopened to the public without toll.

This bridge served satisfactorily until an ice jam destroyed part of the structure in the spring floods of 1888, rendering it beyond repair. The ferryboats were once again pressed into service.

Now there came the argument of who was responsible for the replacement of the bridge. After much litigation, the Wisconsin Supreme Court ruled against Grand Rapids and Centralia, and the two towns were forced to finance the reconstruction.

During the time of litigation and before the new bridge was completed, two ferryboat lines, both run on cables and propelled by the river current, competed for the temporary traffic business, one of them being operated by Eusebe LaVigne of the original ferryboat days.

Difficulty in obtaining a substantially solid foundation for the center pier delayed construction, but the problem was finally solved and in the spring of 1889, a new steel bridge spanned the Wisconsin River at the "twin cities."

The Wisconsin River meant many things to many people. Over its 430-mile course to meet the Mississippi near Prairie du Chien, the Wisconsin showed its many faces ranging from a wide and peaceful sandy-bottomed stream, to raging rapids that challenged the skills of even the best of the lumber raft navigators. Challenged, too, was the task of bridge building over the river with so many personalities. The challenge was met many times, beginning with the first bridge spanning the narrows at the Dells in 1850.

Attracted to the surrounding natural beauty and the tremendous power potential of the river, it is not surprising that the first settlers in 1838 had decided to stay in the area. But the Dells was also a treacherous stretch of the waterway where the entire volume squeezed through a fifty-foot-wide, rock-walled gulch that tested the abilities of lumber and log rafters, and often claimed lives of the daring men.

When that first bridge was constructed in 1850, the raftsmen passing through the narrows became, perhaps, the first entertainment attraction of the Dells. Tourists lined the bridge where they could watch the lumbermen skillfully maneuver the rafts below.

A major flood washed out the bridge in 1866. There was some talk in later years of rebuilding the bridge at the narrows for the benefit of the tourist trade, but that project was never carried out.

Another bridge had been built by the railroad at Kilbourn (present-day city of Wisconsin Dells) in 1857. This was a double-decked bridge serving a dual purpose: trains traveled across the upper deck while the lower deck handled public traffic. Sparks from a passing locomotive in 1866 set the wooden structure ablaze in what was described as a "two-hundred-foot sheet of fire." 1866 was not a good year for bridges at the Dells.

Toll bridges spanning the bigger rivers like the Wisconsin were not uncommon in the 1800s, and many remained in service well into the Twentieth Century. Because the state had no funding for road improvements in those early days, a bridge was the product of private enterprise, just as the ferryboats, and charging a fee for its use was the only means of recovering the construction expense. A boat, perhaps, was a lesser investment and in the long run meant a quicker return and larger profits, but the bridges offered great advantage: season changes did not affect their usefulness; risk factors were reduced; they were less time-consuming and more convenient, as the bridges could provide for a steady stream of traffic – no more waiting for a ferry if it happened to be at the opposite shore when crossing was desired.

Not long after the close of the Civil War, Gen. Jonathan Moore came to Grant County, recognized the possibility of linking the tiny settlement of Muscoda (it was then called English Prairie) to an agriculturally rich area across the Wisconsin River, and it was he who conceived the idea and invested over $24,000 to construct the first bridge. Prior to that time, small boats had been the only means of communication, so the bridge meant a convenient and efficient way for farmers to deliver their grain to the railroad that passed through Muscoda, and Gen. Moore believed that this little town could someday become a mighty grain shipping center.

Although he wasn't the first white settler, Col. William Hamilton, son of Alexander Hamilton, is given credit for the establishment of a settlement at Muscoda, or as it was known then, English Prairie. Two courageous youngsters from New York, John and his brother Cuyler Armstrong had passed by this site in their canoe in 1822 on their quest for the great western American adventure. They continued on to the Mississippi River, and down to Galena, Illinois, where they stayed for a short while. Their attention was drawn to lead mining, and as the mining operations pushed farther to the north, they eventually made their way back to the prairie along the Wisconsin River in 1828. John Armstrong was then married, and while living at English Prairie, his wife bore three children. Their first son, however, died before he was a year old. Two daughters were born in 1830 and 1832.

Cuyler Armstrong and John Aynsley arrived from Mineral Point, established a warehouse on the bank of the Wisconsin at English Prairie, and regularly conducted a trading business with the surrounding Indians, with whom the settlers were on friendly terms at that time. A few other families settled there, too, but in early spring of 1832 the Black Hawk War was heating up to the danger point, and although they had no fear of the local tribes, there was no real safety for the white settlers outside a fort. Hostile Indians floating downriver in their canoes one night was the signal for the English Prairie settlers to flee to the safety of military forts at Montfort. Because of overcrowding by so many settlers, John Armstrong took his family to Fort Elizabeth a short distance into Illinois.

Some of those same pioneers may have returned to their homes at English Prairie after the war, and then Col. William Hamilton came to the place about 1836 and saw this settlement as the perfect location to build a lead smelting furnace. Until then, all the lead mined in the territory was hauled to Galena and sold to commission merchants, who in turn sold and shipped it to St. Louis markets. The cost of hauling the product to Galena from the mines opening farther north became prohibitive, as the price of lead had fallen dramatically. Miners and smelters were somewhat discontented with the treatment they received from the Galena middlemen, spurring efforts to establish alternate shipping routes. Hamilton speculated that a smelting furnace closer to the mines, and right at the steamboat landing at English Prairie could reduce the handling costs and make this a profitable operation, even though the margins were quite narrow.

Hamilton operated the furnace for a number of years, and then finally sold it to Thomas Jefferson Parrish, whose primary mining and smelting business was at Montfort.

By 1847 the white population stood at about fifty, with a trading post and one store, all occupying log cabins. Even the coming of the railroad did not create any rapid growth, as there was still no connection to the rich farmland across the river. Muscoda could only remain as a small trading post village – until Gen. Moore built his bridge.

The first team of horses and wagon crossed the bridge in September 1868, marking the beginning of a new era of prosperity for Muscoda. Within a few years, the population increased and many businesses located there, as this was now the commercial center for a prosperous agricultural district.

Although the original bridge was severely damaged by a tornado in 1896, and agitation in favor of a free bridge had started as early as 1875, it remained in service until plans for its replacement actually occurred in 1926. The new bridge was completed in 1929.

This original toll bridge across the Wisconsin River at Muscoda built in 1868 remained in service until 1929. (From "Muscoda, the First Hundred Years")

A few miles farther down the Wisconsin River, at Boscobel, was the site of another long-enduring ferry service.

Hiram Comstock first saw Boscobel in 1850 on his way to Prairie du Chien. He returned four years later after a short period of employment in Potosi making bricks for the old Grant County Courthouse, and engaged in similar business at Boscobel.

A service known as the Manhatten Ferry had been established to transport passengers and teams across the Wisconsin River at Boscobel sometime prior to 1855, but the steam-powered boat was not a success. Hiram Comstock recognized a great potential, bought out the ferry business, did away with the steam engine, and began operating the ferry with pole power, which proved to be more practical. In time, a cable was stretched across, and the river's current did the work.

This was a time when Comstock could take advantage of a rush of settlers entering the area, and his investment in the ferry became quite profitable. It was a risky occupation, but a similar ferry at Georgetown was his only competition. (When the Wisconsin River was a busy thoroughfare, Georgetown thrived with its hotels and quite a number of grog shops, but now nothing remains to mark its location.)

But the enterprising ferryman saw more potential on the other side of the river at his landing area that was known as Manhatten. There he platted a town and sold building lots. His town, however, didn't gain any popularity, and Mr. Comstock paid back all the money he had collected.

Even though his new town failed, his ferry continued to be successful for seventeen years, until the Boscobel bridge rendered it obsolete in 1873.

Constructed in 1873 with private capital, the original bridge at Boscobel was replaced in the 1930s. It was the last remaining covered bridge in Southwestern Wisconsin. (1932 Milwaukee Journal photo)

McGilvray's Ferry
and the Seven Bridges Road

Alexander MacGillivray first came to Canada from Scotland where he engaged in the logging business for a number of years. Then in 1848 he brought his family to Wisconsin, and after an unsuccessful season of logging in the Wisconsin River valley, he heard of the rich agricultural area near the Mississippi. Leaving his family safe and secure in Portage, he set out alone for La Crosse in search of a homestead. In La Crosse he learned of the Black River valley country and he decided to see what opportunities it offered for a homesteader. Only a blazed trail led him across the bottomland, and he forded the Black River a little north of present-day New Amsterdam. McGilvray (he had shortened his name by then) looked over the surroundings, selected a parcel of land for his future farm, and returned to La Crosse to file the claim. He went back to his homestead and stayed long enough to cut and put up a stack of hay, and then headed for Portage where he remained that winter.

The next spring, 1850, McGilvray brought his family to Trempealeau, which was known as Reeds Landing at that time. Because they were traveling with team and wagon, they had to go a considerable distance out of the way to cross the Black River at Gordon's Ferry near Galesville. The family settled into a house at Reeds, while Alexander went to the homestead and began felling trees to construct a log cabin. The following spring, he moved his family to their new home and began farming.

New settlers kept moving into the area from the south. For anyone living in the vicinity, it was a long trip by way of Gordon's Ferry to the La Crosse markets; McGilvray recognized the need of a ferry crossing at his place to accommodate the increasing traffic on a much shorter, more convenient route. So in the spring of 1854, he and Charles Utter built a scow in the streets of Trempealeau, hauled it to McGilvray's place and launched the first of five boats that would be operated at that location on the Black River until a bridge was constructed in 1892. At times, long lines of stagecoaches and freight wagons waited their turn to be ferried across at this busy landing that was now a part of the newly established road to La Crosse. Many travelers chose to remain at McGilvray's tavern overnight, as there, around the evening fire they were always entertained with good food, exciting stories of pioneer life told by hunters, freighters, and woodsmen, and Alexander McGilvray often treated his guests to music on his bagpipes, which he had brought with him from Scotland.

This is one of the six remaining bridges on the historic McGilvray "Seven Bridges Road," preserved as a hiking trail, and listed on the National Register of Historic Places. The seventh bridge across the main channel of the Black River no longer exists. The steel structures erected by La Crosse Bridge & Steel Co. replaced the original series of wooden bridges in 1905-1908. (Photo by author)

Ferry 'Cross the Chippewa

In 1856 there was only a small village on the site of the now flourishing city of Eau Claire, Wisconsin. The settlement lay on both sides of the Chippewa River, where excellent waterpower had lured some enterprising capitalists to pursue the development of commerce. A bridge was only a dream then, and all communication between the two parts of the village was by means of a ferryboat. There, too, the water flow of the considerably wide river allowed the use of a cable guided craft, propelled by the current's pressure. The long rope was supported at intervals by floating buoys.

Management of the conveyance was entrusted to a man known as Mr. M. He obtained the charter from the village and agreed to keep his boat in readiness to carry passengers to and from their homes and places of business located on either side of the river, at any hour of the day or night. With a novice at the helm, or sometimes even with the master operator, disasters occurred, and the early settlers often found themselves in amusing experiences. The following is just one of the many Chippewa River "ferry tales."

On a bright and chilly autumn day, three gentlemen strolled up from their cabins, a mile below the ferry landing, intending to cross over to the East side, join their wives at a tea party, and return with them later in the evening. Arriving at the landing, they were annoyed to find the boat on the opposite side and deserted by its captain. In vain they shouted: "Halloo-oo. Halloo-oo. The b-o-a-t!"

No response but echoes came from the long line of low bluffs behind the town. After tedious waiting, they saw a Norwegian blacksmith coming down to the opposite bank, his arms laden with packages, evidently eager to come home.

"Come over with that boat, Ole!" they called.

Ole refused, at first, knowing the danger for an unskilled sailor. But at last, he yielded to the urgent request from the three men on the opposite shore. He wound up the rope, set the rudder, and pushed the boat away from the bank. Everything seemed to be going smoothly, at first, but Ole remained nervous with the unfamiliar task, and in mid-stream, the rope broke, allowing the ferry to drift aimlessly down the river.

The men who had lured Ole into the dilemma followed him along the bank, shouting advice and encouragement. Eventually, Ole succeeded in guiding the boat to shore far below the proper landing, and with a sadly demoralized condition. The poor Scandinavian was nearly crazed with fear, as he knew Mr. M was a man of quick temper and would deliver dire penalties on anyone who tampered with his boat.

But Mr. Ingham, the leader of the three-man party, was boldly and expediently inventive, and he would not be one to leave his abettor in the lurch.

"Now, Ole," he instructed, "take your bundles and come along. We got you into this scrape – we will get you out of it."

In the dim light of dusk, they went to the blacksmith's shanty, where Ole explained to his wondering wife that he must be away all night and no one must know that he had been at home that evening. Then, still toting his packages, he followed the three friends, who, by this time were gloating over their scheme to outwit the ferry operator. At the nearby lumber mill, they boarded a skiff, always in readiness there, and rowed across the river.

"Now," Ingham told Ole, "you must stay with your Norwegian friends on the East side until morning, then come down early to the ferry and let the captain know how anxious you are to get home."

Ole hurried away, prepared to play his part; Ingham and his two friends joined the tea party, preserving strict secrecy of their evening's escapade. They listened calmly to the story brought to the table by a latecomer: "The ferryboat is in trouble again. Someone took it without leave and has left it abandoned on the shore down by the bend."

Then followed the condescending remarks from the rest of the partiers, and the unsparing reflections upon the character of the person responsible for such a flagrant deed. The three men's wives didn't remain silent, either, spewing their displeasures toward the evildoers, their sentiments probably heightened by the fear of not returning to their homes that night.

But with unchanging face and guarded conscience, the three delinquents played their role and successfully disguised their identity as the culprits.

After finishing a prolonged chat at the post office, Captain M returned to the river and found his boat gone. Understandably, he uttered a few choice words regarding the incident, and then went about retrieving the lost ferry and making the necessary repairs. By midnight, the boat was safely moored at its proper position.

Remembering that he had ferried Ole, the blacksmith, across earlier that day, he could not recall bringing him back. With his suspicion focused on the industrious Norwegian, Mr. M set out for the smithy's cabin, only to find Ole's wife, who couldn't speak or understand any English, frantic over her husband's absence. Mr. M searched the place, convinced that Ole was the guilty party, but he could find no telltale evidence that Ole had been there that night. Mystified – and annoyed – he returned to his boat.

At early dawn, the captain was enlightened with the appearance of Ole, briskly scolding him for the dreadful fright he must have caused his poor wife to suffer. Captain M, somewhat shameful of his earlier accusations, did not reply.

Later that morning, Mr. Ingham approached and reprimanded the captain further. "Why, in the name of justice, don't you stay by your ferry? We came last night to be ferried over, shouted ourselves hoarse, and then walked a mile to row our own skiff across! I tell you, Captain, a servant of the public must be on hand and attend to his business!"

By this time, the captain was in an unusually meek frame of mind. Never before had he been so baffled, and recognizing some justice in Mr. Ingham's lecture, again, he said nothing.

Several years after Mr. M had retired from the ferry's helm, Ingham revealed the whole affair. The astonished captain could now relish a hearty laugh over the unraveled mystery and the unavailing search for the mischievous culprits who had so cunningly evaded capture.

Mississippi River Ferryboats

When the trend of the pioneers pressed westward, the Mississippi River served as a valuable highway to the emigrants arriving by boat from points south, or from states bordering the Ohio River, another important American waterway. But to those pioneers who came overland across Wisconsin or Illinois, the mighty river presented an almost insurmountable barrier. Oxen-drawn wagons, usually heavily loaded with supplies, household goods, farm implements and tools – virtually everything the family owned – added to the challenge. Smaller streams could be forded, and most traveling obstacles avoided or overcome. But when they reached the banks of the wide, deep, and flowing Mississippi, it appeared as an impassable blockade. On the opposite shore, they could see their destination, and for all their efforts of a difficult journey, they would not be deprived of a new beginning in that new land. From this desire and determination was born the ferry. As the influx of pioneers increased, enterprising individuals and firms built ferryboats to transport the wagons and goods of the emigrants to Minnesota and Iowa shores, and to bring settlers of Iowa and Minnesota to Wisconsin cities to deliver their farm produce in trade for other supplies.

Canoes had served as the earliest type of ferry to the Native Americans long before the white settlers arrived. This mode of transportation was readily adopted and used by the hunters and trappers and fur traders in later years. And even to the earliest settlers seeking the land beyond the river, the canoe still served a useful purpose, although it meant a laborious, time-consuming task. Wagons had to be unloaded and dismantled into manageable pieces, and then the whole cargo and wagon parts transported in small quantities on many trips to and from the distant shore. Horses or oxen were unharnessed or unyoked and swam across, led by a halter beside the canoe. On the other side, the wagon was reassembled, reloaded, and the final miles of the journey continued.

This method of traversing the river became quite inadequate, though, as the parade of emigrants seeking the west hastened. To answer those needs of steadily increasing numbers, regular public ferries came into use. They were barge-like flatboats and skiffs large enough to carry loaded wagon and team, steered with a long sweep, and propelled by manpower with oars or poles. And though the flatboats were a marked improvement over the canoe, these cumbersome craft were not yet the perfect solution, subject to risk and uncertainty, always being carried downriver by a swift current. But now a Mississippi River crossing could be completed in an hour or two, that before, with wagon dismantling and multiple canoe trips had taken sometimes many days to accomplish. Although there may have been others, the first documented ferry of this type was operated by Captain Benjamin Clark in 1833 at Buffalo, just below present-day Davenport, Iowa.

Within a few short years, there were many such ferryboats in operation at various locations to transport settlers and their goods from Illinois and the Wisconsin Territory to the Iowa and Minnesota frontier. And once again, just as their predecessors – the canoes – the manpowered flatboats began showing obvious signs of inadequacy as the traffic demands increased. Introduction of the ingeniously developed "horse ferry" drastically reduced the Mississippi crossing time, thereby greatly increasing the efficiency of the ferrying service. This design utilized the strength of horses (and sometimes mules) upon a treadmill installed on the boat deck that served as a drive mechanism connected to side-mounted paddlewheels. The idea caught on, and the ferry business made its next advancement in the evolution process. The following article in a Bloomington (Muscatine) newspaper appeared in 1841: "A new boat, propelled by horsepower, has lately been placed upon the river at this place, for the accommodation of a ferry; and, though hastily made, all of green oak, and clumsy in its exterior, it swims like a swan and will cross in eight minutes with ease and safety. We may flatter ourselves that a ferry is now permanently established."

The transition to the horse powered ferries was not complete by the time steam power progressed to replace many of the man powered units. This third step in motive power literally revolutionized the ferry business. Again, the travel time was reduced considerably, and carrying capacity increased, in some cases, to as many as eighteen teams and wagons.

La Crosse boasted a number of ferryboats providing that service to La Crescent, Brownsville, and other communities on the Mississippi's western banks. But twenty-five miles to the north, the fast growing Minnesota village of Winona looked on with envy, recognizing its lost share of revenue.

Like many cities along the Upper Mississippi River, Winona was mainly a lumber town. The economic strength and growth of lumber towns were based upon receiving their share of the log rafts coming downstream in the early spring. Sawmills at Winona supplied much of the finished lumber that was used to construct the houses, farms and business buildings across southern Minnesota. But during the last half of the Nineteenth Century, Winona developed a diversified economy with a multitude of industries such as farm implements, carriages, iceboxes, and the medicines and extracts of the Watkins Company. It was also becoming one of the largest ports for shipping wheat from the prairies of southern Minnesota. The lack of a ferry at that point in the river diverted valuable business to other places.

Efforts to establish a ferry from Winona to the Wisconsin side of the river began as early as 1855, but it wasn't until April 1865 that the much-needed service at Winona started taking form. Samuel D. Van Gorder received a charter from the Wisconsin legislature granting the franchise to operate a Winona based ferry service across the river. Under its provisions, and with the permission from Winona County and the authorities of the city of Winona, Van Gorder operated a steam ferryboat for the next three years, at which time he obtained a ten-year franchise from the state of Minnesota.

At the outset, however, there were still no roads across the marshy bottomlands on the Wisconsin side of the river directly opposite Winona. Until that work could be completed, the Wisconsin landing would be located a couple of miles upriver at the "stone house."

Mr. Van Gorder made a trial run on the proposed route with the Steamer *Turtle*. Slow as it was, the appropriately named boat performed flawlessly, and he immediately entered into negotiations for its purchase from the builders in Wabasha. A double hull craft with the paddlewheel in the center to protect it from floating ice, the *Turtle* was capable of carrying four wagons with teams. Its cost was $2,000. Local newspapers printed articles encouraging citizens to give their full support to this enterprise, as its success was sure to boost Winona's economy.

Captain Samuel D. Van Gorder put the *Turtle* into service in May 1865. The maiden voyage carried a number of distinguished guests on board, making the run to the "stone house" in about a half an hour, and returned from Wisconsin with a load of emigrants, destined to settle in the Winona area. No fares were charged.

As a gesture in good faith, Van Gorder ran the ferry for a full week, free of charge to anyone wishing to visit Wisconsin, with anticipation of luring more interest and confidence in the long-awaited service. When the fares were levied, though, he was not hard-pressed for business. Winona finally had its long-overdue ferryboat.

The desire to facilitate better trade conditions between Wisconsin farmers and the Winona merchants swayed the city council to arrange for the survey of a road across the marshland opposite Winona in the fall of 1865. A contract was let, several Winona citizens advanced $5,000 for the work, and by the following summer, the road, at a level with the high water mark, was completed. Three years later, 1868, Captain Van Gorder made his own worthwhile efforts by constructing the first road across the Trempealeau bottoms. But he didn't stop with just the road. He also built a barn and offered its use, free of charge, to the Burbank Stage Line, successfully persuading them to use the Winona ferry crossing. About the same time, a daily mail route was established between Winona and Eau Claire, Wisconsin, and that mail stage used the ferry crossing as well.

It wasn't long until increasing traffic demanded a larger boat. Van Gorder met the challenge by enlarging the *Turtle* to more than double the original capacity; the boat could now accommodate ten teams and wagons. Then tragedy struck: the 1869 spring floods washed out all the Wisconsin ferry road bridges. Van Gorder footed much of the expense for their replacement. And that same season, the *Turtle* caught fire, and was almost totally destroyed. Van Gorder immediately rebuilt the craft and was back in operation within six weeks.

By 1878 it was time to replace the reliable old *Turtle*. Van Gorder built a new, far superior steamer, 95 feet long, 34 feet wide, capable of transporting twelve teams and wagons. He named the boat the *Van Gorder*. Two years later, he entered into negotiations with the City of Winona for the sale of the ferryboat, the charter, and the roadway across the Wisconsin marsh to the bluffs. An agreement was reached, and

Winona then operated the ferry service with the *Van Gorder* until 1887 when a new bridge from Latch Island to the Wisconsin bank was constructed, and a cable ferry was installed across the channel from Winona to the bridge. This system remained in use until the high wagon bridge was completed in July 1892.

This old post card view shows an excursion boat passing under the high wagon bridge at Winona, Minnesota. This bridge replaced the ferry service across the Mississippi River there. In the background is the railroad swing bridge. (Post card from a private collection.)

At Prairie du Chien – Ferry service between Prairie du Chien and McGregor, Iowa commenced in 1836 with a flatboat put on the river by Alexander McGregor. In those early times, the majority of its patrons were emigrants bound for the western plains. They came from the east and south on horseback, afoot, and in heavy covered wagons over primitive roads, chasing the sunset through this "Gateway to the West." Alexander McGregor's flatboat, named the *Rob Roy*, carried many of the first settlers across the Mississippi to northern Iowa.

One account from a white haired woman, years later relating her story of her first Mississippi crossing, illustrates the difficulties encountered by the pioneers: she was only a small child sitting in her mother's lap in the seat of a Conestoga wagon, terrified by the powerful floodwater sweeping past the loaded flatboat. To her, it seemed hours before they reached the Iowa shore. There, the steep bank made landing difficult and as her father, walking beside the wagon, urged his team of oxen up the bank, one of the animals stumbled and the heavy wagon slipped backward pulling the oxen with it. Her father hastily helped the mother and child to the ground, and freed the struggling animals just as they were drawn to the water's edge. The little family stood there, helpless, and watched the wagon and all their possessions being swept away. They had saved only their lives and the team with which they would begin again.

By 1859, after the Milwaukee-Prairie du Chien railroad was completed, the original *Rob Roy* had eventually been replaced with three steam-powered ferries that did bonanza business, bringing Iowa wheat across, and continued to transport settlers, their household goods and supplies bound for the lands west of the Mississippi River. Ownership of the ferry service changed several times, but it remained the oldest business enterprise operating in the Mississippi River valley north of St. Louis. In the late 1920s, a survey showed that 22,500 automobiles and 75,000 passengers crossed the river at Prairie du Chien in a single season.

In 1895 George "Cap" Freeman gained possession of the ferryboat service across the Mississippi connecting the City of Prairie du Chien, Wisconsin and McGregor, Iowa, making twelve round-trips daily for more than forty years.

Then came the highway bridge and ferry traffic was all but killed off. Of the three ferries that had been doing big business at the Prairie du Chien crossing, two were sold down the river. But concerning the disposal of the *Rob Roy II*, Cap's favorite boat, he said, "Nothin' doing."

In the spring of 1935 he took the boat to Dubuque, Iowa to have it refurbished to first class condition. When skeptical Prairie du Chien residents asked him what he intended to do with it, he just smiled and told them, "Oh, there'll be need of it. Ferrying ain't dead yet."

The day following his return to Prairie du Chien with the *Rob Roy* in August, Freeman received an urgent SOS message from the mayor of La Crosse. Traffic crossing the river there had been brought to a standstill when a span of the municipal bridge collapsed after an automobile crashed into a supporting pier. At that time, there were no other alternate routes nearby.

La Crosse ferryboats, too, had suffered from the progress of highway bridges, and they lay rusting away on the banks, their usefulness spent. No one had anticipated such a disastrous occurrence, and the lack of any back up transport across the river left the city traffic-bound.

Although it was a catastrophic day for La Crosse, it was a day that rewarded Cap Freeman's faith. He steamed the *Rob Roy* majestically upriver to La Crosse, and like a hero he came to the aid of a crippled city until the destroyed bridge could be rebuilt. Ferrying wasn't dead… yet!

At Dubuque – Ferryboats running between the southernmost points in Wisconsin and Dubuque, Iowa played an important role in the economic development of that city. A ferry landing at Dubuque meant a great amount of business that would have otherwise been lost to towns on the east side of the river.

The first of these was a big side-wheeler, the *A. L. Gregorie*, built in 1855 and owned by Chas. H. Merry. In later years, the line was sold to Hanson & Linehan of Dubuque, who eventually replaced the original boat with a more "modern" ferry, the *Key City* in 1876.

Another ferryboat, the *J. A. Rhomberg*, went into service in 1870, and it too was replaced with the side-wheeler *Eagle Point* in 1884.

Both boats ran with much success until the river was bridged at Dubuque and the disappearance of business on the levee rendered them useless.

At Potosi – About twelve miles upriver from Dubuque, the city of Potosi, Wisconsin occupies a long valley facing the Mississippi River. It was appropriately named with the Spanish word for "lead" as miners began pouring into the region during the early 1800s. Potosi enjoyed its boom years as a mining town, but in 1849 its population of 1500 decreased dramatically when the Gold Rush of the West lured so many away.

Potosi gained another interest, however. An Englishman, Gabriel Hail came to the town and found the ideal natural resources for a brewery. Sparkling pure spring water gushed from the base of the limestone cliff, and a large cavern extended deep into the hill, providing a valuable ingredient for the product and a naturally cool cellar for aging and storage.

During those early years, horse and wagon transportation limited the market area to the village of Potosi and other near settlements. Then in 1872, the Specht Brothers launched a ferryboat, the *McMershey* that operated between the Potosi landing and the Iowa settlement of Specht's Ferry.

Following the suicide death of the brewer, Gabriel Hail, an energetic young German, Adam Schumacher, who had worked in the brewery for several years and had become an excellent brewmaster, obtained a bank loan and purchased the brewery from Hail's estate in 1886. Schumacher began producing a high quality traditional German lager that quickly gained tremendous popularity in the village as well as the surrounding area.

The *McMershey* continued to move passengers, livestock, and produce from the farms and businesses in the Potosi area to markets across the river. But with the coming of the C.B. & Q. Railroad (Chicago, Burlington, & Quincy), the ferry business declined. The Specht Brothers discontinued the service and sold the *McMershey*.

It didn't take long, though, to learn that the railroad could not entirely satisfy the needs of the local farmers and businessmen. They still needed direct transportation to the Dubuque markets. The Specht Brothers answered the call by building another passenger and cargo steamboat, the *Teal*, which they entered into daily service between Potosi and Dubuque. After several years of operation, they sold the boat to Adam Schumacher.

The brewery owner renamed the craft the *Potosi*, and immediately put it to work hauling beer, opening a vast number of new outlets, as well as adding years of color and excitement to the steamboat era. Captain George Kimbel piloted the *Potosi* on daily trips between the homeport and Dubuque, carrying six or eight horse-drawn wagons loaded with beer or farm produce, and up to 100 passengers. On special occasions there would be excursions to Dubuque for the theater, circuses, and other events.

Eventually the railroad service improved, as did the network of highways and bridges, and the use of the steamboat became obsolete. The *Potosi* was sold to a buyer in St. Charles on the Missouri River.

The steamer *Potosi* ran as ferry service between Potosi, Wisconsin and Dubuque, Iowa during the late 1800s. (Newspaper photo)

At Cassville – Midway between the Mississippi crossing to

Dubuque and the one at Prairie du Chien, the settlement of Cassville held high anticipation of becoming Wisconsin's capital. With that in mind, Nelson Dewey, the state's first governor, built the pretentious Denniston Hotel in the early 1840's; its purpose was to house the legislators and to serve as their offices.

This made Cassville an important location, and demanded a ferry crossing to Iowa, then still a part of the Wisconsin Territory. Even though Madison was chosen over Cassville for the state capital, development of the road system steadily increased the importance of establishing the Cassville ferry crossing, as it was a trip of almost forty miles in either direction to the nearest ferry services at Prairie du Chien or Dubuque.

Horses and mules on a treadmill supplied power to side-mounted paddlewheels. It was a good arrangement; the beasts of burden doubled as the power source for pulling loaded freight wagons to and from the boat at either shore.

When railroads finally paralleled both the Wisconsin and Iowa shorelines, regular passenger and mail service was established, and the flatboat ferry continued uninterrupted operation well into the next century. It wasn't until the early 1900s when gasoline engines replaced the horsepower driven treadmills. Eventually, the wooden hull boat was replaced, too, with a steel hulled craft capable of transporting six automobiles.

At De Soto and Glen Haven – During the 1880s, similar ferryboats were operated from De Soto, Wisconsin to Lansing, Iowa, and from Glen Haven, Wisconsin to Guttenberg, Iowa.   They, too, answered an important transportation need, cutting off many miles of difficult overland travel to reach other ferry landings, but their time of service was shorter-lived with the coming of rail, improved roads and bridges.

The *Belle of Pepin*, Captain P. H. Tuttle in command, ferried freight and passengers between De Soto and Lansing until 1886, when it was moved to the more lucrative Prairie du Chien/McGregor crossing.

At La Crosse – The river ferry business between La Crosse and La Crescent, Minnesota proved successful for many years. Neither location had yet been well established when the first ferryboat was put into service in 1850. William McSpadden (Founder of Houston, Minnesota, 1852) conducted a hostelry, the Black River House, at La Crosse, and began ferrying settlers across the Mississippi with a treadmill vessel powered by a team of blind horses; he christened the boat *Wild Kate*, and it is speculated that one of the horses, perhaps, sported the same name.

A La Crosse syndicate made up of Thomas McRoberts, William McConnell, and John McCann, purchased a Pittsburgh built ferry, the *Honeyeye*, in 1856. The "Micks" had operated their craft only one year when it was cut down by ice flows in the spring of 1857. The *Thomas McRoberts* appeared that fall as its replacement and stayed in successful service until the spring of 1878 when it, too, was lost to the unmerciful ice. Meanwhile, the *Jo Gales* and the *Burlington* were chartered. At one time the town site company that attempted to build a city at La Crescent controlled these boats. Their craftiness did not encourage steamers on the Mississippi to land at the newly developing Minnesota levee, preferring, rather, to earn big profits with their ferryboats, bringing people and goods from La Crosse.

La Crosse witnessed many more ferries coming and going, most of which did a booming business until the wagon bridge was built in 1890.

The eastern end of the Southern Minnesota Railroad ended at a place called Grand Crossing near the mouth of the Root River, downstream and opposite La Crosse. There, a dock and transfer incline permitted rail cars to be loaded onto a ferry and were transported across the river to the railhead in La Crosse. The *McGregor,* owned by Captain Isaac Moulton operated in this trade until quite some time after the railroad bridge was completed in 1876.

At Trempealeau – A few miles upriver from La Crosse, farmers toted their heavy sacks of wheat to Trempealeau, where a treadmill powered ferry that operated for many years took them across the Mississippi River to the La Moille, Minnesota landing. From there, they took their wheat to the nearby Pickwick Mill on Big Trout Creek, to be ground into flour.

At the Chippewa River – Read's Landing occupies a narrow shelf of land sandwiched between high bluffs and the western bank of the Mississippi River. It was the first community to be settled in Minnesota, and although it remains only as a quaint little residential area today, it is truly a significantly historic site. It first achieved importance as a French fur trading post about 1800, and remained so for many years. It was eventually sold to Charles Reed. The settlement attracted more business and grew. By the 1850s it had become a popular and convenient stop for the steamboats bringing supplies by the ton and new settlers by the score to the upper river region. Again, the community turned its attention to the Chippewa River that had once been a busy avenue of the fur trappers, and now was the transportation highway for the rapidly advancing logging industry. Read's Landing became an important staging area for the southbound log rafts, as well as a supply station for the lumbermen of the Chippewa Valley. And for many years the town remained a favorite resort for the lumberjacks – violence and lawlessness on its streets was not uncommon.

The construction of the railroad along the Mississippi drastically reduced the river traffic, and the Chippewa Valley lumber industry eventually played out. Business prospects died and residents moved on to other opportunities. Today, a few of the old structures remain among the more modern residences, and the Wabasha County Historical Society and Museum is permanently housed in the historic school building there.

Opposite Wabasha and Read's Landing on the Minnesota shoreline is the timber rich, vast bottomland of Wisconsin's Chippewa River. Sporadic attempts were made at building a road through the bottoms in the early days, and a cable ferry was chartered and established at Read's Landing. Little business was done during the summertime, but during the winter months, the ferry business boomed. It may seem a bit ludicrous to run a ferry when ice is three feet thick on Lake Pepin, just above, and the entire Chippewa River is covered over with ice just as thick, but because of the rapid flow of water entering from the Chippewa, and perhaps the warmth of the water exiting Lake Pepin, the Mississippi River was rarely closed by ice at Wabasha and Read's Landing. Ferries at both crossings were in operation during the winter for many years, bringing loads of wood and hay over from the bottoms that were almost impassable during the summer.

Captain E. E. Herman's cable ferry at Read's Landing, propelled by the current to move it across the channel, did, however, frequently experience trouble with "slush ice." To combat this problem, he built a vessel that could be considered one of the smallest steamboats on record. *The Joker* was but twenty-five feet long with an eight-foot beam, fitted with propellers at each end. Lashed to the lower side of the re-designed ferry barge, the little steamboat worked perfectly for many years.

Just a mile above Read's Landing, where Lake Pepin ends and the Mississippi reclaims its current, Samuel Shaw ferried for many years with a flatboat that could carry one or two teams. Originally, Samuel used the "armstrong" method for power; the boat was poled upriver the proper distance, and then headed out into the channel. With luck, and providing there was an upstream wind – or no wind at all – the craft would drift down to the proper landing place on the Wisconsin side. Downstream or crosswinds, however, proved hazardous, and the landing point wasn't always the desired one. Shaw later converted his ferry to treadmill power.

The *Belle of Pepin*, piloted by P. H. Tuttle first appeared at Read's Landing and began making its regular five-mile runs to Pepin, Wisconsin in 1877. That trade ended when the Burlington Railroad built through Pepin six years later. Tuttle relocated his steamer to De Soto, Wisconsin.

At Lake City – The *Ethel Howard* was but one of many boats to make the 2½ mile run across Lake Pepin to Stockholm, Wisconsin. Over the years, this trade had been accomplished by large steamers, as well as barges pushed by smaller vessels.

Captain John S. Howard had been operating his new craft only a few weeks when he was called upon for a rescue and recovery mission following the July 13, 1890 killer tornado that struck Lake City, and capsized an excursion boat, the *Sea Wing*, in the middle of Lake Pepin. But the captain hesitated, knowing his small ferryboat was not capable of withstanding heavy seas created by the passing storm, and perhaps wise not to risk another disaster. This was not to the satisfaction of the townspeople, and Captain Howard was forced to defend his boat from would-be mutineers. By the time the lake had calmed enough to suit the little *Ethel Howard*'s safe navigation, half of the *Sea Wing*'s two hundred excursionists had drowned.

At Red Wing – Red Wing, Minnesota was named for a young Indian chief. A trading post was established at "Red Wing's Village" at the head of Lake Pepin, just below the mouth of the Cannon River. Early French explorers and traders viewed the high bluff at Red Wing, and reminded of the thatched barns seen in their homeland, they called it La Grange, which means "the barn." That familiar landmark recognized by all rivermen came to be known as "Barn Bluff."

At a very early time, wheat became an important crop in Southern Minnesota, and a flourmill was built at Red Wing. This port was at one time the largest primary wheat market in the world, Goodhue County being the leading wheat producing county in the state.

The narrowness of the Mississippi at Red Wing was ideal for the successful operation of a cable ferry. The service helped build Red Wing into a popular commercial center for a vast area of Wisconsin, as well as the inhabitants on the western banks. The town became known as "the biggest little manufacturing town in the Northwest," boasting flourmills, shoe factories, large tanneries, linseed oil mill, a furniture factory, and

A view of Barn Bluff from across the river channel. Mississippi River highway bridge is on the right. (Photo by author)

ironworks. Nearby were thick beds of exceptional clay; factories in Red Wing engaged in the manufacture of sewer pipes, bricks, and fine pottery.

Corn eventually replaced wheat as the main crop, and dairy farming led the agricultural interests. Fertile valleys were also discovered to be ideal for raising vegetables, and truck farms soon took their place high in the ranks of the growing Minnesota agricultural industries.

When the steamboat trade declined, primarily with the advent of the railroad, and most of the thriving river towns lost their significance and practically died, Red Wing continued to develop into a manufacturing city, breeding a healthy economy making it a good place in which to live. Citizens proudly called it "The Desirable City."

At Prescott and Hastings – Where the St. Croix River enters the Mississippi from the north, there is a narrow tongue of land between the two rivers. Here was established the town of Point Douglas, named for the statesman who was instrumental in Minnesota becoming a territory. The first post office in what is now the State of Minnesota was established there, even before Point Douglas was a town. Today, Point Douglas is a beautiful county park, with only a population of less than

100 living nearby.

Across the Mississippi River is the city of Hastings, where, in 1855 Alexander Ramsey built the first mill in Minnesota to utilize the roller type machinery for grinding flour. This method was a great improvement over the old millstones, and revolutionized the flour milling business.

It was at the confluence of the two rivers that cable ferries were located across the mouth of the St. Croix River at Prescott, Wisconsin to Point Douglas, Minnesota, and across the Mississippi to Hastings, Minnesota. At Hastings, an unusual bridge eventually replaced the ferryboat service in 1923. In order to reach the low west bank from the much higher east bank without a steep decline, the approach ramp was built in a spiral – a most unique design, indeed.

Old post card view of Spiral Bridge at Hastings, Minnesota. (From private collection)

Captain Daniel Smith Harris commanding the *War Eagle* led the flotilla of seven steamboats carrying more than 1200 passengers up the Mississippi River from Rock Island, Illinois to St. Paul, Minnesota on the grandest excursion of all time. The passengers had arrived at Rock Island on two trains from Chicago.

The Grand Excursion of 1854

The Grand Excursion of 1854 etched a pivotal milestone of great magnitude – a turning point in the development of the "Old Northwest." Although there had been settlements established in the frontier regions of Wisconsin, Minnesota, and Iowa prior to that time, nothing can compare to the influence that this event bestowed upon the pioneer region.

The first railroad to link the Atlantic coast with the Mississippi River reached Rock Island in February 1854. It marked the beginning of commercial travel continuous from the eastern seaboard to St. Paul, Minnesota via rail and steamboat. To celebrate this great milestone, the builders of the Chicago & Rock Island Railroad wanted to introduce a large number of people to this yet unsettled western region, as well as to the new passenger and freight service. They offered a free pleasure excursion from Chicago to St. Paul via the joint efforts of the recently completed railroad to the Mississippi and then by riverboat to St. Paul.

189

Invitations were extended to politicians, newspapermen, artists, businessmen, and prominent community leaders to participate in the excursion to visit the renowned Falls of St. Anthony.

Response from far and wide was overwhelming. Requests for passes were so numerous that the originally planned one train and one river steamer would not be adequate. When all the travelers were assembled at Chicago – to where they had been transported free of charge – two trains of nine coaches each decorated with flowers, flags, and streamers, drawn by powerful locomotives left the station westward bound early on the morning of June 5th.

At frequent stops along the route, they were greeted with speeches, parades, and cannon salutes, and at Sheffield, Illinois, a free lunch awaited the excursionists.

The two trains arrived at Rock Island at 4 P.M. There the Minnesota Packet Company waited with five steamboats for the passengers to board. Leading the fleet was Captain Daniel Smith Harris in command of the *War Eagle*, accompanied by the *Golden Era* (Capt. Hiram Bersie), the *G.W. Spar-Hawk* (Capt. Montreville Green), the *Lady Franklin* (Capt. Le Grand Morehouse), and the *Galena* (Capt. D.B. Morehouse).

With the unexpected number of participants (more than 1,200) two more boats were chartered (the *Jenny Lind* and the *Black Hawk*), and yet a large number of people were returned to Chicago for the lack of adequate accommodations.

Among the participants were former President Millard Fillmore (his term had ended in 1853), former Illinois Governor Ninian Edwards, and future Attorney General Edward Bates. They were in the company of numerous notable eastern businessmen, writers, artists, judges, and professors from Yale, Harvard, and Dartmouth Universities. The press was well represented with reporters sent on the journey from New York, Boston, Albany, Cincinnati, Chicago, and nearly every metropolitan newspaper in the Eastern states.

After the confusion of getting 1,200 passengers situated aboard the fleet of boats, and a speech delivered by Fillmore, the flotilla began its long voyage up the Mississippi in the late night moonlight with a magnificent send-off of music, whistles, bells, and spectacular fireworks.

The splendid June weather was interrupted just after midnight when a violent thunderstorm enshrouded the northbound fleet in impenetrable darkness. Only the sudden flashes of lightning revealed to the passengers brief glimpses of the other boats and vivid views of the forested riverbanks. In a few hours the storm subsided and the travelers were finally able to rest after a long, eventful day.

Because of the number of people aboard the boats, accommodations did not allow everyone a comfortable bed in a stateroom, however. Many of the young men were relegated to mattresses spread out on the main cabin floor that couldn't be put down until after midnight, and had to be taken up before 5 a.m. in order for the stewards to prepare the tables for breakfast. This afforded them little sleep each night, and sleeping during the day was entirely out of the question.

Early the next morning Captain Harris and the *War Eagle* led the procession past Bellevue (Iowa) and steamed up the Fever River where they made their first official visit at Galena, Illinois. There the excursionists were treated to a tour of the lead mines followed with a picnic dinner in the woods, complete with fancy wines from Ohio and France.

Despite heavy rains, a large crowd greeted the boats at Dubuque, where Fillmore and others addressed the onlookers, and then it was off to see more of the wilderness of the sparsely settled Wisconsin and Minnesota.

Frequent landings at the scattered settlements along the river for the boats to "wood up" (load wood fuel for the steam boilers) offered the tourists numerous opportunities to trek ashore and to explore the bluffs that tower in fascinating forms. Cruising up the river they glimpsed real Indian villages and witnessed first-hand the grandeur, the majesty, and the beauty of the west.

Many of the cities we know today did not exist, or were merely a trading post near the river's edge. La Crosse, a city of over 51,000 population today was described as an embryonic village occupying a spot on a wide prairie, marked by Indian trails, here and there plowed patches of the few settlers, occasional oak forests, and inland low bluffs and hills.

For most of the journey, the excursionists enjoyed nearly perfect weather conditions. They were no doubt prepared for much worse with plenty of warm clothing, as Minnesota had already gained a reputation for long, bitterly cold winters. Had the trip occurred a week earlier or later, the participants might have experienced less favorable climes: just prior to the excursion, the Minnesota Territory was bludgeoned with thunderstorms and extremely heavy rains. (This was actually a blessing in disguise, as the rain produced ample runoff that raised the Mississippi water level, greatly improving navigation.) A few days later, Minnesotans suffered through more thunderstorms and extreme heat and humidity. As a Ft. Snelling observer reported on June 15, "The weather is awful hot these days, only good for growing crops and mad dogs."

But instead, the excursionists carried home with them reports of a paradise. Above average rainfall had carpeted the landscape with lush vegetation, and a cool, dry Canadian air mass had provided them the most pleasant temperatures. Anything else might have curtailed the rapid population growth that soon followed.

The responsibility for providing well-prepared meals fell upon the stewards, now called upon to serve quite an array of notable guests. That such elegant meals could be prepared and served in the confines of a steamboat remained a mystery to some, for the fare would have done honor to any first class hotel or restaurant. Meats and vegetables were prepared in one kitchen, while pastries and deserts were made in another. When needed, fish, meat, eggs, and vegetables were obtained at the various settlements along the way. (Two bushels of speckled trout were purchased at Trempealeau – a rare treat for the excursionists.) Supplies of fresh meat (a dozen lambs or pigs) were picked up from time to time. Two cows on the lower deck supplied fresh milk twice a day.

Amusements aboard the boats were plentiful and varied. In addition to the magnificent scenery of the Mississippi Valley and the luxurious dining fare, the passengers aboard the seven boats found other forms of entertainment. Often two or more vessels were lashed together, allowing separated friends to meet, and mingling with new faces. Music and dancing in one cabin lured the lighthearted, while the more intellectual and scientific minded would be attracted to another cabin to listen or participate in discussions or debates on such popular topics as slavery, reciprocity or annexation with regard to Canada, and the impact of the discovery of gold in California. Newspapermen from the east drew highly interested audiences as they expounded on current event subjects with their more complete and up-to-date information like that of the captured slave in Boston who was sent back into slavery, or the rioting of native Americans and Irishmen in Brooklyn. The scientists and University professors present among the group provided special interest with talks about new inventions such as a compact and almost frictionless steam engine, Ralston's portable sawmill, a new patent for making nails, and gas lighting – all of which were on exhibition in New York.

When the Grand Excursion fleet entered Lake Pepin late on Wednesday night, June 7, four of the boats were lashed together. The night was spent in "dancing, music, and flirtations" under a nearly full moon as the boats proceeded upstream.

Rays of the bright June sun glorified the day as the excursion vessels rounded the bend below St. Paul the next day. Two bands on board struck out with lively tunes as the fleet approached the jubilant crowd assembled and waiting on the St. Paul levee. It was excitement like the town had never witnessed.

St. Paul, then, was still a young town – it had existed only six years, but already boasted six thousand inhabitants. As a frontier town, it had advanced quickly – its streets lined with brick dwellings, stone warehouses, a brick capitol with stout, white pillars, a courthouse and jail, several churches, schools, a billiard room and ten-pin alley, dry goods stores, grocers, confectioners and ice creamers, and a numerous array of taverns and saloons. Beyond it lay a boundless, untamed country.

Shortly after arrival, the excursionists were accommodated in every conceivable form of conveyance – from stagecoaches, to lumber wagons, to water carts – and at various rates of speed started on a grand tour of St. Paul, beginning with the Falls of St. Anthony. They visited Lake Calhoun, Minnehaha Falls, and Ft. Snelling. Then in the evening a reception was held at the Capitol, where Territorial Governor Henry Sibley officially welcomed the visitors. As the spokesman for the excursionists, President Fillmore thanked the citizens of St. Paul for their cordial reception.

At eleven o'clock, the tired tourists returned to the landing; the boats lay ready and waiting to begin their journey home.

The people who participated in this "fashionable tour" of 1854 were almost unanimous in their praise for the Upper Mississippi riverboats. And with the number of reporters representing all the major newspapers, the excursion received generous amounts of favorable publicity, for it was, indeed, a brilliant innovation on the part of the railroad and steamboat companies. Millard Fillmore declared it to be one for which "history had no parallel." The *Chicago Tribune* described the journey as "the most magnificent excursion, in every respect, which has ever taken place in America."

When the Milwaukee & La Crosse Railroad was completed to the Mississippi in 1858, a similar excursion party was conveyed to the Falls of St. Anthony aboard the *Northern Belle*, the *War Eagle*, and the *Northern Light*. In the years to follow, individuals, families, and entire organizations embodied the thousands who made pilgrimages to this shining star of the West, and by 1866, at least twenty steamboats ran regular excursions to St. Paul. But probably no other single factor bears the degree of significance in aiding the settlement of the Upper Mississippi River Valley as that of the Grand Excursion of 1854.

Enter: the Railroad

Although much of the vast railroad network that once crisscrossed the country has vanished, it is true that this transportation system provided a tremendous forward advancement in national development. Until the advent of the railroads, the nation's inland commerce moved principally upon canals, lakes and navigable rivers when ice, drought or flood did not interfere. On land, people were dependent upon the stagecoach for long journeys and the Conestoga wagon for freight movement. Travel was slow, and the cost of transporting freight long distances by land was often prohibitive. Where water routes were not readily available, this lack of transportation retarded agricultural and industrial development and confined trade to small areas.

As railroads spread across the nation, distinct changes occurred. Vast new regions opened up to farming, mining, lumbering and manufacturing. In some of the older, already-settled regions, the railroad brought rejuvenation and new, widened outlooks. More and cheaper goods were brought into the towns, and that, in turn, brought more buyers. Industry set new roots as commerce developed and communications speeded up. Agriculture production increased as distance to market was no longer a barrier. Seasonal limitations of handling freight, passengers and mail were greatly diminished.

It should be noted, too, that the railroad became a great industry in itself. The rail companies invested in the communities they passed through by building taxable structures for depots, repair shops and supply stations. And, of course, the construction, maintenance and operation provided a tremendous number of jobs for the local work forces.

Long before Wisconsin attained statehood in 1848, advocates of a canal system linking the Great Lakes to the Mississippi River had their hopes aimed high, in light of the effectiveness that watercraft had proven over the years.

Surveys of the Lower Fox and Rock Rivers were made to ascertain the practicality of constructing a canal system suitable for navigation from Fond du Lac, at the head of Lake Winnebago, to Rock Island on the Mississippi. Thorough study of the planned route between Fond du Lac and Watertown revealed that there would be no great difficulty in connecting those points by a canal that would carry boats drawing seven feet of water, with little comparative cost. Many people were strong in faith that the improvement would be made, and that it would one day do as much business as the Erie Canal, passing through an exceedingly fertile country, connecting the Great Lakes with the Mississippi on the most feasible route. Had this expectation been realized, it would have developed several villages and towns into big cities, providing economic growth otherwise out of reach.

Most of the entire distance would follow the existing river channels and several lakes, although frequent cut offs in the form of independent canals would be required. It was firmly believed that the impending cost was worthwhile, and that the project was not only possible, but also an absolute necessity in the chain of contemplated improvements, and of great national importance.

But spanning the distance with a man-made waterway soon lost the interest of investors, and the failed idea eventually died as the prospect of a more viable railroad link perked their ears. By 1840, more than 2,800 miles of completed railroads were in use, mostly in the eastern states, and the plans for a transcontinental road was nearing reality. The fast growing Wisconsin Territory, with statehood looming on a near horizon, and without a single mile of railroad yet, could not – would not – be left behind in the race into the future.

Businessmen and investors rallied, and the first railroad line was chartered in 1847 as the Milwaukee and Waukesha Railway. The first rail laid by this company was put down in the city of Milwaukee in 1848. At the same time, it was decided to extend the line from Waukesha to Madison, and ultimately to the Mississippi River to terminate at some point in Grant County. A board of directors was elected in May 1849, with Byron Kilbourn chosen as the president of the company. The following year, the name was changed to the Milwaukee and Mississippi River Railway.

An enterprising young pioneer, Anson W. Buttles arrived in Milwaukee with valuable railroad experience. He had gained his education in Pennsylvania and Maryland where he prepared himself for the profession of civil engineering, a lucrative occupation in the days when new territories were still being opened and surveyed. He began work on the Chesapeake and Ohio canal, and was later employed on the Baltimore & Ohio Railroad.

Working as the railway surveyor under the direction of Byron Kilbourn, Buttles laid out the first railroad grade in Wisconsin between Milwaukee and Waukesha (then known as Prairieville). His career continued with Kilbourn in subsequent years when activities were transferred to the Milwaukee & La Crosse Railroad.

From the time the charter was granted in 1847 the officials were busily engaged in locating and financing the project and it was not until February 25, 1851 that the first train rolled over the rails between Milwaukee and Waukesha. The line was then extended in 1852 to Milton Junction, Stoughton, and Madison. Four years later, 1856, the road was in operation as far west as the Mississippi River.

As early as 1843 the subject of a railroad connecting Lake Michigan and the Mississippi River (and more specifically Grant County) had been entertained, to facilitate a means of transit for the vast quantities of lead produced by the mines in the southwestern part of Wisconsin. Galena, Illinois, however, already well into establishing itself as a shipping port, was opposed to the road, worried that the competition would interfere with Galena's trade. As time would prove, though, Galena had little to worry about for years to come.

Two projected routes made Potosi the terminus on the Mississippi, with one passing through Lancaster and Fennimore, and the other via Platteville. The Milwaukee & Waukesha company was authorized to extend its rails to the river, but instead of building on either of the proposed routes through Grant County, the company that had changed its name to Milwaukee & Mississippi followed the Wisconsin River Valley to Prairie du Chien.

Note: Other proposed railroads were to reach Potosi, as well. The Galena & Chicago was to include a branch to Potosi, but it never went into Grant County. A vast system, of which the Illinois Central was a part, was to be extended northward through Potosi. And when it was thought that the Milwaukee & Mississippi would come through Dodgeville, the Potosi & Dodgeville road was chartered. But neither of these railroads ever materialized. It would be nearly thirty years – 1883 – until Potosi heard train whistles. That's when the Chicago, Burlington, & Quincy built its road up the east side of the Mississippi River.

Terminating on the riverbank at Prairie du Chien, the Milwaukee & Mississippi Railroad greatly changed the way of doing business for the settlers of northern Iowa and southern Minnesota, as well as the people on the eastern side of the river in Wisconsin. It opened up new market opportunities for the farmers, but for those in Iowa and Minnesota, the river posed an obstacle.

Now, when there are numerous railroad and highway bridges spanning the Mighty Mississippi, we think little of a time when crossing the river on the winter ice became of great importance. And it was particularly so at McGregor, Iowa, directly across from Prairie du Chien where was located the only reachable railroad in that part of the country. When the word got out that "they are crossing the river on the ice at McGregor," it was the biggest news of the year to the farmers. It meant their best opportunity to reach a market. From the time of the first "thick" ice through December and January there was a rush to get to McGregor and over the river to the railroad with their hogs and wheat. It was the only time hogs could be marketed during the entire year and most of the year's wheat was still on the farms. River navigation had usually closed in the fall before the farmers had been able to haul more than a small percentage of their grain to be shipped south by steamer. Ferryboats ran between McGregor and the Wisconsin side until the ice started to form, and then followed nearly total cessation of business and an anxious wait for the river to freeze. When ice crossing finally was established, Prairie du Chien burst into a furious business stampede. Some Iowa and Minnesota farmers brought their hogs and produce to Lansing, Iowa, then down the 30 miles to Prairie du Chien over the Mississippi ice. Some came 10 miles upriver from Clayton, Iowa. But the greatest bulk of trade came by way of the trails through the hills to McGregor where the loads could be weighed at the city scales.

Only about six weeks of dependable ice could be counted on. Butchering began as soon as word spread through the country that the Mississippi had frozen, and soon trains of wagons loaded with grain or with hogs stacked like cordwood moved along every trail leading to McGregor and Prairie du Chien. Farmers hauled their produce from as far as Albert Lea and Rochester, Minnesota, and from Mason City, Iowa. Taverns and inns along the trails did a booming business, too, during the winter months, providing a place for the teamsters to eat and sleep, and rest their teams on the long, cold journey. By early January the rush was generally at its peak.

A January thaw was the dreaded nemesis of this wintertime business bonanza. Prolonged warmer temperatures meant deteriorating ice, especially at mid-channel where the current was swift. Sleepless nights were many for farmers, buyers and merchants when teams and loads began breaking through the ice, and occasionally some were lost. Attempts would be made to carry the loads across the open water with rowboats, however, that process was slow and impractical and by then, for many, all chances of reaching a market disappeared. Dangerous congestion followed at the McGregor landing: the levee and streets jammed with waiting teams and loads of grain and butchered hogs. All available warehouse space was packed to the rafters. The hogs were the greatest worry. With no place to safely store them, they were stacked by the thousands on the streets and sidewalks and guards placed over them.

The only salvation was a cold snap, but even that did not solve all the problems. Sudden congestion was certain to follow at the Prairie du Chien terminal, and soon the word would come across to McGregor that no more hogs could be accepted, as there were not enough rail cars to load them on. At that point, the bottom dropped out of the market, and the farmers not fortunate enough to have delivered their produce yet were forced to dispose of their loads in any manner they could. This meant tremendous disappointment and devastating losses for many.

A lean period of no shipping always occurred between the ice hauling and the opening of river navigation. The break-up of ice in the river in late March or early April, and the beginning of ferry operation was good reason for celebration, as once again the farmers' produce could be delivered to the railhead at Prairie du Chien. Another grand celebration came with the first southern steamer to touch dock. From that point on, Chicago and Milwaukee no longer held a monopoly on the Iowa, Minnesota, and Wisconsin grain trade.

Leading citizens of La Crosse and other towns across the state became anxious to gain rail communications with the rest of the world. They convinced Milwaukee Road president Byron Kilbourn to come to La Crosse in 1852, and at that time the plan to build the railroad to that city was definitely decided upon. Timothy Burns, S.T. Smith, and B.B. Healey of La Crosse were named commissioners to aid in the completion of this plan.

To the residents of La Crosse, the news of the project was gratifying. With the coming rail connection they began to feel that the day was near when their city would assume a position of importance. By virtue of its location, the completion of the eastern connection would make La Crosse the great commercial distributing point for the Upper Mississippi River Valley. The planned Southern Minnesota railroad project, also masterminded by La Crosse entrepreneurs, now seemed an important one, and the completion of the projected railroads to the north and south would certainly be hastened. It would surely attract the attention of eastern capitalists seeking investments in business and manufacturing to the La Crosse area.

The first public meeting outside the city of La Crosse to promote the building of the railroad from Milwaukee to La Crosse was held at the Village of Beaver Dam in the winter of 1853. It was attended largely by farmers and businessmen from Washington, Ozaukee, and Dodge Counties. Byron Kilbourn starred as the central figure of the group of promoters, and addressed the assembly with his great force of character, resolute will, and giant intellect. The principal subject of his persuasive speech was, of course, raising the money to build the road. Wisconsin was poor, and had not yet gained a financial status among the wealthy

Eastern cities, nor had its name been heard by any of the rich men across the sea. If the railroad were ever built, it had to be done by the local people. As there was no surplus cash in the state, the only way to raise enough money for the project was for the farmers living along the proposed route to mortgage their homesteads and invest the face value in capital stock of the company. These mortgages were to run ten years and to draw interest at the rate of ten percent per annum until paid. This was a poser for the poor man who had come to Wisconsin to make a home for him and his family on government land grants. Kilbourn was ready to convince the farmers that instead of being a hazardous risk, it was really a chance for them to earn big money "as easy as rolling off a greased log." The railroad was to promptly pay the interest each year, and at the end of the ten years when the mortgages came due, the surplus earnings of the road would be sufficient to wipe out the entire debt. The farmers would not only have their mortgages paid off, but would also have their stock in the road, free and clear. All Kilbourn was asking was for the farmers to take the first step, and the railroad company would do the rest.

Kilbourn and his associates in La Crosse did not originate the scheme to raise the money; its design was the invention of Joseph Goodrich of Milton. The plan had worked and helped to build the railroad to Prairie du Chien, and now Kilbourn worked it for all it was worth on the La Crosse line. With the aid of E. D. Clinton, another man possessing a certain rugged eloquence that was taken well among the rural residents, they convinced the farmers to secure the huge mortgages against their land, and the railroad construction commenced.

As with many big business ventures, the railroad companies were not immune to corruption. The State of Wisconsin was still in its infancy, not yet established with any degree of financial power; little means of overland transportation except via the mud roads that were literally impassable in spring and fall; public conveyance was the stagecoach; farmers hauled their surplus produce to distant markets with oxen and wagons, often returning from a week-long trip as poor as when they started; the mail was carried on horseback, and those who could receive letters twice a week were lucky. It is no great wonder that the people were eagerly ready to make almost any sacrifice to attain the benefits the railroad had to offer. In doing so, many fell victim to the corruption ushered in by the coming of the steel rails.

In retrospect, the people of Wisconsin saw and felt the effects of the sensational and disgraceful Milwaukee & La Crosse Railway history with varied perspectives: to the old pioneer who hauled his wheat in a wagon over muddy roads; to the politician who was relegated to private life for having received "a pecuniary compliment" from Byron Kilbourn for his vote in disposing of the famous Land Grant; to the lawyer who was only interested in the legal aspects of the case; and to the former judges of our Supreme Courts, some of whom nearly lost their positions by reason of questions growing out of the railroad agitation.

Unfortunately, the railroad company was bankrupt before the road was one-third finished; by the time most of the mortgages came due, the property had been sold several times over by the United States Marshall, and those now in possession felt no concern for the farm mortgagers. Needless to say, the farmers felt they had been treated fraudulently; foreclosure proceedings went before the Circuit Courts and were eventually handed over to the Supreme Court. Litigations went on for years, but were finally settled in favor of the railroad. All of the farm mortgages were eventually paid, but it cost many of the farmers their homesteads; some moved west, again, to start over and to grow with another new land.

Although this is a disgraceful page in Wisconsin history, the state did benefit tremendously with the building of the railroad that reached La Crosse in October 1858. (By then, the name had evolved to Chicago, Milwaukee & St. Paul) The Milwaukee Road grew and prospered; La Crosse boomed with the added rail service, and it soon became an important commercial hub of the Mississippi River Valley, just as the people had hoped it would.

In time, there would be no less than five railroads entering the city. The CM&St.P was the connection with Chicago, as was the later Chicago, Burlington & Quincy. The Dubuque and the Southern Minnesota divisions of the Milwaukee gave the city a direct outlet through the rich agricultural country of Iowa and Minnesota. The Valley division tapped into the vast hardwood and pinelands of the Wisconsin and Chippewa valleys, making easy access of those resources to the flourishing lumber manufacturers of La Crosse. The Green Bay Railroad brought the city two hundred miles nearer the Atlantic coast markets with its direct connection with Lake Michigan. Direct routes to the west and the Pacific coast were provided by the Burlington Road through its connections with the Great Northern and Northern Pacific at the Twin Cities. The locally owned La Crosse & Southeastern brought the Wisconsin counties of Vernon, Crawford, and Richland into direct communication with the La Crosse commercial center.

An influx of capital and rapid population growth brought about a substantial rise in land values, and certainly influenced the number and quality of improvements made to the city. But this accelerated augmentation was not confined to La Crosse alone; surrounding communities benefited from the effects produced by the added mode of conveyance as well. Much new farmland was developed and people of various professions were attracted to La Crosse and its neighboring communities. Once again, advancement in transportation capabilities proved to be the key factor for progressive development.

But Some Towns Vanished

The concept of railroad development seemed to deliver a certain attitude among the early settlers of young villages and towns in the form of expectations and visions of tremendous economic growth. Populations expanded rapidly where the steel rails were anticipated. Adversely, the census dwindled in many towns when the railroad selected alternate routes, and in some cases the settlements vanished entirely after being bypassed. Although this might be considered overreaction in present times, for the pioneers it was a time when transportation sources were limited, and the land routes were hardly more than dirt paths barely passable during wet seasons, and often bound by snow during winter months. Railroads offered a promise of less restricted connectedness to the marketplace. So it was this attitude that many people believed their community could not survive without the railroad, resulting in entire populations – buildings and all – moving to other towns, sometimes a mere mile or less, to reap the advantages of an advanced transportation system.

Dover

About twenty miles west of Madison, the village of Dover was established in 1844 and rapidly grew to a population of nearly 700. By 1850 Dover boasted a hotel, post office, cooper, blacksmith, shoemaker, wagon shop and several stores. But when the railroad located its depot at nearby Mazomanie and made no stop at Dover, residents there began moving their homes to Mazomanie, and Dover faded into ghost town status. Now, the only visible reminder is a small cemetery at a roadside park.

Newport

The village of Newport once neighbored Kilbourn (now Wisconsin Dells) on the Wisconsin River. Its boom in 1850 was also a result of railroad speculation. A hotel was erected on the site of an old Indian village, and soon, homes, stores and factories sprang to life. In the short period of three years, Newport grew to a population of over 1,500 residents as building lots in this boomtown in the wilderness were sold by the hundreds in New England states. The town expanded on the basis, perhaps, of too much confidence that it occupied the most favorable location for the railroad to cross the Wisconsin River. Railway builders had other ideas, however, and the track bypassed Newport on its course into Kilbourn (Wisconsin Dells). By 1858, residents, storeowners, and factory operators boldly moved their homes and business facilities to Kilbourn, and Newport physically faded away.

Neshonoc

Monroe Palmer, a millwright and speculator, came to LaCrosse county from Vermont in 1851, purchased fifteen acres of land on the La Crosse River and constructed a dam and sturdy grist mill with hand hewed oak timbers. His mill eventually began furnishing large quantities of feed and flour to the many logging camps in the general area. Three years later, he hired a surveyor to plat a village he called "Neshonoc," after the Indian name for the area. The only post office between La

Crosse and Sparta was established there. Mail was carried on foot from La Crosse, but by 1853, a stagecoach delivered it three times a week. Viewed as a location with the advantage of good waterpower created by the dam, the settlement grew with more businesses, churches, a school, and homes. Many people believed that the village was destined for further growth and would become an important commercial center because of this advantage. Neshonoc was considered for the La Crosse County seat, and with the anticipated railroad near in the future, it was expected to become the site for a Milwaukee & La Crosse rail station.

Today, this majestic old mill can still be viewed in its picturesque setting against the tree-covered bluff where State Highway 16 bridges the La Crosse River at the northeastern edge of West Salem, Wisconsin. (Photo by author)

Land donated to the railroad company at the site that is now West Salem became the station site in 1858, however, and because of the dominance of the transportation availability, more people settled at West Salem and more businesses established there. It was only a mile from the thriving village of Neshonoc, but with the lack of direct shipping and transportation facilities, the little village of Neshonoc could not compete with its neighbor. Its residents began moving their homes and businesses nearer the railroad. Palmer finally sold the mill, and it later burned down, but was rebuilt with limestone by its then current owner, Samuel McMillan. By the 1890s Neshonoc had all but disappeared; only the stone gristmill and dam remained.

Dekorra

Seven miles downstream from Portage, the thriving little village of Dekorra once occupied the bank of the Wisconsin River. It was there that the first gristmill of the area was built in 1843. No other mills at the time meant a busy place, as farmers hauled their grain as far as forty miles to be processed there.

Dekorra, named after a Winnebago Indian Chief, was platted in 1837 under the direction of Thompson, Trimble & Morton, and it was they who started the construction of the mill. Others soon followed and the town quickly developed with the addition of two hotels, a post office, blacksmith, general stores, shoe shop, and the barrooms considered necessary for every river town.

Lumber rafting on the Wisconsin River played a large part in making Dekorra the successful place it was. An endless procession of rafts passed by, and the hospitable little milling town became a favorite stop for the rafters. Ox teams hauled a considerable amount of lumber to inland points from the Dekorra landing, and the taverns and barrooms offered a good place for the lumbermen to spend their money before continuing the journey down the river.

The gristmill changed ownership many times over the years, but remained a cornerstone of the community. At peak times, the mill produced as much as 250 barrels of flour per day, and shipped its product by the carload to the logging camps of the northern pineries.

Crossing the river in the early times was by means of a pole ferry. It always proved exciting, and perhaps uncertain, as one could never be exactly sure just where the landing on the opposite shore might be. Eventually, though, a cable ferry was implemented, and a river crossing could be done with a better degree of certainty.

Shortly after the Civil War began, Captain William Ryan organized the Dekorra Home Guard consisting of 100 local men. When the time for the call to duty came, the Guard was not taken as an entire organization, but instead, Capt. Ryan with about half the men joined the Iron Brigade, and the remainder went with various other outfits.

After the war, business revival followed the railroads. Lumber rafting on the Wisconsin diminished. As Dekorra's population gradually slipped away to Portage and Baraboo, the lack of patronage caused the stores and shops to close, one by one. The post office was closed, and the mill stopped its wheels forever. Sadly, Dekorra's dot on the map is only a memory.

Helena

There was a day when the red-shirted raftsmen floated by on their rafts of lumber, and loaded wagons drawn by ox teams rumbled through the streets of a town named Helena just across the Wisconsin River from Spring Green. Not far away was the neighboring community of Wyoming.

The most prominent feature of Helena was the shot tower, and though it did not make Helena, neither did Helena determine the location of the shot tower.

Missouri towers had controlled the entire output of the southwestern Wisconsin mining territory. All the lead was sold at Galena and St. Louis, made into shot, and shipped down the Mississippi to the Gulf, and on to the New York markets. But Green Bay merchant, trader, and riverman, Daniel Whitney saw an opportunity in 1831 for making lead shot, and he had a plan for a cheaper method of reaching the eastern markets. He selected a high bluff along the Wisconsin River to build the tower. The location was in near proximity of the mining district, and the river afforded a natural shipping avenue.

In his employ at his trading establishment at the portage of the Wisconsin and Fox Rivers was John Metcalf, who had previous experience in the Missouri shot towers. He would be put in charge of building and running Whitney's facility.

The small village of Helena already existed near the site when work on the tower began. General Dodge had laid it out, and its location on the river was expected to rival Galena. But so far, after three years, Helena consisted of only a few log huts, a tavern, and a blockhouse – one of the forts ordered by Gen. Dodge to protect the people in case of Indian trouble.

Before the tower was completed, the Black Hawk War in 1832 all but wiped out the town. Military troops demolished the houses, using the timbers to make rafts on which they pursued the fleeing Indian tribe.

The blockhouse was the only structure left.

After the war, work continued. Although the original Helena residents had left, Whitney established a store and a house to accommodate his men, and in 1833 the tower was completed and in running order with six men employed. Not much shot was produced at first. Lead was hauled from Galena, and the finished shot was hauled back to Galena, primarily in exchange for supplies.

In a year's time, the town, once again, showed considerable growth – a new store, cooper shop, blacksmith shop, barracks for the men and a warehouse. Then in 1836, the tower was sold to a Buffalo, N.Y. concern, though Daniel Whitney stayed on as a part of the company. The name was changed from the Wisconsin Shot Company to the Wisconsin Mineral and Transportation Company. Within a couple more years, Helena was a thriving town.

Alva Culver had previously worked as a carpenter on the company buildings. He rafted timber down the Wisconsin from the northern pineries to Helena and built the warehouse. Then in 1839, he returned and built his own hotel. It was the first and largest in Helena – two stories with fourteen large bedrooms, a friendly fireplace in the parlor, and a ballroom that served as a public meeting place, and host to all kinds of entertainment.

Mr. Culver built two steamboats for the Wisconsin River trade – the *Lady Catharine* that he piloted between Helena and Portage, and another small boat that he ran between Helena and Prairie du Chien. He also operated the ferry at Helena for a number of years. That ferry ran under several different owners until 1887 when the Wisconsin River was finally bridged.

By the late 1840s, the population was again growing – settlers were attracted to the valley because of the expected development of navigation on the Wisconsin River. Some of the newcomers settled at nearby Wyoming, and it too soon became a bustling community with saw mill, stores, school, lumber yard, and a post office established in 1848.

Helena Shot Tower at Tower Hill State Park. A 120-foot vertical shaft was dug through sandstone, and accessed through a horizontal tunnel cut into the bluff from the riverbank. A 60-foot tower was then constructed over the shaft to create a total height of 180 feet. Molten lead was poured from the top of the tower through a ladle with holes in the lid, and as the droplets fell down the shaft, they cooled and solidified, and collected in a pool of water at the bottom. The shot was then hauled through the tunnel to the finishing house where it was sorted, bagged, and loaded onto barges to be transported to eastern markets. The current tower and smelting house at the top are close replications of the originals. (Photo courtesy of the Wisconsin Department of Natural Resources.)

But river transportation was greatly retarded by low water and rapids, and the Portage canal had not yet materialized, rendering the water route impractical. Hence, a quite profitable business developed in the form of overland transportation. Farmers and teamsters hauled their produce from the Helena area to Dodgeville and Mineral Point, returned with lead for the shot tower, and many engaged in hauling the shot from Helena to Milwaukee, returning with supplies.

The shot tower business had been sold in 1847 to Washburn and Woodman, a Mineral Point law and real estate firm. They operated the tower for about two years, and apparently abandoned the project. Then, in 1853 John Bradford came in from Illinois and took over. About the same time, an entire colony of emigrants had arrived from Prince Edward's Island, considerably increasing the size of the village. Both

Helena and the shot tower business boomed.

These were probably the most prosperous years for Helena; the shot business was good, and that brought in a lot of business to the hotels and stores. But the railroad from Milwaukee steadily pushed westward on its path toward Prairie du Chien and the Mississippi River. When it crossed the Wisconsin and passed through Spring Green, as would be the similar history of many small towns, the people of Helena and Wyoming firmly believed that the railroad was the only way of the future, and by 1861, the beginning of the Civil War, operations at the shot tower had been suspended – nearly all its machinery was sold to a party erecting a tower in Chicago. Stores, hotels, and homes were moved, and some simply torn down. The shot tower warehouse was torn down, and its lumber used to construct the town hall at Arena. The stone was used to build a smokehouse.

Helena had been revived once after its near total destruction during the Black Hawk War. But this time, nothing would ever bring it back. From rise to fall, it lasted only 30 years, but what grand years they were!

Abandoned RR depot at Avoca, Wisconsin. This station was a result of alternate railroad routing that bypassed Helena. (Photo by author)

Lumber Ghost Towns

Many towns in the northern frontier were created and evolved as a result of the lumber industry. And just as their counterparts father south that depended on mining, a good number of these settlements did not survive when the industries and transportation sources changed. Unfortunately, the Upper Midwest cannot boast spectacular, almost intact ghost towns like those of the gold and silver mining era of the West. In most cases, the decline of the northern lumber towns was gradual; houses, mills, and stores were torn down or relocated in another community, and the land put to other uses. In these places where people once lived and anticipated a prosperous future, the villages are forgotten, and rarely a trace of their earlier prosperity can be seen.

Paper towns – towns that were planned by overoptimistic speculators and given names – were created by the dozens, but failed to attract settlers, thus, they never existed as anything much more than a name on the map.

Twin villages about ten miles above Taylors Falls – Amador on the Minnesota side of the St. Croix River, and Sebatana on the Wisconsin bank – were planned around a flourishing sawmill, and were to be connected by a ferry service across the river. When the settlements did not flourish, the speculators moved away and the towns simply vanished.

Neshodana emerged on the Yellow River in Burnett County, Wisconsin as another town projected around a sawmill built by a Milwaukee speculator. But with no growth, by 1868, nothing remained.

Fortuna, a village expected to show great promise, seemed to meet a similar fate. Located just west of the St. Croix River, where the military road from Point Douglas to Lake Superior crossed the Kettle River, it was thought to have good waterpower, and would prove to be a great lumber depot. Although Fortuna was named temporary county seat of Buchanan County (That county was dissolved in 1862 and is now the northern portion of Minnesota's Pine County.) and the name appeared on state maps until 1881, the town barely existed, and its exact location is still questioned.

The village of Vasa could be considered more than just a paper town. It did disappear, but for a while it seemed that this settlement on the west bank of the St. Croix would develop into a successful city.

Francis Register, a clerk for Judd, Walker and Company, a lumber company in Marine Mills, turned his interest to become a land agent. He made arrangements for a tract of some 300 acres of land adjacent to the St. Croix River just north of Marine that included about two miles of waterfront. He had the land surveyed and laid out streets, and in an attempt to attract Scandinavian emigrants, he named his town Vasa, in honor of the Swedish king. The land was put on the market in December 1856, and when the post office was established the following February, sixty-one building lots had been sold – not a bad start considering it was the middle of winter.

Publicity and advertising in newspapers spoke highly of a good steamboat landing, a steam-powered sawmill, a large three-story hotel, flourishing stores, and a number of substantial houses. The town was predicted "a growing prosperity and first class position among western towns." The *St. Paul Pioneer and Democrat* was so impressed with Vasa that it urged immigrants to look first at this new settlement.

But Vasa fell victim to the panic of 1857 and the following depression years. First the sawmill failed after a partner absconded with what little money was left. Then in 1859 the town's name was changed to Otis (after the original land owner) because it was discovered that another Vasa had already been established in Goodhue County. The final blow came in 1860 when the post office was closed. Vasa reverted back to wheat fields, and its proprietor, Register, still deeply in debt, returned to Philadelphia where he became a prominent lawyer. To what was left, the name Copas – after the family name of an early storekeeper, John Copas – was given to the settlement. It remains today.

Chengwatana (in the Chippewa tongue means "pine village") at the mouth of Cross Lake, were the Snake River starts its final run east to the St. Croix, had been an Indian village and fur trading post for many years. Lumbermen became interested in the Snake River area in the 1840s, and by 1849, Elam Greeley had constructed a dam. The settlement soon consisted of several log houses and a hotel. Judd, Walker and Company of Marine recognized the timber value of the area, and joined Greeley to build a sawmill below his dam. They platted a village and called it Alhambra, which had become a stopping place on the military road being built to Lake Superior. But the village of Alhambra must not have been profitable, for the same Marine company and a group of St. Paul speculators resurveyed the settlement in the late 1850s, and returned the village its original name of Chengwatana. Attempts were made to settle groups of Belgian and German emigrants there, but the population never exceeded a hundred people.

For about a decade, Chengwatana, as small as it was, was the largest valley settlement north of Taylors Falls, and for all practical purposes, it had the potential to develop into a prosperous lumber town. But the town proprietors made the fatal mistake of trying to dictate to a railroad. Soon, tracks were being laid along Cross Lake opposite Chengwatana and toward the new town of Pine City. "Chengwatana should have had the railroad depot," journalist John Trowbridge wrote in the *Atlantic Monthly* magazine, "but it made the common mistake of setting too high a price on what it deemed indispensable to the [railroad] company, which, accordingly, stuck to its own land, and put the track on the other side of the lake... It is the railroad that makes towns," the author concluded, "not towns that make the railroad."

Pine City flourished with steam sawmill, shingle mill, stave factory, hotels, stores, and a school. Three or four hundred loggers arrived every spring with the log drives down the Snake River, and Pine City reaped the benefits. Chengwatana with its ninety-odd residents, its few wooden houses and huts, and a small waterpower sawmill was definitely on a decline. The clincher came with the 1872 election when the Pine County seat was removed from Chengwatana to Pine City. The village that had existed since before the white man arrived, withered and died, and was lost in oblivion. Not a single original building remains.

Sunrise City was also on the government road heading north from Taylors Falls. By 1856, this settlement, situated on the Sunrise River a short distance from its confluence with the St. Croix, had a busy sawmill and was home to some fifteen families. It grew slowly until 1869 when it reached its peak population of 300. By then it had a school, and its business district had grown to include two gristmills, four hotels, two stores, and one saloon, in addition to the original sawmill. Part of its early success was due to the regional land office located there for the public sale of acreage in the St. Croix Valley. The land office, though, was moved to Taylors Falls in 1868, and the following year the railroad missed Sunrise City by ten miles, passing through North Branch instead. When the trains started running between St. Paul and Duluth, traffic on the government road almost ended entirely, and Sunrise City's gradual decline began. Despite occasional attempts to restore the town's economic vitality, like John S. Van Rensselaer's unsuccessful cheese factory in 1874, hopes for the forgotten village faded, and in time, "City" was officially dropped from its name. Sunrise experienced a temporary boom shortly after the turn of the century when another railroad – the Arrow Line – projected its road linking the Twin Cities with Superior, and began grading and laying track nearby. But the railroad never matured, and Sunrise, once again, sank into the sunset.

Franconia, a few miles south of Taylors Falls, was another lively river town that the railroad bypassed. But that was not the only reason the town was reduced to a handful of houses and summer cottages, corn and potato fields. This was a milling town that depended on its lumbering interests, and on the river for transport of wheat and wood to downriver markets. While uninhibited navigation availed, Franconia remained a busy place. But then the St. Croix Boom Company gained its powerful control of the river during the 1880s, and put forth little effort to maintain an open channel for steamboat navigation. With supply lines and market transportation choked off, the lumber and flour milling towns above Stillwater were left to a slow death.

Franconia was not a large city, but its streets were lined with homes, stores, hotels, factories, saloons, and the beautiful four-story stone flourmill built in 1864 by Luxembourg immigrant Paul Munch. At the riverbank stood the sawmill and shipbuilding yards where, in the 1860s, many lumber and grain barges were built, as well as three sizable paddle wheel steamboats. One of those boats, the 130-foot *Viola*, played a small but important role in the St. Croix transportation saga.

Optimistically, everyone expected a great future for Franconia. Struggling for more than a decade with the impaired river transport, however, and compounded by lack of rail service, Franconia announced in the August 1, 1896 *Polk County Press* that it was about to sell its jail and other property and go out of business. A nearly completely abandoned village lay at the river's edge in 1899. Just as transportation had brought the town to life, the lack of it brought on its downfall.

On opposite banks of the St. Croix at its confluence with the Mississippi – Point Douglas on the west bank, and Prescott's Landing in Wisconsin, these two towns had their start during the earliest years of the Minnesota Territory development, and rivaled for about a decade until Prescott, the village with the more advantageous location won the competition for survival.

Point Douglas, though, was the early favorite. When Prescott's Landing was nothing more than a trading post in the 1840s, Point Douglas boasted the best general store in the region. It had a post office, and it became a regular stopping port for steamboats to obtain cordwood fuel, and to transfer passengers and freight bound for points up the St. Croix Valley. The Minnesota Packet Company, with semiweekly service from Galena, Illinois, stationed a full-time agent at Point Douglas, as the town was predicted to be "among the most prominent settlements of the Territory." (*Minnesota Chronicle and Register* of St. Paul, 1850)

Point Douglas reached its peak four years later with two stores, two hotels, a school, a sawmill, and about twenty homes. But Prescott was not just sitting idly by. The town was platted in 1853, and with the development of an improved levee that created an excellent steamboat landing and adequate warehouse facilities, Prescott, Wisconsin soon became the favorite port of call for the Mississippi River packets. St. Croix boats, then, picked up northbound passengers and freight at Prescott, and eventually bypassed Point Douglas.

Overshadowed by the rapidly growing nearby Hastings on the Mississippi, Point Douglas slowly faded away. Railroads and highways played havoc with the limited usable land space on the narrow strip of land between the two rivers (Mississippi and St. Croix) where the village lay. Today it is difficult to tell just where the town was, and it is hard to imagine that on this point there once stood a flourishing sawmill and a busy steamboat landing.

For a settlement to survive in those pioneer days, it needed the combination of the right location, good leadership, money, and adequate transportation was a vital element required to allow the town to advance and prosper. In the St. Croix Valley, Stillwater is fortunate to occupy a site selected by four ambitious young men, with the hope that they could build and operate a successful sawmill there. As it turned out, this site was unequalled anywhere else along the river. John McKusick, Elam Greeley, Elias McKean, and Calvin Leach, came in 1843, organized the Stillwater Lumber Company, and completed the first commercial sawmill to produce the first lumber in Minnesota, thus giving the St. Croix Valley its initial boost toward the great lumber boom era. Although all four men played important roles, John McKusick is credited with naming the village after his hometown of Stillwater near Bangor, Maine.

Stillwater became known as the "Birthplace of Minnesota." Sixty-one delegates met in August 1848 at McKusick's boarding house on Main Street, now the Chamber office. They drew up a petition requesting the U.S. Congress to recognize the new Territory of Minnesota. Because of their initiative, the Minnesota Territory was established in March 1849. Statehood came nine years later.

While in its infancy, Stillwater attracted more wealthy lumbermen, and within a short time, the town had become a leading market center. Its excellent riverboat landing (actually created by a landslide after heavy rains) and strategic location made it the perfect supply depot for the entire St. Croix lumbering region.

As the lumber industry diminished, and was eventually gone from the valley, Stillwater remained, even though it was feared to become just another fading boomtown. Today it is a lively community with a wide variety of business. And one can still walk down the historic, picturesque Main Street and catch a glimpse of an era gone by.

Iron Mining Towns

The state of Wisconsin, in the very early years, held mining interests other than the lead region of the Southwest. In the far north, the Gogebic, Menominee, and Penokee Iron Ranges have produced millions of tons of iron ore. "Red Gold" drew immigrants here to mine the ore needed to satisfy the demands of a growing industrial nation, populating new towns where dense forest and wilderness had once been. Transportation systems like the Milwaukee, Lake Shore, & Western Railway were created to answer the transit needs of the new northern industry.

Although most iron mining in Wisconsin had ceased by the 1960s, the world's industrial revolution benefited significantly from the tremendous contributions of the Wisconsin iron mines, and the industry occupies an important chapter in Wisconsin history. Most noted ranges lie in the far northern part of the state, and extend into the Upper Michigan Peninsula to the east, and into Minnesota to the west. They were discovered by strange variations in magnetic compass readings during geological surveys, and confirmed by visual sightings of the distinctive ore on the surface. Much of the iron ore of these ranges lay close to the earth's surface and forming hills and mountains, making it relatively easy and inexpensive to mine.

Iron ore deposits were discovered and mined as far south as Sauk County, as evidenced in the stories of Ironton and La Rue. Like many towns that were nurtured to life and prospered around mills or mines, Ironton in western Sauk County rose to become an industrial center in the wilderness because of the spirit and efforts of James Towers, an ironmaster from Crown Point, N.Y. He first came to Mayville in eastern Dodge County in 1850 and began the manufacture of iron products. Thoroughly familiar with the entire iron business as it was developed by that time, Towers was seeking an opportunity for business on a larger scale.

He heard the rumors of unlimited iron deposits in the hills of the Baraboo Valley, so he began exploration of the area, and in the rugged bluffs overlooking a beautiful valley near the site that would become Ironton, Towers found the opportunity he was seeking. His trained eye detected the rich mineral deposits in the rock outcroppings and in the soil, and he imagined a prosperous manufacturing city in the valley below him, bustling with the families of the men who would work for him in his blast furnaces and factories.

After purchasing the property, he returned to the East to make arrangements for developing his project in the wilderness. He convinced many of his former employees – mostly Irishmen – to move with him to Wisconsin, and to become the vanguard of settlement in the valley of the Little Baraboo River.

The new town suffered its share of hardships while log houses were erected for the families along the river. Then it was a matter of constructing the blast furnace, iron mill and foundry, while preliminary development of the mine was under way. Machinery for the entire operation was shipped to Portage by rail, and then hauled by ox teams and wagons to the new town site, a long, slow, and laborious task.

Four years later, Ironton's furnaces and foundries were hard at work. Charcoal burners were busy night and day converting the hardwood trees into high quality smelting fuel. Ore from the mine on a hillside two miles away was transported to the mill by cumbersome ox carts, where it was smelted and cast into pigs or saleable merchandise items, and then hauled to the nearest markets 20 or 30 miles away.

The superior quality pig iron from the Ironton foundries always found a ready market at Milwaukee, Chicago, Rockford, and other manufacturing cities for the best prices. Prosperity was at its peak as the output yielded a profitable income.

James Towers did not live to see the greatest success of the business, nor the tragic decline that came as the ore bed began to run out. The property changed ownership several times, and each owner, expanding the scope of the plant, realized a profitable success. But the advance in timber value and a corresponding increase in the cost of producing charcoal, and the plummeting price of pig iron that came in 1890, made the manufacture of iron at a furnace lacking all the modern facilities highly unprofitable.

When James Towers located his mine, he had not discovered an inexhaustible "drift," but rather a deposit of unusual high quality ore of limited quantity. By 1895 the supply was depleted and the company was dissolved. Iron works gave way to agriculture and dairying, and the great gash in the hillside that was once a mine was soon overgrown in brush.

Ironton still remains, although it is no longer the great steel town in the woods.

You won't find La Rue on any current Wisconsin road map, although if you ride the vintage steam-powered train from the Mid-Continent Railway Museum at North Freedom, Wisconsin, you will pass, and perhaps stop briefly for a glimpse of what remains of the town. (Photo by author)

La Rue didn't emerge as an actual town until 1903, and its short life ended in 1914. Mining of a low-grade iron ore used for paint pigment had begun near there in the 1880s, and the Douglas Iron Mining Company was actively probing for higher grade ore, but with little success.

Then in 1900, W.G. La Rue arrived, bringing with him the diamond drills, and plenty of experience gained in the Minnesota iron ranges. He and his partners incorporated the Sauk County Land & Mining Co. in 1902, and within a short time they had brought up samples of 53 percent iron from several hundred feet below the surface. They leased the land to the Deering-Harvester Co., and by 1903 the mining boom was under way.

This new beginning of successful iron ore production meant business for the railroad, prompting the Chicago & North Western Railway to extend a spur line three and a half miles south to the mine from the main line at North Freedom. Tons of the red rock were loaded into the wooden ore cars and carried away to blast furnaces in Chicago.

The operation seemed to be a sure bet, so by the end of that year, La Rue and his partners incorporated the La Rue Townsite Company. Hotels and a row of company-built cottages soon provided housing for the Norwegian, Swedish, and Finnish miners. Saloons, stores, and a church were established on streets named Iowa, Illinois, Wisconsin, Indiana, and Deering Avenue. A busy little town, La Rue was on the map.

The ore was rich, but as the mines probed deeper, in time another problem became insurmountable. Water filled the mineshafts faster than pumps could take it out. Eventually, the cost was too high to compete with the Minnesota iron ranges, and the operation was simply shut down in 1914.

The miners left to seek work elsewhere, and with no population, businesses closed. Buildings fell into ruin, and La Rue quickly became a ghost town.

When the need arose for an extremely hard quartzite rock in 1917, work trains once again made the rusty rails of the Quartzite spur to La Rue creak and groan. A mile farther south from the remains of the abandoned town lay a vast deposit of quartzite at a place called Rattlesnake Den, and once again the tracks were extended and quarry operations began that continued another 44 years, but the town was never revived. The Harbison-Walker Co., owners of the operation, shipped the material via the Chicago & North Western to plants in Ohio for blast furnace lining and the making of firebrick. But as the steel production process changed, the demand for the quartzite rock diminished, and in 1962 the Baraboo range was again abandoned.

Today, the Mid-Continent Railway Museum, located at North Freedom, Wisconsin maintains the Quartzite spur line and operates vintage steam-powered trains to the mining site as tourist excursions. Adjacent to the authentic 1890s depot that houses railroad memorabilia and gift shop, one can view a host of steam locomotives and cars from the Golden Age of railroading.

Mid-Continent Railway Museum Depot at North Freedom, Wisconsin where many restored vintage railroad cars and locomotives are on display. (Photo by author)

Southern Minnesota Railroad

The pioneer businessmen of La Crosse, possessed with visions, civic ambitions, and adequate abilities to carry out their plans, took a leading and exceedingly active part in building the Chicago, Milwaukee and St. Paul to this point, thus giving the struggling little lumber town the opportunity it had craved since Nathan Myrick erected his trading post on this all but vacant river bank prairie. Construction of this first line of railroad to La Crosse and the subsequent building of the Southern Minnesota Railroad, also planned and fostered by local citizens, combined to establish one of the most important railroad centers in the Middle West.

The old newspapers indicate that building a railroad across southern Minnesota with its eastern origin at La Crosse would be an important factor to further develop a healthier economic climate in that town. It meant a solid connection with a growing new area of settlement west of the Mississippi River where a budding agricultural industry showed great promise, arising the need of commercial transportation – for produce to markets as well as incoming supplies to support merchants, mills, and manufacturers.

Settlers in the Root River Valley depended on that waterway as a primary transportation artery, as canoes, flatboats, and keelboats served them better than the marshy overland trails from the Mississippi. The heavier cargo transported up the Root River, however, was slow and labor-intense, and in 1855 the Root River Steamboat Company was organized in Houston, Minnesota. The vessels constructed for use on the Root had to be small, as the river was not adequate to accommodate the larger Mississippi packets, but even with their small size they provided faster and easier transportation of freight and passengers. The first steamer was put into service in 1857.

Edward Thompson had first come to the Root River Valley from Illinois in the fall of 1850. He journeyed by stagecoach to Galena, steamboat to McGregor, Iowa, and then by team by way of Decorah over the hills to the mouth of the South Fork of the Root River. There he built a canoe and paddled his way toward the Mississippi where he engaged the season's last steamer back to Illinois. He must have liked the country he saw on that first exploring visit as he returned the very next spring to the mouth of the South Fork, built another canoe, and once again set out on the Root River in search of a new home. Eventually, he discovered the possibility of a good waterpower source where another stream emptied into the Root – Thompson Creek, the site that is now Hokah, Minnesota. There he settled, built a log cabin, a dam and a mill, and the village of Hokah was born. Although it was not constituted as an independent village until 1871, a post office was established there in 1850, and by 1855 it had a school, churches, and a volunteer fire department.

A few years later, the population had grown and more settlements had been established along the Root River. Although the river was not ideal for navigation, the lack of better transportation had spurred some successful attempts. Edward Thompson and his brother, Clark, commenced the construction of a sidewheel Root River packet at Hokah, and launched it at the mouth of Thompson Creek, but it sat idle, lacking engines and machinery. In late fall, 1857, the *Key City* and the *Ben Coursin*, two Mississippi steamers collided near Dresbach, Minnesota. The *Ben Coursin* sank. Its wreckage was purchased for $300 and salvage operations went on all that winter to retrieve the engines and boilers. They were hauled to Hokah on sleds and installed in Thompson's new boat.

By spring, the vessel had been christened the *Wenona,* and it began its work on the Root River. One account claims that Rushford was the destination of its first trip, while another states its maiden voyage, piloted by C. Martin, was to Stewart's Mill at Cushon's Peak (now Money Creek) for a cargo of black walnut lumber destined for Winona, Minnesota. Whichever destination is correct, the Root River presented numerous navigational hazards, as it had not yet been "improved" for use by the larger craft. The *Wenona* encountered sandbars, snags, ticklish maneuvering around sharp bends, and suffered considerable damage by overhanging tree limbs. But the trip was deemed a success, and the *Wenona* continued, with regular service between La Crosse and Hokah.

About that same time, the Douglas Brothers of Melrose, Wisconsin were determined to prove that the Black River northward from La Crosse was navigable, and had a small steamer constructed for that purpose by a prominent boat builder in La Crosse. The *Little Frank* made one trip to Black River Falls in June of 1858, but heavy use of that river for log driving made steamboat navigation impractical. The craft was later transferred to the Root River, where, with the steamer *Wenona* made its first trip upriver as far as Rushford, and continued to make regular runs between La Crosse and Hokah.

More vessels were constructed at Houston: the *Itasca* that was accidentally sunk at La Crosse due to carelessness on the part of the captain and crew. The craft was recovered by new owners, and served on the Mississippi transporting troops and supplies during the Civil War. The *Express*, a small sternwheeler, made regular runs to La Crosse, but it too sank near the La Crosse harbor, was re-floated and later sold to G.W. Winslow who ran it on the Black River. Competition from the developing railroad finally brought an end to the short-lived glory of the little steamboats on the Root River.

The Southern Minnesota Railroad, masterminded by T.B. Stoddard of La Crosse, was planned to begin with an interstate bridge across the Mississippi at La Crosse, traverse the southern tier of Minnesota counties, and continue on to the Rocky Mountains, and eventually to the Pacific Ocean, thereby making La Crosse the eastern terminus of this great railroad. Stoddard began securing land for this project as early as 1852, and in 1855 formed a company in Hokah, Minnesota to build the road. It would be known as the Root River Valley and Southern Minnesota Railroad. The Minnesota Territory granted a charter, but it expressly stated that Hokah was to be the eastern terminus. This did not prevent Stoddard from continuing his elaborate plans; a channel of the Root River would be improved from Hokah to the Mississippi River, adequate to accommodate any steamboat plying the upper Mississippi, thus completing the continuity of the transportation system.

The concept of a railroad passing through the southern counties of the Minnesota Territory, linking the new frontier with eastern industry and markets, was received with great anticipation. However, national financial difficulties plagued the company; very little grading had been done on the roadbed by 1858 – the year Minnesota gained statehood – and by the time Civil War bullets were flying in the South in 1861, no railroad tracks had been completed in Minnesota.

Although they had failed to meet their obligations to Minnesota, a new charter was issued in 1864 as the result of reorganization of the bankrupt company. T. B. Stoddard of La Crosse was elected president of the Southern Minnesota Railroad Company, and its board of directors successfully lobbied the state legislature for the franchises and lands of the old company.

Again, congress issued additional land grants to help finance the road with the stipulation that completion of ten miles of operational railroad was required within one year.

Grand Crossing, opposite La Crosse on the west bank of the Mississippi and just south of present-day La Crescent, Minnesota, had become the eastern terminal of the Southern Minnesota Railroad. Construction began westward from there in 1865, but because of so much trestlework required due to the marshy bottomland along the Root River, progress was slow. Once again the company failed to complete the required ten miles, however, the legislature saw fit to grant an extension of another year.

Hokah, Minnesota, a small but thriving village of 300 people five miles west from Grand Crossing was chosen for the Southern Minnesota Railroad's foundry and machine shops. Hokah already was a busy place with several stores and shops, and three hotels, and now was added the distinction of a major railroad operation. Over the next few years, more than 300 railroad cars including elegant passenger coaches were built there. (In 1872, though, these shops were moved to Wells, Minnesota.)

When construction of the road had reached Hokah, a number of platform cars and locomotives were ferried across the Mississippi; the use of a construction train accelerated the progress, and in January 1866, locomotive whistles sounded in Houston, eighteen miles west of the Mississippi. By January of 1867 trains began arriving regularly at Rushford, thirty miles beyond Grand Crossing. Rushford remained the western terminus for nearly two years, and then in 1868 the village of Lanesboro began enjoying the benefits of rail service. Within four more years, the road was complete to Winnebago City, a total distance of 167 miles.

Over the years of development, the Southern Minnesota suffered its share of troubles and setbacks. Even after the road was operational, expansion efforts were plagued with problems.

The town of Chatfield voted bonds of $65,000 to finance a branch of road from Fountain to Chatfield. Work began in 1870 to excavate the deep cuts required, and when $70,000 had been expended and the project still far from completion, it was abandoned, reportedly due to the extreme expense involved.

After the railroad was completed across Fillmore County, extensive litigations ensued, resulting once again in reorganization under Minnesota law in 1876. During the following year the Southern Minnesota Railway and Southern Minnesota Railway Extension Companies were formed. By 1880 they had deeded the entire line from the Mississippi River to Sioux Falls (including a branch from Wells to Mankato) to the Milwaukee & St. Paul Railroad Company.

The people of Caledonia, Minnesota must have been aware of the difficulties they would face, but in 1873, determined to combat their handicap of no railroad, they organized the Caledonia & Mississippi Railroad Company, procured a right of way to the Mississippi and did some grading. But no substantial progress was achieved, though, until the Chicago, Clinton, Dubuque & Minnesota Railroad Company conceived the idea of building a road westward from their line along the Mississippi through Caledonia. Their offer to complete the road, including equipment for operation, received vigorous response, and the old company reorganized as the Caledonia, Mississippi & Western. Purchase of right of way was extended and surveying began.

Originally, the planned route passed through the towns of Canton and Harmony, and then to the south of Preston. However, because of the initial lack of financial cooperation from Canton and Harmony, and after much bitter argument and persuasion, those commitments were fulfilled and Preston was assured of becoming the western terminus of the branch.

Once started, construction of the narrow gauge road from Reno, on the Mississippi, to Preston did not take long; grading began in June of 1879, and in late September the first train chugged into Caledonia. The construction gang was within sight of Preston by Christmas Day. But extreme frigid temperatures suspended their work, and on December 26, 1879, the work train pulled into Preston. Passenger trains began running on a regular schedule in January 1880.

That spring, the Chicago & Northwestern Railroad Company

examined this stretch of road with great interest. Their intension was to purchase the line and extend the tracks to Chatfield. But when the Chicago, Milwaukee & St. Paul company got wind of their competitor trying to move in on their territory, they immediately struck a deal with the eastern stockholders and bought the Reno-Preston route.

This line retained its narrow gauge tracks until 1901. That meant a great deal of delay-making inconvenience and quite often, poor service, as all freight arriving at Reno bound for the Caledonia and Preston stations required unloading and transfer at Reno.

A bill was introduced in the Minnesota legislature authorizing the railroad and warehouse commission to order the gauge broadened. People living in the towns along the line agreed and supported the bill. Eventually, the company had no choice but to comply. Work commenced in the summer of 1901 and the first standard gauge train consisting of an engine, a combination mail, baggage and smoking car, a day coach and the superintendent's private car occupied by several company officials, arrived at Preston on November 11, 1901.

Several settlements along that pioneer stretch of the Southern Minnesota Railroad "boomed" with the arrival of the steel rails, and some were created during or after the railroad construction. Each one grew to significance as a commercial center for its surrounding agricultural community. By the 1860s, wheat farming was the leading industry, which had led to the establishment of many flour-milling operations throughout the Root River Valley. And in many of the small but expanding towns there was located a wagon builder to answer the farmers' needs. Each had the usual general commodity merchants for groceries, hardware, farm supplies and domestic goods, and some gained the one important service that had been lacking – a post office.

Houston, Minnesota, located approximately twenty miles up the Root River Valley from the Mississippi, is a prime example of an entire settlement re-locating as the result of railroad influence.

William McSpadden settled with his family there in 1852, and soon more settlers followed. McSpadden named the settlement Houston after the famous general under whom he had served in the Mexican War. By 1854 there were stores and a school among about 40 buildings. Smaller steamboats began making their way from the Mississippi up the Root

River to Houston and beyond with regularity, bringing freight and more emigrant settlers.

When the Southern Minnesota Railroad arrived in 1866, an area resident, Mons Anderson donated land to be used by the railroad for the location of a station depot. But this land lay about a mile to the west of the little settlement of Houston. Within a short time, the post office building was moved to its new location near the depot, as now the mail was arriving daily on the train. Soon, the entire village followed, and the new Houston blossomed.

Arrival of the railroad drew attention to Houston, and within a year or two, the community boasted hotels, churches, lumber and flourmills, livery stables, a variety of merchants, and a booming population.

Some towns along the route boomed more significantly than others. Even before the railroad's arrival, just the anticipation started a vigorous growth at Rushford, some thirty miles west of the Mississippi River. By the time the road was completed to Rushford early in 1867, the town had emerged from a tiny river crossing settlement with only a handful of residents occupying mere shanties, to a busy metropolis supporting all forms of business, and its population rapidly increasing to more than 1,600. Rushford remained the western terminus of the Southern Minnesota for nearly two years, creating the atmosphere of a true frontier boomtown.

Baggage wagon and mail cart displayed outside the old Rushford depot that now serves as the Rushford Historical Society Museum. (Photo by author)

The arrival of the railroad in Rushford required more hotels. The Northwestern, built in 1868 by Hiram Adams and George Onstine, became one of the most popular hostelries along the Southern Minnesota Railroad. (Photo courtesy of Rushford Historical Society)

The Rushford City Mill established in 1858 by Hiram Walker, later owned by D.J. Tew, 1876-1917. This mill produced 30,000 barrels of flour annually. (Photo by author)

Abram Hanson constructed this stone building in 1870 for Rushford's first hardware store. It still stands today, and houses a fine restaurant and lounge. (Photo by author)

A huge celebration was thrown in December 1868 when the Southern Minnesota Railroad completed its line into Lanesboro. The citizens there might have been celebrating the birth of their town, as well; Lanesboro was only a few months old at the time.

The first loads of lumber were hauled from Rushford by ox team in July 1868. The town quickly sprouted as the result of efforts of an investment group influenced by the railroad's intensions of routing through this valley, and locating a station in the vicinity that became the city of Lanesboro. The railroad had selected that place mainly because of their discovery of an ideal location for a dam on the Root River where it flowed through a narrow, rock-walled gorge. A railroad plus an excellent source for waterpower added up to the perfect site for a town. The Lanesboro Townsite Company, comprised of eleven investors, purchased 500 acres of land from several farmers who had settled there earlier, and commenced to plat their project. By the time the Southern Minnesota RR arrived that December, Lanesboro boasted business places, hotels, homes, and a grand beginning for a successful town.

The Townsite Company had one simple objective, and that was to attract more permanent residents as well as summertime vacationers from the east, who would surely find pleasurable times in this resort setting. But if their goal was ever to be realized, several areas of concern required immediate attention.

A dam on the Root River would satisfy more than a source for waterpower necessary for mills; it would create a lake that would in turn create the desired resort atmosphere. Visitors could enjoy all the recreational benefits, and Lanesboro business owners could enjoy the added income generated from them. Col. W.H. Walrath of Rushford supervised the crew of men hired to build the dam.

Next on the list of concerns was the creation of first-class accommodations for travelers. A large, luxurious hotel was planned, and William Listman of La Crosse, Wisconsin was contracted for its construction near the town's center. The resulting Phoenix Hotel, completed in 1870 at a cost of $50,000 to the Townsite Company was destined to gain a reputation of presenting the finest accommodations and the most splendidly furnished hostelry in Southern Minnesota. Upon its completion, the Phoenix housed business offices, the Bank of Lanesboro, and a saloon, in addition to the comfortable parlors and suites of rooms. Its lower level also served as the railroad ticket office and baggage room.

Col. Van Fleat was put in charge of a crew to excavate and grade the needed roadway up the west bluff. It would provide an avenue of commerce for the farmers, and allow settlers to continue the journey westward after replenishing their supplies in Lanesboro. Crude as it was, not wide enough for teams and wagons to pass except in two or three places, it was a road, and adequately served its purpose until later improvements could be made.

All of the concerns were addressed and satisfied. The town was well planned, and the plan was well executed. During the next few years, Lanesboro boomed, and for several decades to follow it remained a favorite summer resort for families from the east.

Two smaller towns sprouted in the valley shortly after the railroad had built through. A few miles west of Rushford, a Norwegian immigrant, Peter Peterson Haslerud gave 15 acres of land to the Southern Minnesota Railroad for the purpose of securing a depot and warehouse. Thus, the town of Peterson was nurtured to a thriving community. A host of businesses as well as a wagon builder lined Main Street. Two flourmills operated in Peterson: a water-powered mill was built in 1872, but was destroyed by fire just five years later; a steam-powered mill erected in 1876 was quite productive, however, it only remained in operation for three years. The mill closed in 1879 and the structure was used for other purposes. The tall chimney for the steam generator still stands today, and is one of the highly visible monuments of yesteryear remaining in Peterson.

The Quickstad Farm Implement Company manufactured wagons and sleighs and provided blacksmithing services from these buildings in Peterson. The company expanded to produce other agricultural equipment, and operated until 1954. (Photo by author)

The wagon shops, as well as many other Main Street buildings can be seen, and the railroad depot, constructed in 1877, has been moved one block from its original location. The station is wonderfully preserved and houses an interesting display of Peterson area history.

The Peterson train station built in 1877 remained an active depot until 1965. It has been moved from its original location and is now used as a museum for the community. (Photo by author)

A few miles east of Lanesboro the town of Whalan came to life when an Irish immigrant settler, John Whaalahan (his name was shortened to Whalan) offered 200 acres of land for a town. The first house was built in 1868. That same year, the Walker flourmill, located ½ mile east of the town, began operation, and Whalan soon had a busy Main Street. Within a couple of years, a second flourmill appeared, as well as other business places and more homes. Although not a large city, Whalan had grown to significance: six trains stopped at the Whalan depot daily to deliver mail and shipments of grocery and other supply items for the local merchants. Outbound freight of grain, flour and cheese was loaded, destined for the eastern markets. The Southern Minnesota provided the all-important passenger service, too, as the people of Whalan depended on other communities for doctors and dentists, and La Crosse, Wisconsin still remained the major commercial hub.

Whalan's short Main Street still has a few of the original structures. This was the post office, established in 1869. It is now a private residence. (Photo by author)

This historic railroad across southeastern Minnesota is gone now. The route has been converted to a wonderfully scenic bike trail. The Chicago, Milwaukee, St. Paul & Pacific ended its operation with little fanfare in 1980. The passenger service had stopped years earlier, and many of the quaint little station depots had already been closed, leaving only the freight business to slowly dwindle away as a result of the greatly improved highway systems of modern day. Just as the stagecoaches and riverboats could not compete with the speedier railroad, the railroad died a similar slow death with the coming of motorcars and trucks providing more convenient and efficient means to move passengers and freight.

Southern Minnesota Railroad
c. 1870

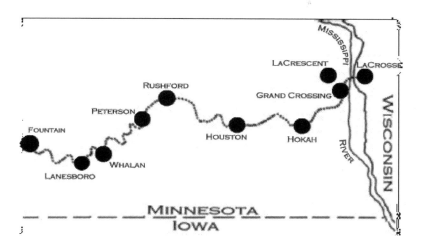

Bridging the Mississippi

The need to connect the railhead at La Crosse with the Southern Minnesota was accomplished by transferring the cargo by barges. Until 1870, all freight was loaded and unloaded by hand, but then the barges were constructed so that entire freight cars could be ferried across the river. One barge carried four rail cars, and eventually two barges were towed on each trip. In later years, the McDonald Brothers of La Crosse built larger barges that held six cars each.

When the barges could not operate during the winter months, temporary trestles – "winter bridges" – were constructed across the ice to connect the two railroads. With piling driven through the ice, these tracks were laid in late fall, and removed before the ice break-up in the spring. The first winter bridge between Grand Crossing, Minnesota and La Crosse was constructed in 1870, but by 1879, both the winter bridges and the rail car ferries would become a thing of the past.

In the years following the railroad's arrival at La Crosse, the Chicago, Milwaukee & St. Paul Railroad had extended the line to St. Paul. The Southern Minnesota railroad project was completed and had been in operation for five years. A short line between Dubuque, Iowa and La Crescent, Minnesota, terminated its tracks on the Mississippi banks just opposite La Crosse. But the struggle was not yet over, by any means.

In 1868 the Southern Minnesota Railroad sought to construct a bridge over the Mississippi River; congress authorized it, but their business didn't warrant such an undertaking and the project was abandoned. A short time later, the Chicago, Milwaukee & St. Paul petitioned congress and was granted a charter to bridge the Mississippi at La Crosse. However, their choice of location for the construction did not suit the Secretary of War, who maintained the authority over such matters at that time. The Secretary feared that it was a detrimental safety factor, not only to river navigation, but also to the city, having its terminal located in the business district, creating hazards to the public. The people of La Crosse, though, did not view it as a hazard. Moving the bridge and terminal location far to the north of the city, as the Secretary suggested, meant many added miles of track, lost time for the trains that would have to travel beyond the downtown area at a slow rate of speed, and an inconvenience to public access.

The railroad building engineers further defended the location choice by pointing out that it was on a good straight stretch of river with adequate entrance to the draw, both above and below.

But the government was not ready to give in, claiming more objections: the selected location presented obstructions for highways, and that construction of the bridge would be damaging to the riverbank.

Persistence of the people of La Crosse who supported the location choice compelled the railroad to continue its battle with a response that provided ample remedies for all the government's objections.

After several long years of controversy, heavy hitters among a group of Wall Street speculators who owned commercial property in La Crosse suggested a per car tariff be charged to the railroad companies using the bridge. A decree from the U.S. Circuit Court approved the bridge under that stipulation. The railroad had finally won out, and construction commenced in June 1876.

At a cost of $500,000 the structure was completed in late November of that same year – record time in bridge building over the Mississippi, considering the monumental undertaking for that era. The total length of the bridge from the eastern bank of the Black River to the Minnesota shore was nearly two miles, 1688 feet of which crossed the main channels, with a draw span of 360 feet. In addition to the bridge proper, the project included more than a half-mile of trestlework approaches.

Upon completion of the river bridge, La Crosse soon boasted service of five railroad lines entering the city, and connections to other cities in all directions. Chicago had been added to the list, as in 1873 tracks stretched there from Milwaukee. Rail service

A paddlewheel steamboat passes through the opened railroad swing bridge across the main channel between La Crosse and Grand Crossing. (Photo courtesy of La Crescent (Minnesota) Area Historical Society)

southward from Fond du Lac with Chicago as its ultimate terminus had been in operation since 1860. Although some of the short lines still remained isolated, the bigger companies absorbed many, and connections to the main lines soon followed. Extensions to the west rapidly appeared – to Omaha in 1883, and Kansas City in 1887.

By the 1880s-90s, La Crosse was literally connected to the rest of the world.

Note: The railroad swing bridge at La Crosse/La Crescent on the Mississippi River is still in operation, however, the ironwork was reconstructed in 1902 and the operating mechanism converted from steam power to electric motors in 1952.

Expanding Network

From its meager beginning with twenty miles of completed track connecting Milwaukee and Waukesha, the Chicago, Milwaukee and St. Paul Railroad grew to be one of the great American railway systems extending over a vast country. That first twenty miles was a mammoth undertaking in itself, but the project gained even more momentum as the road (then known as the Milwaukee & Mississippi) soon extended another forty miles to Eagle. A year later, it reached Milton, and encouraged by the success thus far, another company built a spur line from Milton to Janesville. By 1854, the road had penetrated through Stoughton and into Madison, and only two years later, the steel rails stretched all the way to Prairie du Chien on the Mississippi, a total distance of 194 miles. Just as the stagecoach lines had developed routes northward to meet the needs of a spreading population, providing the best means of transportation at the time, the railroads gradually penetrated farther into the vast wilderness. Speculation on the part of town promoters greatly influenced businessmen to locate their facilities in new settlements based on the anticipation of a soon-coming railroad. This growth, in turn, was hoped to further entice the railroad companies to recognize a higher potential of freight and passenger business to and from the rapidly developing commercial centers. In some towns this scheme worked successfully.

During those earliest days of development, the railroads were financially hard-pressed and could little afford to build depots or other amenities where needed. Such was the case between Stoughton and Madison; a small depot was constructed at a place called Door Creek. The grade was rather steep, and the wood-burning locomotives had difficulty getting their trains started on the westbound trip after stopping at Door Creek. But the railroad company couldn't afford to build another depot in a more suitable location.

About that same time, William H. McFarland decided that he wanted to spend more time with his family and submitted his resignation to the railroad company after several years' employment. He had built the first boxcar used on the line, and had been promoted to construction foreman.

McFarland came from London, England at the age of thirteen, learned the carpentry trade in Charleston, South Carolina, and later moved to New York. He eventually became intrigued by the western movement to the Wisconsin Territory, boarded a steamer at Buffalo destined for Milwaukee, where he secured employment with the railroad as a carpenter.

Upon his resignation, the company asked him if he would purchase land west of Door Creek and construct a depot, water tank, windmill, and stockyard. In return, the railroad agreed to make him station agent, and pay him a salary and rent for the buildings. McFarland bought 160 acres there, and the bargain was carried through, even to naming the station McFarland. A village sprang up around the depot, and McFarland soon became a major grain shipping point in the area.

The Old Stamm House at Pheasant Branch was built in 1847 as an Inn to serve travelers on Old Sauk Trail, the main overland route between Milwaukee and St. Paul. It also housed a store and served as the post office, and during the Civil War, it was a safe stop for escaped southern slaves on the Underground Railroad. Pheasant Branch is now part of Middleton, and the Stamm House on Century Avenue, the oldest tavern in Dane County, is still serving as a fine restaurant. (Photo by author)

Several small communities had emerged on the west side of Lake Mendota by the time the Milwaukee & Mississippi Railroad started building westward from Madison toward Prairie du Chien on the

Mississippi River. W.B. Slaughter had platted an area as early as 1836 that he called "City of Four Lakes," intended to be the site of the Territorial Capitol. However, maneuvering by more influential politicians located the capitol a little farther east at Madison. As more settlers arrived in the area, the communities of Pheasant Branch and East Middleton developed, and the residents of these small towns anticipated a prosperous future with the coming of the railroad. But both towns were bypassed as the railroad company chose to lay their tracks through an unpopulated area between the two settlements. People became more interested in settling near the newly erected station, and by 1856 the City of Middleton boomed forth, quickly flourishing with businesses and homes. Large grain elevators along the tracks soon became the important factor, as wheat production was the mainstay of the area economy. A full array of enterprise including blacksmith, tin shop, stone quarry, lumberyard, stockyard, factories, stores, and even an opera house, among many others made Middleton an important commercial center. One of its hotels – the American House – was quite popular: people came from Madison on the train just to enjoy the hotel restaurant's Sunday chicken dinners for 25 cents.

This stone building on Middleton's Branch Street was the first blacksmith shop built by Henry Prien in 1851. James Dohr, a German immigrant joined him that same year and established a wagon shop, and with nearby lodging, Pheasant Branch was a prominent stop for travelers. (Photo by author)

The American Hotel began operation in 1870 and became quite famous for its 25-cent Sunday dinners. The building still remains in historic downtown Middleton. (Photo by author)

The original depot in "Middleton Station," built by W.B. Slaughter in 1856, was located across the street from the present depot shown here. Many stores and homes were constructed near the depot, and Middleton quickly flourished as a commerce center. (Photo by author)

By the late 1800s all the mail arrived by train. Now a café on Parmenter Street in the historic downtown district, this was Middleton's first post office outside a private home. The first telephone company began on its second floor, and the city's first public library was started in this building. (Photo by author)

The Southern Wisconsin Railroad was chartered in 1852. After purchasing the Milton-to-Janesville line and extending it thirty-three miles to Monroe, it was generally understood that this road would be carried through to the Mississippi opposite Dubuque, but it never transpired. Some time later, however, it was completed to Mineral Point with spurs running to Platteville, Shullsburg, and Warren, Illinois.

While the Milwaukee and La Crosse Railroad Company struggled its way across the state, another company, the Milwaukee, Fond du Lac & Green Bay Railroad formed. Money was raised, construction began, and locations for depots selected. But the company was unable to carry the project to completion, and in 1854 consolidated with the Milwaukee & La Crosse. Construction was then hurried forward, and by the end of 1855, the rails had reached fifty miles to Horicon, and another forty miles to Portage by the end of 1856.

Competition evolved between rival companies as many smaller organizations were chartered, and some of these ambitious undertakings had the same destination cities in their sights. Such was the case with the Milwaukee & Watertown Railroad Company, chartered in 1851, which began its work on a line from Brookfield to Watertown, and was subsequently planned to extend to La Crosse. At the same time, a line was in the planning stages that would run from Madison by way of Portage to the St. Croix valley, and from there to the west end of Lake Superior. This intensified the bitterness between the rivals, however the struggle didn't last long. The Milwaukee & Watertown was soon absorbed in a merger with the more powerful Milwaukee & La Crosse Railroad. Consolidation of the two companies combined the congressional land grants of 1856, as well as other resources, and by 1858 rail lines of nearly 400 miles were completed from Portage to La Crosse, from Watertown to Columbus and Sun Prairie, and from Horicon to Ripon and Berlin.

Consolidations among the railroad companies occurred almost as rapidly as the companies were chartered. The Racine, Janesville & Mississippi Railroad was chartered to build a line as the name would imply, but when Janesville did not contribute its financial share, the route was altered to pass instead through Beloit, as the citizens there raised a $100,000 donation for that purpose. The company then consolidated with the Rockton & Freeport, and continued as the Racine & Mississippi. That line was in active service to Beloit by 1856, to Freeport, Illinois by 1859, and to Savanna, Illinois on the Mississippi by 1860. Another consolidation at a later date brought about another name change – the Western Union Railroad Company – and in 1870 the St. Paul Road took charge of its operations and eventually it became known as the Racine & Southwestern division of the Chicago, Milwaukee & St. Paul.

The Milwaukee & Western Railroad was still another result of consolidations and acquisitions. It was formed after the Madison, Fond du Lac & Lake Michigan bought from the La Crosse company a portion of road it had acquired from the Milwaukee & Watertown, and was chartered to build a road from Madison via Fond du Lac to Lake Michigan.

When the La Crosse & Milwaukee and the Milwaukee & Horicon companies defaulted in payment of the interest on their bonded debts in 1858, the bondholders instituted foreclosure proceedings on the various trust deeds given to secure the bonds. Litigation in both the state and federal courts resulted in a final settlement by a decision of the United States Supreme Court, but not until 1868. In the meantime, both roads were sold to an association of the bondholders who organized the Milwaukee & St. Paul Railway Company. The new company succeeded to all the rights of the La Crosse and Horicon companies, and soon afterward purchased the property of the Milwaukee and Western, thus gaining control of a large portion of the existing railroads in Wisconsin. This company continued to expand in southeastern, central, and northeastern areas of the state, extending into the Wolf and Fox River Valleys. The directors of the Milwaukee & St. Paul had secured a majority of the common stock, and in 1867 obtained control of the Milwaukee & Prairie du Chien – the first Wisconsin railroad to reach the Mississippi River.

Wisconsin Central On Its Way Northward

Some 500 people crowded about the little depot in Stevens Point to see a locomotive and train of cars steam into the town for the first time on November 15, 1871. The arrival of the railway was a grand event for the residents at that time, for it meant expansion and progress, and linking the northern community with the outside world.

Until that time, people wishing to travel to metropolitan areas like Milwaukee or Chicago had to take a tedious ride in a stagecoach over rough roads to Gills Landing, and then a stuffy little steamer down the Wolf River and across Lake Winnebago to Oshkosh, where they could finally board a train to the big cities. The arrival of the railroad also meant cheaper hauling of food, clothing, dry goods and other freight necessities that came from the outside.

But it had been a long, costly wait. Many roads were planned – on paper – to pass through Stevens Point. One of the railroads, the Horicon, laid such plans, and sold stock to the residents along the proposed right of way. Farmers were given stock for mortgages on their property, but the road was never built, and many land owners lost considerably.

Then the Wisconsin Central Railroad received valuable concessions from the government in the form of land. Its right of way included a strip of land twenty miles wide northward to Ashland at Lake Superior. Villages, cities, and counties along the proposed route voted and pledged large sums of money to aid the railroad construction: Portage County voted in favor of $200,000 in bonds, and the city of Stevens Point gave the railroad its right of way through the city, a large parcel of land on which to build machine shops and other facilities, and an additional $25,000. The county and city received stocks in the company in return.

Work began in June 1871 at Menasha. The Colby Construction Company, having been awarded the contract to build the road from there to Stevens Point, sublet much of the work to numerous small contractors along the way, so the grading and laying of track was started at various points simultaneously, and the road was completed rather quickly.

The Stevens Point Cornet Band assembled on the public square, and followed by a large crowd, marched to the little depot and started playing as the wood-burning locomotive steamed into town with its train of cars carrying railroad officials, a number of other important men about the state, many news reporters, and a large contingency from the private sector of citizens. Two hours of ceremony followed, including a dinner served at the Curran House in downtown Stevens Point, and plenty of speeches offering ample praise to this all-important accomplishment.

In the far northern reaches of Wisconsin, the village of Ashland had experienced its share of problems while its citizens anticipated the rail connections with the rest of the state.

Situated at Chequamegon Bay on Lake Superior, Ashland had been the focal point of mineral excitement and a strong prospect of a forthcoming railroad, and had attracted quite a few settlers. But hard times drove them away to other towns and by 1863, Martin Roehm, with his wife and son were the only remaining residents. They were the "Swiss Family Robinson" of Ashland until 1871 when some of the old residents returned and the town began to restore, probably due to a survey made by the Wisconsin Central Railroad that located the proposed route for tracks to Ashland, and the expectation that the Wisconsin Central road being built northward from Menasha would soon connect with the Ashland project. The work actually began in

1872, and during that year Ashland enjoyed sizeable growth as reconstruction of the city progressed rapidly. Eugene Prince established an express line to Duluth to serve the growing business and population, via Lake Superior during the summer and overland stage during the winter. The line continued operation until the railroad was completed, but that would take five long, trouble-infested years to accomplish.

The thirty-mile rail route to Penoka, just south of Mellen, crossed rough country making for difficult construction and requiring some of the best engineering skills available. Six miles out of Ashland, a 1,560 feet long, 103 feet high bridge crossed the White River. Seventeen miles of the survey followed the course of the crooked Bad River, requiring seventeen bridges within a distance of nine miles. After several delays and shutdowns during a financially depressed time suffered by the entire country, the line was completed to Penoka Gap in 1873, leaving that the only railroad communication into Ashland for the next four years.

The incidents following that day in late December 1872 when construction superintendent Capt. W.W. Rich received orders to notify the crews to stop working and to remain in camp until the paymaster arrived are sometimes referred to as the "Ashland War." Here was a settlement of some twelve hundred people that had developed order out of chaos, opened streets, built bridges, stores, hotels, saloons, shops, homes, docks, and warehouses. The population was of a quickly brought together mixture of rough railroad builders, a large number of true pioneers, and of course, the camp followers – those bad men (and women) who preyed upon the wage earners with their less-than-honorable ways. From March to November of 1872, over 200 new buildings had been erected, and over 800 men were in the camps engaged in the challenging task of clearing a path through the rugged wilderness and building a railroad. Almost everyone in Ashland, at that time, depended on the wages from the railroad company, so naturally the order of a shutdown caused a tremendous stir.

Two weeks elapsed before the paymaster arrived. When Rich escorted him and his assistant to what was known as Kelly's camp, the laborers demanded pay "to date," but the funds available were only to the date of suspension. Capt. Rich held off the angry railroad men from attack with his revolver, while the paymaster, his assistant, and Rich retreated to a waiting team. They managed to reach Ashland ahead of the mob and reported the matter to the town's officials. However, there was only one deputy sheriff and one constable at Ashland, hardly an adequate force to handle a confrontation of this magnitude. Messengers were sent to Bayfield to alert Sheriff Nelson Boutin of the situation.

Boutin arrived in Ashland that night (January 1, 1873) with forty-two men armed with rifles, under the command of Capt. Pike. They immediately took charge, closed all the saloons tight, and posted sentinels on the street. The Sheriff and his men remained for ten days, until a settlement was reached and all the railroad workers were paid.

June 2, 1877 was a great day, for after the long four-year delay, the Wisconsin Central work crews finally reached Penoka Gap; the golden spike was hammered in, and the first train from Milwaukee passed over the road on its way to Ashland. Although it was late on a Saturday night, the whole town turned out to welcome the train in a crazy excitement. The event was worth celebrating – Ashland was finally connected to the rest of the world!

The Wisconsin Central passing through Stevens Point came with much disappointment from the people of Wausau, however. Originally, that railroad was planned to cross the Wisconsin River at Wausau, but because of political and financial influence, it was diverted to Stevens Point.

The lumbermen, as well as other business owners of Wood and Marathon Counties recognized the need of rail service, and organized the Wisconsin Valley Railway to run from Tomah to Grand Rapids (Wisconsin Rapids). But with only the grading completed to Port Edwards, they ran short of financing, and outside help would be required. Little success came until encouraging negotiations started with the Chicago, Milwaukee & St. Paul. An agreement was finally reached to turn over 200,000 acres of land to aid the company in building the road. Construction began, and by July 1873 the railroad was operating to Grand Rapids, and the right of way graded to Junction City.

Once again, the wealthy and influential businessmen of Stevens Point nearly ruined Wausau's efforts to gain their railroad connection. With substantial financial offerings, they had convinced the railroad company to alter the route to Stevens Point instead of Wausau. Fortunately, for Wausau, their officials got wind of the debauchery, made a counter offer, and persuaded the builders to retain the originally planned route.

The railway was built to Wausau and formally opened to traffic on November 4, 1874. Despite the schemes by Stevens Point to make its neighbor to the north no more than a trading post, (according to an article by J.C. Clark in *The Wausau Record,* October 1905) Wausau developed into a significant city with a population of about 15,000 people by the turn of the century. Another contributive factor in that accomplishment came with the arrival of a second railroad – the Milwaukee, Lake Shore & Western – in 1880. Wausau finally had its connection to the entire country.

The West Wisconsin Railroad started building its line from Tomah to St. Paul in 1869. This was a land grant affair, there being thousands of acres of prime timberland given the company by the government to be sold for the purpose of financing the construction. Following a northwesterly course, it crossed the Black, Chippewa, Menomonie, and St. Croix Rivers, touching the small villages of Black River Falls, Merrillan, Augusta, Eau Claire, and Hudson. Several small mill towns were started between Tomah and Black River Falls, the principal ones being Millston and Warren. But one thriving lumber town had been missed by all the railroads.

Chippewa Falls had risen from a battleground of the Sioux and Chippewa tribes since John Brunett, the first white man to visit the valley, arrived in 1832 and later returned to open a trading post for furs and erected a sawmill. But it wasn't until 1856 that the town was laid out. By 1874 the population there had reached 6,000; a new courthouse, jail and sheriff's house had just been completed, and plans for other substantial buildings were being made. New streets were in progress, and the Union Lumbering Company's mill was producing thousands of feet of lumber every day, and already new industries were contemplating a Chippewa Falls location. But the most important event for the town had not yet been realized – Chippewa Falls still didn't have a railroad.

All efforts to secure the construction of eleven miles of track from Eau Claire had been defeated. Outside support was not forthcoming, and County aid had been continuously denied. The citizens, however, were determined to build these eleven miles of road to connect with the West Wisconsin Railway, which ran between Chicago and St. Paul through Eau Claire. The Chippewa Falls and Northwestern Railroad Company was formed with T.C. Pound as its president and the city issued $25,000 in bonds to aid the $160,000 project. Once the road was completed, it was to be turned over to the West Wisconsin Railway for continued operation. Work commenced in the fall of 1874, and the road was officially opened in June 1875 with a great celebration. Chippewa Falls finally had its long-awaited railroad.

Prior to the mid 1700s the Chippewa and Sioux (Santa Fe Dakota) Indians were the only major inhabitants of Western Wisconsin and Eastern Minnesota. Their activity greatly influenced the exploration and development of vast portions of this bountiful woodland region.

Although the Indian nations collectively contested the white man's intrusions into their hunting grounds, the Chippewa and the Sioux were also bitter enemies, and often confrontations erupted in battle between them to gain territorial dominance. But eventually, the warring tribes would come to an agreement, in order to avoid the hostilities that were killing their people. A neutral territory that included much of present-day Buffalo County, bordered on the west by the Mississippi River, designated a zone in which neither side was to hunt, trap, or fish. The early French explorers and fur traders learned of the neutral ground, took advantage of the absence of Indian interference, and safely moved into the area to harvest abundant quantities of fur bearing game. Subsequently, their exploration and knowledge of the area hastened settlement once the threat of hostile Indians began to further subside in the early 1800s.

Mondovi is one of the little towns that emerged from this. Harvey Farrington first visited the area in search of new farmland in the spring of 1855. He was quite impressed with the richness and the beauty of the valley. Everything he, or any other pioneer could want, was readily available: good farmland soil, waterpower, streams filled with trout, and plenty of elk and deer to provide an ample supply of food. Farrington convinced his three brothers and another friend to settle there as well, and soon after, they persuaded still another group to stake claims. It was first known as "Pancake Valley," but when Harvey Farrington registered the claims for him and the others at the U.S. land office in La Crosse, the area acquired the name "Farrington." Three years later, 1858, the village was platted and building lots were offered for sale at $25 each. The name Mondovi was chosen for the village, after the site of a 1796 Napoleonic battle in Italy.

A hotel and a general store were among the first commercial buildings to appear, and the first postmaster assumed a 16-mile route to Durand and return. Later, the mail arrived by stagecoach from Eau Claire, and the stage departures were coordinated with the railroad schedules there. Four hours were required for the stage run to Mondovi, a distance of about 20 miles.

A school and churches were established, and Mondovi's population grew to 300 by 1876, bringing with it more businesses typical of a pioneer town: gristmills, blacksmiths, livery stables, wagon shops, and even a cheese factory was built in 1875. And due to a rich clay deposit nearby, a brick factory started operation about the same time. Local farmers marketed prosperous wheat crops at Alma on the Mississippi River.

Then the lumber industry began to render its economic influence on the area. Much of the farmers' produce was sold to the logging camps on the Eau Claire and Chippewa Rivers, and all the other local businesses reaped the benefits of increased sales, as well. Mondovi boomed.

By the time the Sault Ste. Marie and Southwestern Railroad reached Mondovi from Osseo in June 1890, the population had grown to over 500. Just five years later, that figure was rapidly approaching 1,000, and in another three, Mondovi residents were enjoying the convenience of electricity in their homes.

And a six-hour stagecoach ride was still the best means to get to Alma.

About 1875 the citizens of Lancaster began to feel the need for railroad connections. With great determination they displayed their willingness to give support and aid to any company that would build a road to almost any possible connection. Several different routes were discussed and plans were made, but for various reasons the plans failed, and the routes to Dubuque and Platteville never became reality. Then, in 1878, when a railroad facility through Lancaster seemed almost unattainable, the president of the Chicago & Tomah road, D.K. Williams appeared on the scene and proposed to complete a line from the Milwaukee & St. Paul, which was to run from Woodman through Fennimore and Lancaster, and then extend east to Montfort where it would connect with the Galena Road coming northward. Naturally, his proposal was well received and he easily gained the support from towns along the proposed route. The money was raised and work commenced. Construction superintendent Patrick Flynn hastened the work along despite the usual obstacles encountered with such an undertaking. On New Year's Day, 1879, the first locomotive puffed into the town. Lancaster had finally gained its heart's desire.

The Chicago & North Western Railroad purchased the Galena to Montfort and the Woodman to Lancaster roads in the following year.

The Chicago & North Western was chartered by the State of Wisconsin and the State of Illinois in 1859, and its principal lines connected much of Iowa, Minnesota, and Wisconsin to Chicago. It called itself the "Pioneer Railroad" when in 1864 it acquired by merger The Galena & Chicago Union Railroad, the first road in operation out of Chicago (and all of Illinois) in 1848. By 1864 it had a line completed and in operation from Chicago to the Mississippi River at Fulton, Illinois, and had leased track extending across central Iowa built by the Cedar Rapids & Missouri River Railroad with anticipation of soon reaching Council Bluffs. It also leased the Chicago, Iowa & Nebraska RR, which had build from Clinton, Iowa to Cedar Rapids.

Daily trains were running from Chicago through to Evansville, Wisconsin by 1863. The ultimate plan was, of course, to connect Chicago with St. Paul, and by acquiring two other uncompleted roads, started by fledgling companies – the Baraboo Air Line (so named for its straightness of route) and the La Crosse, Trempealeau and Prescott Railroad – the C&NW completed rail service through Madison, Baraboo, North Freedom, and Reedsburg to Elroy, Wisconsin in 1872. The route from Winona Junction through La Crosse, West Salem, Bangor, Sparta, Norwalk, Wilton, and Kendall to Elroy was completed the following year, thus giving the C&NW its first line connecting Chicago to the Twin Cities.

This was a very busy railroad, as the new route had opened more markets to the farmers and merchants of a large area. Shipping grain and livestock via rail greatly increased efficiency over the wagonload quantities, and meant increased profits for the farmers. Merchants could now take advantage of carload shipments delivered in less time and with greater safety. In the 1870s, twenty or thirty daily trains passed through Evansville, which had become one of the main stops. Forty or fifty trains ran between Sparta and Elroy daily. The larger number of trains on that portion of the route was probably due to the hilly country and shorter trains. At Kendall, the railroad stationed "pusher" engines to assist the regular locomotives to negotiate the hills and tunnels between there and Sparta.

One of the few Chicago & North Western depots remaining in its original location at Kendall, Wisconsin. C&NW tracks were abandoned here in the 1980s and the route is now part of the Wisconsin State Bike Trail. (Photo by author)

The line soon became quite successful, and a second mainline track was laid (double-track) to handle the increasing traffic. Repair shops were built at Baraboo, designated at that time the new division headquarters, and nearly 500 railroad employees lived there.

There were so many trains scheduled to meet at Evansville, by 1879 the company had to construct sidetracks to accommodate them. Business boomed and within a few short years the Evansville depot was the nucleus of all transportation activities, surrounded by numerous warehouses, lumberyards, and factories. Hotels, liveries, and other enterprises prospered, as now the town attracted a great deal of business interest.

Advancement in agricultural progress was a key factor in Evansville's prosperity. Because of the railroad, local grain and livestock dealers could negotiate better prices with the larger markets in Chicago and St. Louis, and arrange for cheaper, mass-quantity shipping. Farmers were no longer limited to single crops suitable for just local consumption, but could now grow and raise various crops and livestock, knowing there was a ready market. Tobacco became an important cash crop in the area, and even though there were cigar manufacturers in Evansville, much of the product was warehoused, sorted, and shipped to other markets, creating many additional jobs in the city.

Evansville became an important manufacturing center, as well, with wagon builders, harness makers, cheese factories, and among the largest were the Lehman Brothers furniture factory, the Baker Manufacturing Company, maker of the "Monitor Vaneless Windmill" that was marketed throughout the western United States, and the Evansville Manufacturing Company that made tacks and provided employment for both men and women.

A fire completely destroyed the Baker Manufacturing Company and the adjacent Lehman Furniture Company in 1884. The loss was tremendous, but the Bakers engaged in rebuilding immediately. The Lehmans, however, decided not to replace their ruined business and sold the land to the Baker firm, allowing them some expansion room.

The railroad continued to expand. The "Janesville cut-off" was added, providing that town with a much-wanted connection with the C&NW, and Evansville continued to boom through the 1880s, growing to a thriving metropolis. By the end of that decade the growth had leveled off, and then an economic depression halted it completely. That growth would never again resume the lively momentum of the 1880s.

The Chicago, St. Paul, Minneapolis & Omaha Railroad, better known as the "Omaha Road," was a successful subsidiary of the C&NW. A small regional railroad with most of its track in northern Wisconsin and Minnesota, it eventually extended into Iowa, Nebraska, and South Dakota.

It started as the Minnesota Valley RR in 1865, but was acquired by the stronger West Wisconsin RR just two years later. By 1876 its network had expanded and through trains ran between St. Paul and Chicago via Elroy, Wisconsin where the line connected with the C&NW. The following year, the West Wisconsin defaulted on its debt, and the Chicago, St. Paul, Minneapolis & Omaha Railroad Corporation was formed, which fell into the control of the C&NW in 1882.

The Omaha Road served Minneapolis-St. Paul, Duluth-Superior, Eau Claire, Ashland, Hudson, and extended south and west to Omaha, Nebraska and Sioux City, Iowa.

Another railroad originating in Minneapolis in 1870 – the Minneapolis & St. Louis – ran between he Twin Cities and Peoria, Illinois. Because it was meant to allow freight to bypass the congestion in Chicago, it was sometimes referred to as the "Peoria Gateway." Its sister company, the Iowa Central, had been in operation since 1866. The two railroads merged, and were eventually absorbed into the Chicago & North Western.

It was an agent for that railroad, Richard Sears of North Redwood, Minnesota, who received a shipment of watches in 1886. The cargo was unclaimed, and a short time later, he started the mail order business that became Sears, Roebuck, & Co.

In time, America again began to change the way it transported passengers and freight. The arrival of the motorcars, trucks, and buses rendered the most profound impact on the stability of the railroads. The C&NW completed a new, more direct line north of the Wisconsin River between Milwaukee and St. Paul in an effort to increase speed and efficiency, and from then on, the road through Baraboo declined. By 1924 the company had closed all the shops there. As the popularity of shipping goods by truck increased, and as the public cultivated its fondness for the automobile, the demand for rail transportation diminished. When the superior highway systems developed after World War II, railroad usage declined so drastically that railway companies started to abandon some service, and even some rails. The C&NW mainline was reduced to a single track again in 1954. Passenger service had fallen to just a single train per day, and ended with little notice in 1963. Tracks between Beloit and Evansville were abandoned in 1977, and west of Reedsburg in the 1980s. The Chicago & North Western

Railroad would survive for only a few more years before being absorbed[1] into the vast Union Pacific system in 1995.

After more than 150 years without interruption, the Illinois Central Railroad is the only major rail carrier operating in the United States under its original name. Founded in 1851, the IC was chartered to build a road from the confluence of the Ohio and Mississippi Rivers at Cairo, Illinois to Galena in the northwest corner of the state, with a branch from Centralia (named for the railroad) to Chicago. It was the first railroad to receive a land grant under the Federal Land Grant Act signed by President Millard Fillmore in 1850. The road was completed in 1856, giving Chicago a direct shipping route to New Orleans via a railroad-operated Mississippi steamboat line from Cairo. During the Civil War the IC transport system played an important role in moving Union soldiers and supplies.

Following the Civil War, the Illinois Central progressed across the Mississippi to Dubuque, and by 1870 reached Sioux City, Iowa. It expanded farther west across Iowa in 1886 with branches to Cedar Rapids, Omaha, Nebraska, and Sioux Falls, South Dakota. During that same time, it incorporated the Chicago, Madison & Northern, to construct a connection with the IC line at Freeport, Illinois northward to Dodgeville and Madison, Wisconsin. The route required a 1,260-foot long tunnel through solid limestone near Belleville, Wisconsin that plagued the company with trouble for over a year.

Construction began at each end of the Stewart Tunnel on December 13, 1886. It was named after James Stewart who had been awarded the contract to build the road from Monroe to Madison. He died from injuries when he was thrown from a buggy while driving over the proposed rail route.

Then in September 1887, the workers went on strike for higher wages. When management didn't give in to the demands, many left. New crews were brought in at a 50-cent increase over the beginning wages – now workers were earning $1.75 per day.

At first, all the work was being done without the aid of power equipment. Holes to hold the blasting powder were bored with hand-operated drills. Eventually, steam-powered compressed air drills, and two large steam shovels – one at each end – were brought in. A small locomotive named "Stella" and six cars each holding two cubic yards were used to haul the 155,000 cubic yards of limestone out of the tunnel to Lynn Valley where it was needed for fill.

In mid-November, a stream of water began flowing from the roof of the tunnel, halting the work for two days until the water flow stopped. That portion of the roof had to be shored with timbers and bricked over to prevent any possible cave-ins.

Winter weather presented constant problems – January temperatures reached lows of 54 degrees below zero. The north end of the tunnel had to be boarded up to make labor efforts inside the tunnel possible. Snowdrifts up to fifteen feet deep blocked the tracks for several weeks.

Despite all the tribulations encountered during the tunnel construction, when the two crews boring through the rock from opposite directions finally met, their courses aligned within one inch on either side. The final rail was spiked into place January 26, 1888.

The first train steamed through the tunnel at ten miles per hour on its February 1st run from Freeport to Madison. But the tunnel woes weren't quite over, yet. As a train passed through on April 21st, cave-ins damaged the locomotive and derailed one car, the engineer and fireman narrowly escaping injury. It was not until August that year when repairs were completed and regular service was resumed on the Chicago, Madison & Northern Railroad.

James Hill – A Railroad Man
Who Made a Difference

During the Nineteenth Century, Minnesota, as with any newly developing region, was subject to profound changes. Of all the forces creating change, the railroads made the greatest impact. Their influence determined where towns would locate and in time, provided the means of measurable success for Minnesota industries. Perhaps the most influential was the Great Northern Railway that evolved from one of the first railroad charters to be granted by the Minnesota Territory.

The Minnesota & Pacific Railroad Company was incorporated by act of the Minnesota Territorial Legislature in May 1857. It was one of four such companies created to take advantage of the federal land grant act, with the stipulation that it would construct a railroad line from Stillwater on the eastern boundary to Big Stone Lake at the proposed western border of what would soon be the State of Minnesota.

But the panic of 1857 took its toll. Money disappeared from the streets, and banks closed. Minnesotans looked to a bountiful harvest to revive their economy, but the depression continued throughout 1858, despite the news of statehood in May. The people wanted speedy and reliable transportation, so they voted in an amendment to their new constitution providing four railroad companies access to public bond money in the amount of $5 million.

The Minnesota & Pacific Railroad surveyed a route from Stillwater to St. Paul, graded and bridged the line from St. Anthony to Crow Wing, and acquired ties. But it fell short of affording rails, engines, or rolling stock, and could not meet its share of obligation regarding the Five Million Dollar Loan. The Minnesota Legislature granted an extension because of the hard economic times.

By 1862, with the help of New York investments, the first operating railroad in the state ran from the levee at St. Paul to the Falls of St. Anthony, a distance of ten miles.

It was Colonel William Crooks and the Hon. Edmund Rice who journeyed to the East in May 1861 to carry out negotiations with potential investors. Their ploy began in Philadelphia, and finally in June, while in New York, they struck a deal that would finance the St. Paul to St. Anthony Falls line.

Work began in the fall of 1861, but suffered long delays over a right of way dispute. Further legislation during the winter months finally enabled the company to proceed, and the first ten miles of railroad in Minnesota was finished and put into operation the following July.

The company was later reorganized as the St. Paul & Pacific Railroad, and following bankruptcy after the economic panic of 1873, it would become part of Jim Hill's Great Northern Railway Company.

James J. Hill had emigrated from Ontario, Canada to St. Paul, Minnesota at the age of eighteen. He started working as a bookkeeper for a steamboat company, and used the opportunity to learn everything about the freight and transportation business. During the winter

First locomotive used in Minnesota in 1862, it is one of few Civil War era engines to still exist today. It is restored and kept at the Railroad Museum in Duluth, Minnesota. (Great Northern Railway photo)

months when the riverboats couldn't run, being quite ambitious and aggressive, Hill began engaging in more endeavors, and by 1877 he had virtually monopolized the coal business, was in the steamboat business, and had become Member of the Board of several major banks. Hill also found great success in acquiring bankrupt businesses, reviving them and then reselling, usually at a huge profit.

Hill's brilliance, hard work and dedication, and his pride in being the best at everything he did, raised him to great power. He learned any new business quickly, and just as quickly formulated a strategy for it. His entry into the railroad industry is evidence of his uncanny ability to predict the future of business.

Jim Hill studied and researched the bankrupt SP&P Railroad for three years, considering it a golden opportunity. He finally concluded that there was a lot of money to be made with a railroad in Minnesota if it were properly capitalized, and he teamed up with a former steamboat business partner, Norman Kittson, along with Donald Smith, George Stephen, and John S. Kennedy, and together they bought the failing railroad and vastly expanded it, negotiating with Northern Pacific Railway for track use rights. James Hill became the general manager of the new company – the St. Paul, Minneapolis, & Manitoba Railway Co., formed in May 1879. By then the road had been expanded to connect with the Canadian Pacific. Timing was perfect; two great harvest seasons followed, bringing even more business to the road.

During this time, Hill also got involved with the construction of the Canadian Pacific Railway. He contributed greatly to the success and quick completion of the road to the Pacific coast, but because the Canadian Pacific would soon become a competitor to his own transcontinental route, Hill resigned from the company and sold all his stock.

Under Hill's skillful management, the SPM&M Railroad Company prospered. He encouraged immigrants to settle along his lines by selling them homesteads and then transporting the families and their belongings to their new home. By 1889 Hill had built his railroads across Montana, North Dakota, Wisconsin, and around the Great Lakes. When there wasn't enough industry in the areas where he was building, he bought out companies and placed factories along his railroad lines.

Then Hill determined that the future was all about transcontinental railroads, and his greatest project began. He planned to build the best road possible, the shortest distance and the lowest grades, avoiding the costly development through the Rocky Mountains. He would get what he wanted, for in 1893 the road became reality.

But it didn't come without complications. Just a few months after the project started came the depression of the 1890s. Hill handled the crisis brilliantly, though. To retain his patronage during the hard times, he lowered freight rates for the farmers and gave many businesses credit so they were able to continue paying their employees. By economizing operations, he stayed in business *and* increased the net worth of the railroad by nearly ten million dollars, while every other transcontinental road went bankrupt. The most incredible part of this story, however, is that this railroad was built without public funding.

Hill created the Great Northern Railway Company, and the St. Paul, Minneapolis, & Manitoba became a part of it. The transcontinental road reached Puget Sound at Everett, Washington in 1893. That same year, the Northern Pacific was in a financial disaster. Hill made arrangements to gain its control, and in 1896 it became part of the Great Northern.

Now that he had a successful railroad that could transport lumber products from the far west, Hill knew he needed to expand farther into the Midwest. He had had his eye on the Chicago, Burlington & Quincy that stretched from the Great Lakes to the Rocky Mountains, and into the southern states, as well. With this addition, he would gain the cotton hauling business to St. Louis and Kansas City, and a route to the smelters at Denver and the Black Hills. And he would have a direct line into the lumber consuming prairie states. Hill recruited the assistance of J.P. Morgan and successfully purchased the Chicago, Burlington & Quincy. From that evolved the Burlington & Northern.

Jim Hill came to be known as the "Empire Builder," (as did the Burlington passenger trains later in the Twentieth Century) and with good reason. He took a small, struggling railroad and developed it and the country it passed through beyond expectations. Because of Jim Hill, Minnesota and the Dakotas became popular places for immigration, and the little town of Seattle, Washington became an international shipping port linking America to the world via the most successful railroad network in the country.

From humble beginnings, February 1849 in Aurora Illinois, the Chicago, Burlington & Quincy became the second railroad to serve Chicago. Over track laid with secondhand strap iron spiked to twelve miles of wooden rails, the first train chugged its way from Batavia, Illinois to Turner Junction, and then eastward to Chicago on the tracks of the Galena & Chicago Union RR. The locomotive and cars were borrowed from the Galena company, as their own equipment had not yet been delivered.

By 1864, this railroad had 400 miles of track, all in Illinois. Its name properly described the main routes stretching to Burlington, Iowa, and Quincy, Illinois, both on the Mississippi River. It completed bridges over the river at both towns in 1868, connecting with already operational tracks in Iowa and Missouri. By 1869, its road reached the Missouri River at the western Iowa border. Locomotives were small wood burners, only capable of pulling about a dozen cars. The passenger cars of that time were built of wood, and didn't provide a great deal of comfort to the long distance traveler.

As the Burlington expanded westward, more Midwestern segments were built, including links to St. Louis and Rock Island, and by 1886 the CB&Q had extended its network up the eastern bank of the Mississippi River through Wisconsin to St. Paul, Minnesota. By this time, the steam locomotives were fired with coal, and had become much larger and considerably more powerful. Greater emphasis was placed on the comfort and safety of the passengers with larger, more comfortable coaches, and dining cars for meals in route were commonly used.

Through the years, agricultural products were essential to the CB&Q, and it became recognized as the "Granger Railroad." Representatives worked closely with the farmers and ranchers, promoting the latest techniques in crop and livestock improvement, irrigation and soil conservation, and often advising new settlers on the most successful crops to raise. The Burlington often employed farmers for shop work during the winter months until they were able to establish and attend to their farms full-time.

Near the close of the century saw the purchase of the CB&Q by railroad "Empire Builder" James Hill, founder and developer of the Great Northern, but the Chicago, Burlington & Quincy name remained intact until 1970.

Green Bay Route

The railroad had proved its value as a means of transportation, and in 1853 the Green Bay & Minnesota Railroad was granted a charter to build and operate a road from Green Bay to some point on Lake Pepin, or opposite the city of Wabasha, Minnesota over the most feasible route. This railroad was never built because the company failed to generate adequate capital.

Another charter was granted in 1866 to a company calling itself the Green Bay & Lake Pepin Railway. Although progress was rather slow, construction did actually begin in 1869, and two years later, regular rail service began on the forty-mile route between Green Bay and New London.

Westward progress continued more rapidly after that, and by December 1873, the Mississippi River was reached at East Winona, Wisconsin. By then, the name had been changed to Green Bay & Minnesota, as the company realized that their tracks were not, in fact, going to Lake Pepin.

Anticipation ran high that this road would connect to the Winona & St. Peter and gain further expansion into Minnesota, but unfortunately that line had already fallen into control by the Chicago & North Western.

As with most young railroad companies of the time, financial difficulties plagued the Green Bay line, and it was sold in foreclosure in 1881 to the Green Bay, Winona & St. Paul, a company that was established for the sole purpose of taking over its bankrupt predecessor, and was owned by Eastern railroad interests. The new company didn't expand much during the next fifteen years, however, the Eastern owners developed several subsidiary lines that later became part of the Green Bay Route, and in 1883 became part owner of the Winona Bridge Railway, giving the Green Bay Route access to Winona, Minnesota. This company would not survive long, either, due to continuing financial problems. It, too, went into bankruptcy, and still another new company, the Green Bay & Western was formed to take over in 1896. At last, the Wisconsin Central purchased the company that had remained in tact for nearly a hundred years and merged it into its Fox Valley & Western subsidiary in 1993.

One of the more significant subsidiary lines was the Kewaunee, Green Bay & Western incorporated in 1890 with track from Green Bay to Kewaunee on the shore of Lake Michigan. Freight was transferred to steamships for the trip across the lake, but then in 1892, a ferry service began transporting the loaded freight cars to direct connections with Michigan lines at Frankfurt and Ludington. This proved a major step, promoting the Green Bay & Western from short line to a Class I railroad operating scheduled freights between Lake Michigan and the Mississippi River.

Also incorporated in 1890 was the Ahnapee & Western. This line, actually built in 1892, ran from Casco Junction to the port city of Algoma, and then to Sturgeon Bay. It was eventually merged into the Green Bay Route, as were many other short lines and spurs throughout northern Wisconsin.

Several attempts were made to extend the railway from Sturgeon Bay into northern Door County, but each attempt was successfully blocked by the ship interest. The final effort came in 1914; just when it seemed certain there would be a railroad north, World War I began. Because of the tight money situation, promoters were unable to raise sufficient funds and were forced to abandon the project. They returned all the money to those who had invested. Unlike residents in other parts of the state, the people of Door County didn't look upon this failure with disappointment. With Lake Michigan at its east shore, and Green Bay on its west shore, the narrow Door County peninsula had always depended on the water routes for shipping and passenger service, and with the coming of the automobile, trucks and buses, there seemed little need for a railroad, and a railroad appeared to be a doubtful financial venture.

A railroad into Door County had been a sore issue long before the Ahnapee & Western finally built into Sturgeon Bay in 1894. The people were satisfied without one, and Sturgeon Bay is where the rails stopped. Two stage routes were established northward from Sturgeon Bay – one along the west shore, following the approximate same course as present Highway 42, and the other following the path of present Highway 57 on the east shore.

During the summer months, stage drivers used a combination freight, mail, and passenger vehicle, and in winter, as soon as there was a good snow cover on the ground, an enclosed sleight with a small wood burning stove for passenger and driver comfort was put into service.

Automobiles, trucks, and buses eventually replaced the horse-drawn vehicles to carry freight, mail, and passengers. Washington Island, naturally, was the only part of the county still relying on ships and boats.

Private to Public

Some railroads in Wisconsin started from privately owned lines built for a specific purpose. Two such railroad companies were the Wisconsin & Northwestern, and the Wisconsin & Michigan Railway.

The Wisconsin & Northwestern Railroad began operation in 1889 as the private road of Bird & Wells Lumber Company in Wausaukee. They sold a portion of their track to the Milwaukee road that ran northwest from Wausaukee and connected with the Dunbar & Wausaukee at Girard Junction. Bird & Wells retained their rights for track usage, though, so their log trains could reach the mill. Several new spurs were built off the D&W for logging operations, and some new mainline track was constructed, too. Wells incorporated the Wisconsin & Northwestern in July 1906, as a common carrier serving local transportation needs in Forest and Marinette Counties. It was abandoned in 1921.

The first railroad constructed north of Green Bay was the Peshtigo Harbor Railroad. Built in 1862-63, it consisted of about eight miles of track from Peshtigo Lumber Company's mill to a harbor on Lake Michigan. Its sole purpose was to haul finished lumber to the harbor for loading onto ships. This line was originally laid with strap iron mounted on wooden rails, but in 1869-70 was converted to regular steel rails.

Another private logging railroad running from Marinette county into Michigan incorporated as the Wisconsin & Michigan in 1894, and in the following year had over fifty miles of track laid between Bageley Junction, Wisconsin and Faithorn Junction, Michigan where it met the SOO Line. It also extended south to Peshtigo, and wanted the Peshtigo Harbor line for the purpose of ferry connections. In September 1895, the W&M took over the private line of Peshtigo Lumber Company. The ferry was only a limited success and was discontinued in 1905, but Peshtigo Lumber remained the railroad's biggest customer.

The W&M expanded its operation with more tracks to serve the iron mines; the iron mines along the route played out by 1910. Not willing to give up, the W&M bought the Holmes & Son Railroad and built a link to connect the two roads at Miscauno Island in Florence County. The W&M tried to break into the resort business by building a hotel on Miscauno Island and hauling passengers there. That project, too, resulted in failure.

A temporary revival of the logging industry brought the Wisconsin & Michigan back to life for a while, but when regional logging was completed, once again, the railroad was without a chief source of revenue and went into bankruptcy in 1918. In its reorganization, much of the track was torn up, and the line managed to find limited success during the next few years, but finally succumbed to the Depression in 1938.

Iowa Railroads

Railroad fever started taking hold in Iowa when the Chicago & Rock Island Railroad reached the eastern bank of the Mississippi River in February 1854. The constantly increasing westward movement of civilization drew the attention of the railroad companies with speculations of a tremendous volume of business attainable from the rapidly growing agricultural territory west of the Mississippi. It didn't take long for every community with growing ambitions to establish an interest, and to gain a berth within the western railroad network. Many lines were projected westward from the Mississippi, but very little construction was actually completed before the beginning of the Civil War.

As Iowa's population grew, stagecoaches and steamboats provided transportation, and as the agricultural production increased to beyond that consumed locally, farmers relied on the steamboats to get their crops downriver to markets at New Orleans. But passenger traffic by stage was limited by weather conditions, and the riverboats could not run at all during the winter months when the river was frozen. With little doubt, the people were eager to welcome the coming of the railroads.

City officials in the river cities of Dubuque, Clinton, Davenport, and Burlington knew that railroads would soon extend from Chicago to points along the Mississippi River opposite their towns, and in the early 1850s they began organizing local railroad companies. Although there were several small railroads operating around Iowa's river towns, the Mississippi & Missouri Railroad – later known as the Chicago, Rock Island & Pacific – was the first to cross the Mississippi River in 1856, and not until 1867 did the Iowa & Nebraska – later known as the Chicago & North Western – complete the first tracks reaching all the way across the state of Iowa to Council Bluffs. A single-track railroad bridge was built across the Mississippi between East Burlington (now Gulfport, Illinois) and Burlington, Iowa in May 1855. (That bridge was replaced with a double track structure in 1892.) The Burlington & Missouri River Railway had been incorporated in 1852 at Burlington. Operations began over their first few miles of track on New Year's Day, 1856, and had reached Ottumwa by 1857, Murray by the fall of 1858, and the route was completed to the Missouri River by November 1869. A short time later, the Chicago, Burlington & Quincy Railroad Company, the Illinois Central Railroad Company, and the Chicago, Milwaukee, St. Paul & Pacific Railroad Company all reached the western end of Iowa with their tracks. Council Bluffs had been designated as the eastern terminus of the Union Pacific Railroad that would eventually connect with the Central Pacific to form the first transcontinental road.

Five railroads completing tracks the full distance across Iowa meant tremendous economic growth for the state. Passengers could travel year-round, and the farmers now had a continuous direct connection to the closer markets of Chicago, where their corn, wheat, beef, and pork could be shipped to eastern seaports, and anywhere in the world.

With the arrival of the Milwaukee & Mississippi Railroad at Prairie du Chien in April 1857 came the intensified efforts in Northeast Iowa. The McGregor, St. Peter & Missouri River Railroad had been incorporated in June 1856, and preliminary surveys made of several optional routes westward to Clear Lake City.

When the final decision was made on the selected route, the estimated cost for the first 50 miles was in excess of two million dollars. A campaign was launched to raise the necessary funds: towns, cities and counties were persuaded to purchase stock in the company, and farmers were urged to invest the full value of their land, as property values would surely multiply many times over with an adjacent railroad.

The company managed to grade nine miles of the route up a valley called "Bloody Run" that headed west from the Mississippi River a mile upstream from McGregor. But progress was slow on the crooked, steep route that required twenty-three bridges. A supply point was established at the mouth of Bloody Run, and a village quickly grew up there that would serve the needs of construction crews. It was named North McGregor, and within a year, the infant town contained several business places with more being prepared for the following spring trade – warehouses, three fine hotels, a school and church, a steam-powered grist and sawmill, a sash, door and blind factory, a foundry, several mechanic shops, stores, a livery stable, and about fifty dwellings occupied by a population of about 300.

The economic panic of 1857, however, had brought the project to a standstill. Money supplies, both locally and from the east, were drying up, and a bad crop year contributed to a poor outlook. Renewed hope came a couple of years later with new ownership. Reorganized as the Northern Iowa Railroad Company, promises were made to complete the road to Monona by January 1, 1862, and more local financial support came quickly. But very little construction was accomplished. To add to the problems, one of the subcontractors absconded with the payroll, and a riot led by angry railroad construction workers ensued in McGregor. Had it not been for Father Richard Nagle, priest of St. Mary's Parish, who galloped his horse into the mob and settled the tension, a lynching of railroad company president Jack Thompson may have taken place. It was then that Thompson appeared to announce that he had secured a personal loan from the bank to cover the unpaid wages.

The onset of the Civil War again put the project on hold. Then new owners – George Greene and Associates – took over the McGregor, St. Peter and Missouri River Railroad, and reorganized the company as McGregor Western Railroad. A contract was let to Greene's Iowa Construction Company to complete the first fifteen miles of road. The steep grade to Monona was completed in 1863, and by November 1865, the Iowa and Minnesota Construction Company extended tracks to Cresco.

The McGregor Western acquired the Minnesota Central Railroad Company in 1867. By then it had completed road to Owatonna, and with the new acquisition, the McGregor company now had a through route to Minneapolis-St. Paul. Later that same year, the company was sold to the rapidly expanding Milwaukee & St. Paul Railway Company that also controlled the Milwaukee & Prairie du Chien. With the exception of the unbridged Mississippi River, this formed the first rail route between the Great Lakes and the Twin Cities.

For a while, the connection of the Wisconsin and Iowa railroads was effected by the use of steam passenger ferry and freight boats. Then in the early 1870s, railroad agent Joseph Lawler constructed fixed spans on the riverbanks and intervening island. In order to connect the approaches without obstructing riverboat traffic, shipwright Mike Spettel designed the pontoon rail bridge. Two structures were built to span the two channels of the Mississippi between Prairie du Chien and North

McGregor. Constructed of fir shipped from the state of Washington, the main channel pontoon was 408 feet long and 40 feet wide. It was designed to pivot at one end on a piling, allowing it to swing completely out of the channel and making enough room for a steamer and large log raft to pass through. The bridge opened with the current's force, and was closed with a cable and winch operated by a 21 horsepower steam engine.

The unique construction was considered to be the world's first permanent pontoon bridges, and viewed as a structural success, floating railroad trains across the Mississippi for many years. But in the 1950s railroad commerce to Marquette (the town's name was changed in 1920) was greatly diminished, and in 1961 the old pontoon bridge was dismantled. Today, a highway bridge crosses the river in about the same location, and although the railroad activity is not what it used to be, and the steep bluffs literally restricted the physical growth of the town, Marquette remains a well-preserved village with a spectacular view of the Mississippi River.

Paddle wheel tug guides a lumber raft past the opened pontoon railroad bridge at North McGregor, Iowa. This unique bridge remained in use until 1961. (Photo from ISG Annual Report XVI)

Changing Times

La Crosse, Wisconsin once enjoyed the distinction of having the biggest river packet business, and supported the largest shipyard on the entire Upper Mississippi River. A couple of years after the railroad reached La Crosse, the Davidson "White Collar Line" of freight and passenger steamers contracted all the traffic for the La Crosse & Milwaukee Railroad the rest of the distance to St. Paul, Minnesota. At that time, La Crosse was the western end of the line for the railroad, and homeport for the Davidson steamer fleet. At the wharf located at the mouth of the Black River where it converges with the Mississippi, the boats were loaded to their capacity to handle this enormous daily business. Combining their freight business, shipbuilding yard and log rafting, the Davidsons had more significantly created the city's leading industry.

La Crosse had not just happened by chance. When Nathan Myrick planted his trading post there, he had good reason, intimately associated with transportation. The enterprising and aggressive Myrick sensed the great potential of the pine forests in the north, and he recognized the Black River as the logical route to move men and supplies to lumber camps, and a natural means of conveyance for the resources to find their way to civilization and use. The Mississippi River represented the one great highway on which civilization marched; men and goods had moved through the wilderness on that course since the earliest times. Naturally, where the Black and Mississippi Rivers met, there should be a city. Just as a merchant would choose a busy intersection to locate his store, Myrick picked Prairie La Crosse for his trading post.

Events that followed justified Myrick's foresight. In time, La Crosse came to be the market central for lumbermen of western Wisconsin. It was their trading center; mills were established to process the raw logs into marketable lumber; supply dealers located their distribution stations there; emigrants seeking the opportunities of the Northwest gathered there; for the remaining life of the lumber industry, the north-south corridor offered by the Mighty Mississippi made La Crosse the up-and-comingest town in the state.

The Davidsons began their shipping empire in 1859 with their first two steamers, the *Frank Steele*, and the *Favorite*, using La Crosse as a homeport. From that small beginning grew a magnificent fleet serving the needs of commerce between La Crosse and St. Paul. Only one other boat purchased and operated by John M. Levy had claimed La Crosse as its homeport until that time. However, the river traffic and travel was a constantly increasing factor in the growth and importance of La Crosse, a mere village at that time.

The Galena Packet Company was the first to operate a line of steamers regularly as far north as La Crosse in 1847, but fierce competition among rival steamboat companies soon erupted on the Upper Mississippi. The Northern Line of St. Louis, Missouri, established regular routes to La Crosse with an array of boats: the *Minneapolis, Rock Island, Davenport, Minnesota,* and *Muscatine,* as well as scores of independent "wildcat" boats. Despite his affiliation with a packet company, Captain Daniel S. Harris displayed his independence by running boats such as the *Frontier,* the *Smelter,* the *Pizarro,* the *Pre-emption,* the *Relief,* the *Sutler,* the *Otter,* the *War Eagle* (first), the *Time,* the *Lightfoot,* the *Dr. Franklin No. 2,* the *Senator,* the *West Newton,* the *War Eagle* (second), and the *Grey Eagle.* Only a few of these boats did he run for more than one season before selling them to his competition, and then acquiring the next one.

Then in 1866, after several mergers and re-organizations, the Northwestern Union Packet Company headed by William Davidson as its president was formed at La Crosse, adding a number of boats to their fleet including the *Belle of La Crosse, Phil Sheridan, Northwestern, Tom Jasper, Alex Mitchell,* and *City of St. Paul.* Strong businessmen as well as accomplished steamboat pilots, William and Peyton Davidson's aggressive characteristics allowed them to all but dominate the trade routes on the Upper Mississippi and on the Minnesota tributaries.

The Diamond Jo Line had the *Ida Fulton,* the *Arkansas,* the *Tidal Wave,* and the *Diamond Jo.* It could be said that Joseph Reynolds became the king of the Upper Mississippi river men. His impressive fleet of steamboats known as the "Diamond Jo Line" outlived its staunchest rivals, and operated under the name of its originator until 1911 – two decades after his death.

By the time Joseph Reynolds made McGregor, Iowa his home in

1860, he had already acquired the trademark and nickname of "Diamond Jo." The diamond-shaped logo inclosing the letters JO had been established during the time he operated a tannery in Chicago, as the result of confusion in identifying his goods among those of other shippers. It didn't take long for the nickname to become Reynolds' common identity as well.

While traveling extensively through Wisconsin, Minnesota, and Iowa, buying hides and furs for his Chicago tannery, he recognized the need among the farmers for someone to buy their abundant grain production. He also recognized a good business opportunity – buying the grain and shipping it to Chicago markets for resale could prove profitable. His success in several previous business ventures in his home state of New York, and then in Illinois, gave Reynolds the confidence to once again make a career change, and to pursue his ever-growing interest in the West. He sold his business interest in Chicago, made his home in McGregor, Iowa, and established an office in Prairie du Chien, Wisconsin, where was located the shipping terminal of the Milwaukee & Mississippi Railroad. There he engaged in the grain trade, shipping the corn, wheat, and oats that he bought at Lansing, Iowa, DeSoto, Ferryville, and Lynxville, Wisconsin, to the railhead at Prairie du Chien.

The endeavors of newcomer Jo Reynolds must have appeared as a threat to the grain traders already established and doing business along the Mississippi River. (In time, he would certainly offer a generous share of competition.) His competitors owned stock in the dominant Minnesota Packet Company, and often the Reynolds shipments were left behind on the levee to suffer great loses from adverse weather conditions. These attempts to put him out of business only drove him into keener determination; Diamond Jo had never been one to settle for defeat. To solve the shipping problem, he decided to build his own steamboat, thereby eliminating his dependency on the competitors who were just as determined to eliminate him.

Reynolds began his riverboat career with the *Lansing*, a comparatively small craft at the command of J.B. Wilcox. In addition to moving his own grain shipments, Reynolds quickly advanced into carrying other freight as well.

When the Minnesota Packet Company offered to buy the *Lansing* and made a promise to provide Reynolds with good shipping service, Diamond Jo took them on their word. He had not been necessarily interested in the transportation business, anyway, so he sold his boat to them. But this turned out to be just another attempt to discourage Reynolds and drive him out of the grain trade, as he soon discovered the discrimination against his business was still present, and once again his shipping problems mounted. Faced with unsatisfactory transport services again, Reynolds saw his only option in building another boat. Christened as the *Diamond Jo*, this second, larger steamer and several barges went into service in 1863.

About that same time, the Minnesota Packet Company reorganized as the North Western Packet Company. The new firm made its promises and guarantees to Reynolds, and once more, Diamond Jo trusted that he would be treated fairly with dependable shipping service if he sold his boat to them. They honorably fulfilled their obligations for three seasons.

But then in the spring of 1866, that company was reorganized again into the Northwestern Union Packet Company, headed by William F. Davidson. Discrimination against Diamond Jo Reynolds soon began. But this time, efforts to squelch their competition magnified it instead. Reynolds would soon have a fleet of steamboats (and he would eventually regain ownership of the *Diamond Jo*) competing successfully with the Davidson "White Collar Line."

His company was first known as the *Chicago, Fulton and River Line* after he made arrangements with the Chicago & North Western Railway to carry grain to their terminal in Fulton, Illinois. But the significance of the "Diamond Jo" name seemed more prevalent among the public, and particularly the press, when they announced the arrivals at various ports of the heavily loaded "Diamond Jo Line" boats. So Reynolds changed the name to the commonly popular one that he had used for many years. Joseph Reynolds was once again a leading player in the grain trade, and the *Diamond Jo Line* was destined to outlive all its competition.

The Davidsons, as was the case with an enormous number of businesses of the time, fell into bankruptcy in the 1880s. Of all the packet companies on the Upper Mississippi, the Diamond Jo Line was the only one to survive the changing times. Joseph Reynolds, in his persistent but calm demeanor, had the foresight to recognize the coming changes in the transportation industry. Steamboating was already on the decline when Reynolds moved his main office to Dubuque in 1874, and by the time grain transport by riverboat had virtually ceased in 1890, Diamond Jo had long since turned his attention to the passenger and excursion trade. The *Libbie Conger* began carrying passengers between St. Louis and St. Paul in 1879, and in the following year the magnificent *Mary Morton* stern-wheeler, the finest boat in the line, (named in honor of Reynolds' wife) entered into regular passenger service to St. Paul, as well. More steamers would be added to the popular passenger line that remained successful into the Twentieth Century.

Hundreds of the big boats steamed their way up and down the great waterway, and by 1860 the arrivals at La Crosse numbered in excess of 1,000 per season. So rapid was the expansion of river traffic, the Mississippi River Valley soon became one of the nation's leading commercial avenues.

The glamorous success of navigation, however, did not come without tragedy. In those early days, the river was a treacherous byway. Improvements for navigation had not yet commenced; shallow water, sandbars, rocks and reefs continually plagued the riverboat pilots. Fallen trees carried downstream by floodwaters lodged in the river bottom mud, created "snags" hidden just below the surface, and were often deadly to a boat's hull when struck. The mere "low draft" design of the boats was not enough to combat all these hazards.

Fires and boiler explosions posed a constant threat to the longevity of a riverboat's service. They were largely constructed of wood, highly susceptible to the shower of sparks often emitted from the smoke stacks. Stringent enforcement of safety standards was still in the future, and the lack of available propulsion technology left the vessels vulnerable to destruction by their own power source – steam engines with boilers fired by cordwood and coal.

Scores of boats fell victim to the many hazards, often claiming lives, the vessels, and their cargo. One such disaster occurred in La Crosse on May 15, 1870; the Union Packet steamer, *War Eagle*, burned while at the dock adjacent to the Milwaukee railroad station. It was said to be the most disastrous fire in the history of the city. The tremendous blaze claimed total destruction to the craft, the railroad station, a string of warehouses and several rail freight cars. Six lives were lost.

The steamer was bound for St. Paul, and had arrived at the La Crosse dock at midnight to discharge a cargo of barreled kerosene, and to load over a ton of mail that had arrived by rail from Milwaukee. Several of the oil barrels had leaked, and the flammable contents saturated a large portion of the lower deck. Captain Tom Cushing instructed the steamer's cooper, William Bennett, to try making repairs to the leaking barrels. Bennett immediately went to work while a deckhand held a lantern to provide light. The assistant was called away, and Bennett placed the lantern on one of the barrels. Whether it was a spark from the cooper's hammer and chisel, or that the oil fumes eventually rose to the lantern's flame, or that the lantern was defective or damaged is not certain. Just minutes after Bennett began the work, the spilled oil ignited, and within seconds the deck was ablaze. In a failed attempt to remove the leaking barrel and roll it overboard, Bennett's trousers caught on fire. By the time he managed to jump into the water, he had suffered only minor burns, but within minutes, the entire boat was engulfed in flames, hopelessly beyond control.

About fifty cabin passengers were aboard, and the large majority of them escaped in their nightclothes. Crewmen heroically assisted many to safety before diving into the river themselves.

Frank Hubbard and Dr. Sam Bugh were engaged in sorting the up river mail in one of the forward staterooms assigned for that purpose. Bugh managed to save the money pouches and registered letters, and barely had time to get ashore; all of the rest of the mails were lost. Mr. Hubbard made his escape by jumping from the front main deck into a wagon. The *War Eagle's* clerk, C. Burrage, as well, had no time or opportunity to retrieve the ship's books or passenger list, but managed

c.1870 Members of La Crosse Fire Dept. and some of their equipment perhaps used to fight the *War Eagle* conflagration. (Photo courtesy La Crescent Area Historical Society)

to save the boat's money.

Two other steamers tied up alongside the *War Eagle*, and because they had just arrived a short while before the fire broke out, they luckily had enough steam to get out of the way, but they were both badly scorched.

Within a few minutes the fire had jumped to the railroad station and then quickly spread to the joining warehouses, stores, grain elevator, and rail cars.

The fire department of La Crosse was promptly on the scene and feverishly at work within fifteen minutes after the alarm bell sounded. Having first attempted to save the warehouses and grain elevator, they found that to be a hopeless task. The intense heat from the fire drove the firemen back, and they directed their efforts to save the express passenger train that had just arrived. Two of the finest passenger coaches were spared, but several other cars were consumed by the blaze.

Shortly after the turn of the Twentieth Century, ideas fostered by pessimistic rivermen and encouraged by congressional agitation indicated that the Upper Mississippi River would never again revive its prestige as a major channel of commerce. The coming of the railroad had superseded the steamboat mainly because it was a time saver, and nothing could restore the prestige that the steamer once enjoyed. The freight and passenger transportation industry was quickly demanding speed as the population grew and its needs became more urgent. Restricted by the confines of the waterways, the slower steamships could no longer compete with the swiftness of the iron horse.

Efforts were under way by the Upper Mississippi River Improvement Association with the vital interests of the river's future welfare. Mr. J. J. Hogan, the pioneer wholesale merchant of La Crosse, supported those efforts and disagreed with the pessimists. No one had a deeper regard for the river, or would have rejoiced more, had the busy days of the steamboat traffic been restored. From his private office at the rear of his immense warehouse, he had daily viewed the broad expanse of the river flowing almost at his feet, and had watched the city's harbor filled with the big boats and the scores of men loading and unloading boxes and barrels of merchandise. It was a time when the nation was recovering from the setback it received during the Civil War, and the Middle West was the Mecca of thousands of home seekers who were quick to see the opportunities offered in the Upper Mississippi Valley.

Mr. Hogan had more than a platonic friendship with the river; he had a deep, all abiding faith in the good it had done for the territory, and his city. He recognized in the murky channel a power that had done more than any other element in building up the great northwest. With tender significance, he recognized, too, that it was a factor that entered largely in the rapid growth of his own business in the early days. It was those sentiments that prompted Mr. Hogan to place his office at the rear in the handsome, new wholesale house, overlooking the river, away from the hum of industry, so that he could sit at his desk, and with the slight turn of his head, a panoramic view of the busy harbor lay before him.

Sadly, the Mississippi River would not see the good old days when freight and passenger steamships provided the bulk of travel accommodations. By the early 1900s, the railroad had thrust its shiny steel rails far beyond the reaches of the riverboats, and the romance with the river, in terms of commerce, slowly declined.

But as the population continually increased along the banks of the Upper Mississippi, so did their interests increase in the natural beauty that had been bestowed upon the river valley. Even though the commercial freight and passenger business on the river had all but died, the demand for pleasure and recreation excursion vessels rose. Many of the old steamers that would have otherwise rusted and decayed were revived for use as excursion boats. Their popularity steadily gained momentum, just as their counterparts in the Southern states had enjoyed for many years.

Although the economic circumstances enhanced by pessimistic attitudes generated the demise of their original usefulness, the steamboats on the Upper Mississippi River lived on.

The years passed. Railroads had shifted the transportation directions from the north-south main currents established by waterways to the east-west routes dictated by the relatively new transcontinental lines. Instead of having a thriving establishment on America's Main Street, La Crosse found itself off on a side street. River traffic was dying by virtue of the deliberately discriminatory rates offered from the unregulated competition of the railroads that were anxious to kill off their water rivals. But there had been time enough, by then, to get a perspective on it all, and to closely examine the changes that had developed. Although there were those who still thought a river revival as impractical and visionary, advocates of the emerging barge systems recognized and enthusiastically endorsed the importance – the necessity – of La Crosse establishing itself as a river terminal once again.

As the discussions and debates would soon reveal, transportation is the lifeblood of a nation. One of the main arteries had been shut off. The men who rated as among the biggest shippers in La Crosse began to see the potential of the river in terms of their business growth; the railroads had not completely satisfied the prospects for improvement in the economic prosperity. A new deal in importance was overriding the developments of the last generation.

In terms of economic advancement, La Crosse had fallen in the ranks among the cities of the state. The reason for this setback clearly pointed to the decline in its dependency on water transportation. The eastern lakeshore cities of Racine, Kenosha, Milwaukee, Sheboygan, and Green Bay, for example, still enjoyed the advantage of cheaper shipping via the lakes, and had developed the opportunities to distribute coal, steel, and other raw materials inland through their ports, just as La Crosse had done in earlier years.

River Transportation Restored

River transportation suffered a few lean years while the railroad was gaining momentum in leaps and bounds, and low water levels made navigation on the river difficult. But during that time, the government was hard at work making the river navigable, and because of faster time and lower rates, freight in large lots was being offered over the river route. All indications pointed to a return of the old days when there was great transport activity on the upper river.

While private shipping lines were promoting and restoring river transportation, the federal government moved ahead to improve navigational conditions on the river and to provide a minimum 6-ft. channel for the low draft vessels as far north as St. Paul. Considerable work was done to keep the river open, even at the lowest stages of water level. Using the lowest measurements of 1864, which became the baseline to maintain the 6-ft channel, the depth standard had been set.

The canal constructed around the rapids of the Mississippi above Keokuk, Iowa had been in use since August 1877. Seven and a half miles in length, three hundred feet wide, with three locks each three hundred fifty feet long, the canal had cost nearly $4.4 million to build.

Snag boats, too, had been kept active on the Upper Mississippi for many years. They removed boulders, boat wrecks, trees, sandbars, and other obstructions from the river, an operation that Mark Twain called "pulling the river's teeth." The crews of these specially built boats, while patrolling the river, located snags, or the captains of other vessels reported sighting them. The snag boat was equipped with hoists and chains that lifted the underwater hazards free of the river bottom and towed them to the bank opposite the navigational channel, where they were pulled ashore, secured, or cut up into pieces as not to become a navigational hazard again. By the mid-1880s, damage to a riverboat due to striking sunken obstructions had become a rare occurrence, while previous to the snag boats, the sinking of steamers was quite common.

Wing dams constructed of brush and rock were already in place at short intervals south of La Crosse, and more were constantly being added. These dams extended from the banks out into the river 200 to 1,800 feet. Their purpose was to hold back the water flow along the shoreline and to direct the water into the main channel, creating greater depths. In addition, they serve another function: sand and silt carried downriver, mostly during times of flooding, is contained by the dams, preventing it from filling up the main channel.

But it was at the northern end, above Lake Pepin, where the most trouble was encountered in maintaining an adequate channel depth. Plans were soon under way to install several dams with a locking system to assist boats across the dams. Such systems were already in use on the Ohio River, and had proven quite effective there. Now, it seemed essential that a similar system was needed on the Mississippi in the vicinity of Hastings and St. Paul. In 1932 construction began, and in subsequent years, twenty-four locks and dams were constructed between St. Paul and Alton, Illinois.

The River Transit Company, headquartered in St. Paul, Minnesota, and whose stockholders were businessmen in cities along the river, was the pioneer in the effort being made to revive river shipping. The company was formed through the efforts of J. S. Brodie, who conceived the idea of using low draft barges to handle the freight. Low draft towboats with gasoline and oil burning engines were designed and built to power the barges, and in a short time, they had proven successful in the shallow conditions of the Mississippi.

When the company began operation, it used only one barge. So much freight was offered that more carriers had to be put into service; by 1925 the fleet had grown to five barges running week-long round trips between St. Paul and St. Louis, making stops at towns along the river.

The popularity of this new transportation system proved overwhelming. More freight was being offered for transport than the barges could handle. They were filled to capacity in both directions, and once again, the river route was proving itself as a faster, more efficient means of conveying freight than the railroads. The rates were lower, giving businesses an added incentive.

That the barge line was not operating at its highest potential, however, was greatly due to the lack of dock facilities with railheads in river towns. Much of the freight consigned to inland points suffered delays, and now it was up to the railroads to develop the necessary improvements.

The barge line accepted through freight between St. Paul and New Orleans, and points between. Several other lines were already operating on the Lower Mississippi, and would relay the barge freight from St. Paul southward from St. Louis. Northbound barges were picked up at St. Louis and brought upriver by the Northern towboats.

Other entities soon followed suit: by 1925, Henry Ford was preparing to operate a fleet of barges between St. Paul and St. Louis. This fleet would not carry general freight, but was intended to haul coal, raw materials and parts to the Ford automobile manufacturing facility in St. Paul, and to transport the finished cars back to St. Louis.

Launching the river transportation service again seemed hardly open to argument that La Crosse had restored its favorable position. True, the lumber industry had dwindled; the northern pine forests were thinned and depleted; the mills gradually ceased operations with the lack of raw material supply. But in place of that one industry, many others could be served, and the greatest of all – agriculture. From the earliest days when there were but a few pioneer log huts scattered throughout the region, there were now stretches of highly developed, prosperous and thickly settled farmland – some of the richest sections in the state – rendering abundant quantities of produce needed in other parts of the country. Effective and cost-efficient shipping became a major issue. Reopening the river vitalized the trade that could now move at low cost up and downstream, to and from the La Crosse port, and complimented the rail system that radiated in all directions. In essence, it was the same setup that had propelled La Crosse forward so rapidly in its youth. To provide adequate transportation service to the surrounding territory was not visionary – it was sound sense, coming from the proverbial voice of experience.

With the steel barges came a rebirth of commercial transportation on the Upper Mississippi. Although the diesel engine towboats of today don't possess that same kind of charm of their steam powered, paddle wheeled predecessors, it is comforting to know that Old Man River – that mighty waterway that played such an important role in the development of our great nation – was not ignored, but was nurtured and maintained to continue its age old prestige.

References and Sources:

In addition to the countless personal visits by the author to the many towns, cities, and historical sites named in this book, the following is a list of information sources. It is sincerely hoped that no one was inadvertently omitted.

(Listed in no particular order.)

<u>Various historical markers</u> in Wisconsin, Minnesota, and Iowa.

<u>Organizations and websites</u>: Wisconsin State Historical Society; Iowa State Historical Society; Minnesota State Historical Society; Houston County (Minnesota) Historical Society; La Crescent (Minnesota) Area Historical Society; Rushford (Minnesota) Historical Society; La Crosse County (Wisconsin) Historical Society; Portage (Wisconsin) Public Library; La Crosse (Wisconsin) Public Library; McGregor (Iowa) Public Library; Marquette (Iowa) Railroad Museum; Mid-Continent Railroad Museum at North Freedom, Wisconsin; Illinois Central Historical Society; Middleton (Wisconsin) Public Library; Mondovi, Wisconsin; Shullsburg, Wisconsin; Mineral Point, Wisconsin; Mississippi River Museum (Dubuque, Iowa); Chippewa County Historical Society; Wisconsin Department of Natural Resources.

<u>Newspaper archives</u>: The Boscobel Dial Enterprise; Green Bay Press-Gazette; Wisconsin Rapids Tribune; La Crosse Tribune; Westby Times; Milwaukee Sentinel; The Muscoda Democrat; Milwaukee Journal; Viroqua Censor; Wisconsin State Journal (Madison); Portage Democrat; Eau Claire Leader; Berlin Courant; Daily Northwestern (Oshkosh); Appleton Post; La Crosse Leader; Eau Claire Daily Telegram; Dunn County News; Rice Lake Chronotype; Chicago Herald; Chippewa Falls Independent; La Crosse Chronicle; Wabasha County Herald; Eau Claire Weekly Free Press; Baraboo Weekly News; Milwaukee Free Press; Two Rivers Chronicle; Burlington Hawkeye; Superior Telegram; Stevens Point Journal; Sheboygan Daily Press; Janesville Gazette; Beloit Daily News; Madison Democrat; Racine Times-Call; Stoughton Courier; Mauston

Chronicle; Beaver Dam Citizen; Hartford Times; Baraboo Daily News; Kaukauna Sun; Mount Horeb Times; Galesville Republican; Telephone News (Milwaukee); Fond du Lac Commonwealth; Prairie du Chien Press; River Falls Journal; Wausau Record; Milwaukee Evening Wisconsin; Waupun Leader; Sheboygan Press-Telegram; Capital Times (Madison); Lancaster Herald; Chippewa Falls Herald; Manitowoc Herald; Fennimore Times; Weekly Home News (Spring Green, Wisconsin).

Books: *History of Northern Wisconsin, 1881*; *History of Fillmore* (Minnesota) *County*; *History of Houston* (Minnesota) *County*; *History of Rushford: The First Decade* by Alden O. Droivold; *Stagecoach and Tavern Tales of the Old Northwest* by Harry E. Cole; *Steamboats on the Upper Mississippi* by William J. Peterson; *The St. Croix* by James Taylor Dunn; *Bella Danger – Steamboat Disasters on the Mississippi River* by Patrick J. Rash.

ABOUT THE AUTHOR

Born into a farm family in the late 1940s, J.L. Fredrick lived his youth in rural Western Wisconsin, a modest but comfortable life not far from the Mississippi River. His father was a farmer, and his mother, an elementary school teacher. He attended a one-room country school for his first seven years of education.

Wisconsin has been home all his life, with exception of a few years in Minnesota and Florida. After college in La Crosse, Wisconsin and a stint with Uncle Sam during the Viet Nam era, the next few years were unsettled as he explored and experimented with life's options. He entered into the transportation industry in 1975.

Since 2001 he has five published novels to his credit, and one non-fiction history volume, *Rivers, Roads, & Rails.* He was a featured author during Grand Excursion 2004.

J.L. Fredrick currently resides at Madison, Wisconsin.

Made in the USA
Charleston, SC
08 November 2014